Fourth Edition

THE MARKETING PLAN HANDBOOK

Marian Burk Wood, M.B.A.

Prentice Hall

Boston   Columbus   Indianapolis   New York   San Francisco   Upper Saddle River
Amsterdam   Cape Town   Dubai   London   Madrid   Milan   Munich   Paris   Montreal   Toronto
Delhi   Mexico City   Sao Paulo   Sydney   Hong Kong   Seoul   Singapore   Taipei   Tokyo

Editorial Director: Sally Yagan
Editor in Chief: Eric Svendsen
Executive Editor: Melissa Sabella
Editorial Project Manager: Kierra Kashickey
Director of Marketing: Patrice Lumumba Jones
Marketing Manager: Anne Fahlgren
Marketing Assistant: Melinda Jensen
Senior Managing Editor: Judy Leale
Project Manager: Debbie Ryan
Operations Specialist: Clara Bartunek
Creative Art Director: Jayne Conte
Cover Designer: Mollica Design

Manager, Visual Research: Beth Brenzel
Manager, Rights and Permissions: Zina Arabia
Manager, Cover Visual Research & Permissions:
  Karen Sanatar
Cover Art: Getty Images, Inc.
Full-Service Project Management:
  Shiji Sashi/Integra, Inc.
Composition: Integra Software Services Pvt. Ltd.
Printer/Binder: RRD/Harrisonburg
Cover Printer: RRD/Harrisonburg
Text Font: Garamond

Credits and acknowledgments borrowed from other sources and reproduced, with permission, in this textbook appear on page 203.

Library of Congress Cataloging-in-Publication Data

Wood, Marian Burk.
  The marketing plan handbook / Marian Burk Wood.—4th ed.
    p. cm.
  Includes bibliographical references and index.
  ISBN-13: 978-0-13-608936-0 (alk. paper)
  ISBN-10: 0-13-608936-4 (alk. paper)
  1. Marketing—Management—Handbooks, manuals, etc.   I. Title.
HF5415.13.W66 2011
658.8'02—dc22

2010000740

10 9 8 7 6 5 4 3

Prentice Hall
is an imprint of

www.pearsonhighered.com

ISBN 10:   0-13-608936-4
ISBN 13: 978-0-13-608936-0

BRIEF CONTENTS

CONTENTS

PREFACE

WHAT'S NEW IN THIS EDITION?

- **Your Marketing Plan, Step by Step.** A special new feature to guide you through the development of an individualized marketing plan.
- **Model of the Marketing Planning Process.** A new conceptual model of the planning process that also serves as an organizing figure for the book.
- **Examples of Marketing Planning in Action.** Dozens of new examples of consumer and B2B marketing, traditional and online marketing, U.S. and global marketing, not-for-profit marketing, and marketing by governmental agencies.
- **Latest Marketing Developments.** New coverage of Twitter and other social media, use of crowdsourcing to engage customers, growth of mobile marketing, and much more.
- **Helpful Checklist in Every Chapter.** In addition to the new "Understanding the big picture for marketing planning" checklist in Chapter 1, every checklist has been revised and updated.
- **New PowerPoint Presentation.** Revised for this edition to emphasize the latest marketing concepts and tools, including more about metrics.

Whether you're marketing a new product, a special service, or *yourself*, a creative, well-researched, and practical marketing plan can make a real difference to your success. Although marketing textbooks often discuss the general use of a marketing plan or contain a brief outline of one, they don't explain exactly how to develop an effective plan—yet that's what marketers, marketing students, and entrepreneurs really need.

The Marketing Plan Handbook fills this gap by taking you through the entire planning process, one step at a time. The emphasis is on applying basic concepts of marketing strategy, tactics, and metrics to develop a marketing plan that is both effective and adaptable. Chapter by chapter, you learn how to formulate a good plan and gain valuable insights from reading about the marketing-plan successes (and occasional missteps) of organizations around the world. At the same time, this updated edition will give you a good overview of the latest marketing developments, including social media, customer-influence strategies, crowdsourcing, and mobile marketing.

YOUR MARKETING PLAN, STEP BY STEP

Don't know where to start or how to approach all the decisions you face in preparing a marketing plan? Each chapter now ends with a special "Your Marketing Plan, Step by Step" feature that takes you through every step in the planning process. By answering the questions in these features and following up on the suggested data sources, you'll have a head start in gathering information and analyzing alternatives for your plan. You'll also find fresh perspectives on the practical application of key marketing concepts. No matter what kind of marketing plan you're creating, these features can help you generate ideas and think about critical issues.

REAL-WORLD VIEW OF MARKETING PLANNING

What happened when Tropicana implemented a marketing plan to change its orange juice packaging (see Chapter 1)? How did Nintendo's marketing plan for the Wii help it outsell Sony's and Microsoft's video game consoles (Chapter 2)? Why would Hewlett-Packard and Xerox plan to price their laser printers and replacement ink cartridges so differently (Chapter 7)? How are the Centers for Disease Control using social media to spread the word about health matters (Chapter 9)? How does Procter & Gamble use metrics to evaluate marketing plan performance (Chapter 10)?

These and dozens of other new examples illustrate how marketing planning is actually conducted in consumer and business markets, in large and small companies, in traditional and online businesses, in U.S. and international firms, and in not-for-profit organizations. *The Marketing Plan Handbook* contains more than 100 examples of marketing in organizations such as the following: Amazon.com, Big Brothers Big Sisters of America, Costa Farms, Dell, Ericsson, Ford, Google, Harley-Davidson, IKEA, John Deere, Kogi Korean BBQ, Li & Fung, Merlin Entertainment, Nintendo, Procter & Gamble, ReCellular, Staples, Teletón, UNICEF, Verizon Wireless, Walmart, Xerox, and Zappos. In response to instructors' suggestions, most examples go into some detail to illustrate the diverse challenges and opportunities that marketers face in preparing a successful plan.

SPECIAL FEATURES HELP YOU LEARN TO PLAN

The Marketing Plan Handbook supports the hands-on development of imaginative yet realistic marketing plans through a series of special features.

Model of the Marketing Planning Process

So much goes into the making of a marketing plan . . . yet it's not always easy to see the big picture when you're working on the details. A new conceptual model, introduced in Chapter 1, guides you through the process and is repeated in all 10 chapters, to serve as a "you are here" organizing figure for the book. Use this model to visualize the connections between the steps and to focus on the three key outcomes of any marketing plan: to provide value, build relationships, and make a difference to stakeholders.

Sample Marketing Plan

What does a marketing plan look like? The appendix presents a sample plan for the SonicSuperphone, a multimedia, multifunction smartphone. This hypothetical sample plan, based on current conditions in the cell-phone market, illustrates the content and organization of a typical marketing plan. In particular, the plan demonstrates how a company might analyze market needs and trends, examine environmental factors, look at the competitive situation, and set objectives to be achieved. It also touches on segmentation, targeting, and positioning; the variety of marketing strategies and programs needed to launch a new product; and some of the metrics used in evaluating marketing performance.

Checklists

How can you be sure your plan covers all the basics? Checklists in every chapter summarize key areas to be examined during the planning process. Topics include the following:

- Understanding the big picture for marketing planning
- Analyzing the current marketing situation
- Analyzing markets and customers
- Identifying and evaluating market segments
- Setting marketing plan objectives
- Analyzing and planning product strategy
- Planning pricing strategy
- Channel and logistics issues
- Planning marketing communications
- Planning a marketing audit

Practical Planning Tips

What important points and pitfalls should you be aware of? Each chapter includes a number of special tips, shown in the margin, to help you make the transition from theory to application. These tips emphasize various practical aspects of planning and mention specific issues or questions to consider when developing a marketing plan.

Powerful PowerPoint Presentation

Created by John Newbold of Sam Houston University, the updated PowerPoint presentation is a powerful supplement to *The Marketing Plan Handbook*. Expanded content and eye-catching graphics make this a high-impact presentation package for instructors to download.

Online Features

Visit this book's Web site, www.prenhall.com/wood, for access to a variety of additional materials: a complete glossary in two convenient downloadable formats; hotlinks to selected online marketing resources; discussion questions for each chapter; an outline showing the main sections of a marketing plan; and faculty materials, including the updated PowerPoint presentation.

MARKETING PLAN PRO SIMPLIFIES PLANNING

Palo Alto Software's highly rated *Marketing Plan Pro* software, which comes bundled with this book, is a professional, user-friendly program for documenting marketing plans. The software includes an introductory video, help wizards, and other valuable features to guide you through the process of preparing a written plan, getting ready for implementation, and comparing actual results with projected results.

Marketing Plan Pro offers a structured plan format and dozens of spreadsheets, tables, and charts to help you organize and present data about your marketing decisions. It also includes sample marketing plans from a variety of organizations, including manufacturers, retailers, consulting firms, service businesses, and not-for-profit groups. Once your marketing plan is complete, you can print it, translate it into a read-only document, export it to other programs, or export it to share with colleagues online.

ACKNOWLEDGMENTS

My sincere gratitude to the knowledgeable faculty reviewers who provided insightful feedback and suggestions for making this new edition even more valuable to students: David Andrus, Kansas State University; Cynthia Brooks, Cleveland State Community College; Valerie Ellis, Santa Barbara City College; Tom Gruen, University of Colorado-Colorado Springs; Talai Osmonbekov, Northern Arizona University; Jeff Periatt, Auburn; Michelle Rai, Pacific Union College; Torsten Ringberg, University of Wisconsin, Milwaukee; J. Alexander Smith, Oklahoma City University; and Bob Veryzer, Rensselaer Polytechnic Institute.

Also, I deeply appreciate the comments and recommendations of the following reviewers, whose involvement helped to shape the first three editions of this text: Mel Albin, University of Maryland University College; Ismet Anitsal, Tennessee Tech University; Tim Becker, University of San Diego, University of Phoenix, Webster University; Cathleen Behan, Northern Virginia Community College; Normand Bergeron, Bristol Community College; Robert Blanchard, Salem State College; Brian Bourdeau, Auburn University; Michaelle Cameron, St. Edwards University; Ravi Chinta, American University of Sharjah; Yun Chu, Frostburg State University; Patricia Clarke, Boston College; Earl Clay, Bristol Community College; Greg Combs, Methodist College; Mary Conran, Temple University; Larry Crowson, University of Central Florida; Brent Cunningham, Jackson State University; Don Eckrich, Ithaca College; William Fillner, Hiram College; Douglas Friedman, Penn State Harrisburg; Ralph M. Gaedeke, California State University, Sacramento; Dennis E. Garrett, Marquette University; B. Christine Green, University of Texas at Austin; Tom Gruen, University of Colorado at Colorado Springs; James Hansen, University of Akron, John Carroll University; Harry Harmon, Central Missouri State University; Betty Jean Hebel, Madonna University; Jeffrey Heilbrunn, Columbia College of Missouri; David Hennessey, Babson College; James Hess, Ivy Tech Community College; Stacey Hills, Utah State University; Mahmood Hussain, San Francisco State University; Lynn Jahn, University of Iowa; Michelle Jones, NC State University College of Textiles; Kathleen Krentler, San Diego State University; Michelle Kunz, Morehead State University; Ron Lennon, Barry University; Ada Leung, University of Nebraska at Kearney; Nancy Lowd, Boston University; Terry Lowe, Heartland Community College; William Machanic, University of New Hampshire; Gordon McClung, Jacksonville University; Byron Menides, Worcester Polytechnic Institute; Margaret Mi, University of Mary Washington; Chip Miller, Drake University; Peter Mooney, Embry-Riddle Aeronautical University; Charlene Moser, Keller Graduate School of Management; Michael K. Mulford, Des Moines Area Community College; Keith Nickoloff, Rochester Institute of Technology; Ralitza Nikolaeva, University of Wisconsin–Milwaukee; Bernadette Njoku, College of Saint Rose; Margaret O'Connor, Penn State Berks Campus; Carol Osborne, University of South Florida; Peggy Osborne, Morehead State University; Joseph Ouellette, Bryant University; Henry O. Pruden, Golden Gate University; Elizabeth Purinton, Marist College; Ruby Remley, Cabrini College; Scott D. Roberts, Northern Arizona University; Mark Rosenbaum, University of Hawaii, Northern Illinois University; Bennett Rudolph, Grand Valley State University; David Saliba,

Duquesne University; John Schibrowsky, University of Nevada, Las Vegas; Gary R. Schornack, University of Colorado, Denver; Camille Schuster, California State University San Marcos; Chris Shao, Midwestern State University; Annette Singleton, Florida A&M University; Allen Smith, Florida Atlantic University; Jim Stephens, Emporia State University; Bala Subramanian, Morgan State University; Michael J. Swenson, Brigham Young University; Ronald Thomas, Oakton Community College; Scott Thorne, Southeast Missouri State University; Beverly Venable, Columbus State University; Ven Venkatesan, University of Rhode Island; Edward Volchok, Stevens Institute of Technology; Kathleen Williamson, University of Houston-Clear Lake; Katherine Wilson, Johns Hopkins University; Wendy Wysocki, Monroe County Community College; and Mark Young, Winona State University.

I want to express my gratitude and my admiration for the talent and dedication of the outstanding professionals at Pearson Prentice Hall who have contributed so much to this book's success: Sally Yagan, Vice President and Editorial Director; Eric Svendsen, Editor in Chief; Melissa Sabella, Executive Editor; Patrice Jones, Director of Marketing; Anne Fahlgren, Marketing Manager; and the entire sales team. An extra-special, heartfelt "thank you" to Kierra Kashickey, Editorial Project Manager, who has been an absolute joy to work with. My thanks to Clara Bartunek for shepherding my manuscript through production with great skill and good cheer, and to Suzanne DeWorken for all her hard work on clearing permissions. Finally, a tip of the hat in appreciation to Tim Berry, Sabrina Parsons, and all the folks at Palo Alto Software who are responsible for *Marketing Plan Pro*.

This book is lovingly dedicated to the memory of my parents, Daisy and Harold Burk, who encouraged excellence in everything. Words on a page aren't adequate to convey what's in my heart as I thank my husband—the love of my life—Wally Wood; my beloved sister, Isabel Burk; and all the members of my fantastic extended family. A great big hug to the Biancolo, Burk, Goodwin, Hall, Mazzenga, Werner, and Wood families—you're the best!

—*Marian Burk Wood*
e-mail: MarianBWW@netscape.net
blog: http://marketinghandbook.blogspot.com/

ABOUT THE AUTHOR

Marian Burk Wood has held vice presidential-level positions in corporate and not-for-profit marketing with Citibank, JP Morgan Chase, and the National Retail Federation, as well as management positions with national retail chains. In addition to *The Marketing Plan Handbook*, she is the author of *Essential Guide to Marketing Planning* and *Marketing Planning: Principles into Practice*, both geared to the European market.

Wood has extensive practical experience in marketing planning, having formulated and implemented dozens of marketing plans for a wide range of goods and services. She has also developed numerous chapters, cases, sample plans, exercises, and print and electronic supplements for college textbooks in marketing, advertising, and related disciplines. Wood holds an MBA in marketing from Long Island University in New York and a BA from the City University of New York. Her special interests in marketing include social media, ethics, segmentation, channels, and B2B marketing.

For more about marketing, please visit her blog at http://marketinghandbook. blogspot.com.

1 Marketing Planning: New Urgency, New Possibilities

PREVIEW

Despite the many forces altering the marketing environment at an unprecedented pace, marketing planning is far from obsolete. You saw, in the recent economic crisis, how quickly customers can change their buying habits and brand attachments. You've seen technology evolve in new and sometimes surprising directions, with the latest online phenomena—such as the YouTube video site and the microblogging site Twitter—taking the marketing spotlight from yesterday's tech darlings, such as the virtual world in Second Life.

You've seen competitors shake up the old order by entering and exiting markets at unexpected times and in unexpected ways. In the retail world, long-established chains such as Circuit City are going bankrupt at a record rate, while younger businesses such as Zappos add customers day by day. You've heard about customers creating personalized products and making commercials—some of which have even been aired during the Super Bowl, as well as on YouTube and beyond. Finally, you'll continue to see financial pressures and governmental actions having far-reaching, unpredictable effects on both buyers and sellers.

All of these complexities have brought a new urgency and new possibilities to the process of marketing planning. That's why, more than ever before, your success in marketing will depend on knowing how to research, develop, implement, revise, and evaluate a marketing plan that is creative, flexible, comprehensive, and—above all—practical.

In the first part of this chapter, you'll learn about marketing, value, the purpose of marketing planning, and the contents of a marketing plan. Next, you'll be introduced to the basic steps in developing a marketing plan. The chapter closes with a look at how to prepare for marketing planning.

CHAPTER 1 CHECKLIST   The Big Picture for Marketing Planning

As you begin the marketing planning process, prepare yourself for the big picture:

✔ What sources of information will help me uncover, follow, and anticipate major developments affecting my product, customers, and competitors?

✔ What do the latest technological and social trends mean for marketing in general? For my industry and my product in particular?

✔ What global and legal changes are likely to help or hurt my product and marketing in the coming years?

✔ What lessons about marketing can I learn from existing products, campaigns, organizations, and leaders that will help my marketing plan?

✔ Which stakeholders are most important to the success of my marketing plan, and why?

✔ How can I get customers and employees to be more engaged with my brand and product?

✔ How can I use marketing to make a difference to my customers and organization?

✔ What value will I be providing to my customers, and how?

✔ What resources and experience do I have to support marketing?

✔ How can I generate new ideas and build on my knowledge and background to do a better job of marketing planning?

MARKETING PLANNING TODAY

Marketing planning has never been more important than it is today. Why? First, marketing is everywhere in our everyday world—at home, at work, at play, in the streets, in stores, and in all the media we see and hear. Marketing can be entertaining and informative, but it can also be irritating and intrusive. Still, businesses must fight simply to capture the customer's attention before they can start to demonstrate the value they provide and, over time, gain customer trust. None of this will happen without careful planning.

Second, thanks to technology, global competition, and new media, customers have more information, more choices, higher expectations, more power, and more involvement with marketing than at any time in the past. *Citizen marketing* is the trend toward consumers becoming involved in marketing through such activities as making a commercial or video about a product, engaging in verbal word-of-mouth (or online word-of-mouse) communications about a product, submitting product or label ideas to the marketing organization, and rating or reviewing a product online.

These days, a good product, brand, commercial, price, Web site, Facebook page, or store display is simply not good enough. This is where reputation really counts: Customers (and distributors) prefer to buy brands that have credibility and a positive image; they want to deal with organizations they trust. The public is increasingly demanding *transparency,* pushing organizations to be more open and honest about their decisions and activities—including their marketing.

Third, customers, employees, and other stakeholders are looking to organizations to make a difference (for instance, by improving quality of life or contributing to society at large). A company with a larger purpose can really stand out, even when competition is fierce and money is tight. Of course, building a great reputation requires meticulous planning, especially now that compliments and criticism can ricochet around the world in an instant through tweets, texts, e-mails, and blogs. Consider the success of Web-based retailer Zappos (see Exhibit 1.1).

Zappos. For the decade that Zappos has been selling shoes and then clothing and electronics online, the company has focused on giving customers the best possible experience. Unlike some Web-based merchants, Zappos gives customers the option of contacting the company by phone, e-mail, or live chat, because "the telephone is one of the best branding devices out there, if you get the interaction right," says CEO Tony Hsieh. Shipping is free, and every purchase is backed by a one-year money-back guarantee. Despite the expense, the company keeps its warehouse open 24/7 and rewards loyal customers with faster shipping and other perks. Zappos' playful TV ads play off the company's "Powered by Service" tagline to showcase the customer focus.

Zappos has also earned a reputation for transparency. More than 400 of its employees use the microblogging service Twitter to share ideas and converse with customers and each other. Nearly 2 million people follow the CEO's tweets. Another way Zappos stays in touch with its customers is by inviting them to post product reviews, good or bad, on its Web site. By emphasizing superior customer service and satisfaction, Zappos has pushed annual revenue above $1 billion.[1]

Marketing and Value

Zappos could not have prospered in the crowded and competitive retail industry without effective marketing. **Marketing,** as defined by the American Marketing Association, is "the activity, set of institutions, and processes for creating, communicating, delivering, and exchanging offerings that have value for customers, clients, partners, and society at large." This definition emphasizes the importance of **value,** the difference between the perceived benefits received (to satisfy a want or need) and the perceived total price. The way a company prospers is by providing value through satisfying customers' needs.

PLANNING TIP

Marketing is all about creating, communicating, delivering, and exchanging offerings that provide value.

Thus, effective marketing covers everything the company is and does to consistently provide value to win customers and earn their ongoing loyalty, as Zappos has worked hard to do over the past decade. Every day brings new decisions about using marketing to profitably acquire, retain, and satisfy customers in a competitively superior way. Online

EXHIBIT 1.1 Marketing Zappos

businesses such as Zappos have the added complications of developing, updating, and operating a Web site; handling customer service; and managing order fulfillment as they work on all the other elements of marketing strategy. Still, marketers in any type of organization are most effective when they plan for marketing in a systematic way.

The Purpose of Marketing Planning

Marketing planning is the structured process of determining how to provide value to customers, the organization, and key stakeholders by researching and analyzing the current situation, including markets and customers; developing and documenting marketing's objectives, strategies, and programs; and implementing, evaluating, and controlling marketing activities to achieve the objectives. The outcome of this process is the **marketing plan,** a document covering a particular period that summarizes what the marketer has learned about the marketplace, what will be accomplished through marketing, and how.

PLANNING TIP

A structured process helps you identify, assess, and select appropriate marketing opportunities and strategies.

The purpose of marketing planning is to provide a disciplined yet flexible framework for guiding the company toward its value and relationship objectives. Because marketing managers are accountable for achieving results on time and within budget, the process must include milestones for tracking progress toward results and control mechanisms for tweaking tactics without abandoning sound long-term strategy. In fact, when the marketing environment is particularly challenging, "clarity of strategy becomes even more important," emphasizes strategy expert Michael Porter of Harvard.[2]

Marketing planning holds the key to customer understanding. Companies now recognize that they have to engage their customers and respond to their concerns, behavior, attitudes, and emotions in a timely way or risk losing their loyalty and goodwill. Tropicana, owned by PepsiCo, faced just such a situation when it recently introduced a new package design.

Tropicana. The marketing plan called for "modernizing" Tropicana's half-gallon container to communicate that the orange juice inside is fresh, pure, and contains no added sugar. "We wanted to create an emotional attachment by 'heroing' the juice and trumpeting the natural fruit goodness," Tropicana's president explained. After 30 specialists worked on the new packaging for five months, the company introduced it with an expensive multimedia ad campaign.

Loyal customers were outraged at the change, however, and bombarded Tropicana with complaints by phone, e-mail, and regular mail. Even worse, sales plunged 20 percent after the repackaging. "We underestimated the deep emotional bond" that loyal customers had with the original packaging, said Tropicana's president. "Those consumers are very important to us, so we responded." And quickly: Barely two months after its introduction, the new juice packaging was gone and the original packaging was back. The ads continued to emphasize the juice as "hero"—but with updates to reflect the packaging change.[3]

As Tropicana's experience indicates, no marketing plan is ever really final. Rather, you need to update and adapt your marketing plan as the market and customers' needs evolve and the organization's situation, priorities, and performance change. Although

Tropicana's marketing managers had done some consumer testing as they developed the new packaging, the flood of complaints from loyal customers was completely unexpected, as was the drop in sales. They also recognized that keeping the new packaging would only add to customer anger and very likely continue to hurt future sales.

Tropicana's managers didn't scrap the marketing plan or ignore the planning process when they received complaints about the new packaging. Instead, they used the feedback as input for further analyzing the current situation and deepening their understanding of customer behavior. Based on this new information, Tropicana fine-tuned its marketing plan by switching back to the original packaging and changing the advertising to be sure the product, not the packaging, was the "hero." Tropicana was back on track to achieve its objectives, as documented in its marketing plan.

Exhibit 1.2 illustrates the overall marketing planning process. As the exhibit indicates, the marketing plan resulting from this process should explain how the company will provide value, build relationships, and make a difference to its stakeholders. This exhibit also serves as an organizing figure for this handbook's coverage of how to develop a viable marketing plan, such as those used by Tropicana, Zappos, and other successful marketers.

Contents of a Marketing Plan

The best way for any organization to move toward its goals is to prepare and implement one marketing plan at a time, over and over. Start-ups, multinational corporations, and charitable foundations all need marketing plans to chart paths to their goals

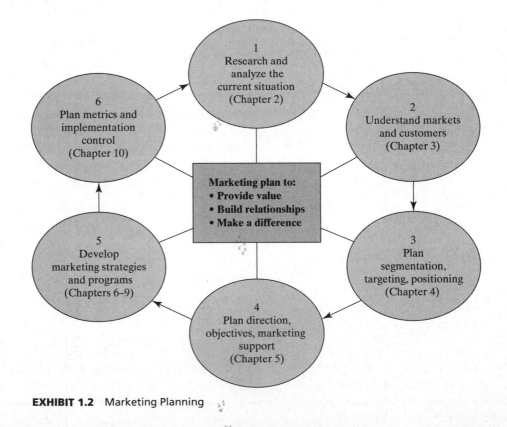

EXHIBIT 1.2   Marketing Planning

(whether defined by profits, donations, or people helped). A marketing plan is one of several official planning documents created by a company.

The company's strategic plan lays out the broad strategies for all units, divisions, and departments over a three- to five-year planning horizon. The business plan, which usually covers a one-year period, outlines the organization's overall financial objectives, including profit projections and funding requirements, and explains the overall strategy for achieving those objectives. It also describes all products and services, explains the marketing strategy, identifies key management personnel and their qualifications, and discusses the company's operations.

PLANNING TIP

Get a fresh perspective by creating a new plan every year rather than adapting last year's plan.

The marketing plan contains much more detail about the coming year's marketing strategy and implementation than is included in the business plan. Created at a lower level than either the business or the strategic plan, it provides shorter-term, specific operational direction for how the organization will use marketing to achieve the targeted results. Often a marketing plan is developed for the entire company; based on this, separate marketing plans may then be prepared for each product or line, new product introductions, each geographic area served, one-time projects, and so on.

Although the exact contents, length, and format may vary, most marketing plans contain the sections shown in Exhibit 1.3. The sample plans accompanying the *Marketing Plan Pro* software and the sample in the appendix show how a plan's contents and length differ depending on the organization and its purpose.

The executive summary is actually the final section to be written, because it serves as a brief overview of the plan's main points. The other sections are generally drafted in the order in which they appear in the plan, with each successive section building on the previous one. Managers can't prepare marketing budgets and schedules, for example, until their objectives, strategies, and action programs have been set. Note that when a company changes one part of the plan, it may have to change other parts as well (such as programs and budgets), because of the interrelated nature of the sections.

In the past, the marketing plan often was sequestered in the marketing department until it was reviewed by upper management, revised, and then distributed to sales and other departments. These days, however, the creation of a marketing plan involves organization-wide input and collaboration—sometimes including partners, suppliers, and customers. Electronics retailer Best Buy is a good example.

Best Buy. Best Buy's CEO and CMO (chief marketing officer) actively seek marketing ideas and reaction from managers and employees throughout the retail chain. The CEO visits stores to get inspiration for new store marketing and to discuss with salespeople how Best Buy can better differentiate itself from Walmart and other rivals. The CMO uses Twitter and his blog to discuss a wide variety of marketing questions with colleagues, customers, and the public. Once, he asked for comments on his SWOT analysis; another time, he requested comments about Best Buy's online marketing strategy. The company also consults partners when looking at sales trends and planning for expansion. In addition to building consensus and cooperation, this two-way flow of information provides valuable input for strategies and implementation at all levels. Careful marketing planning is one major reason why Best Buy has done well, while competitor Circuit City has gone out of business.[4]

Help!

This is in the DYS right?

EXHIBIT 1.3   Main Sections of a Marketing Plan

Section	Description
Executive summary	Reviews the plan's highlights and objectives, linking the marketing effort to higher-level strategies and goals.
Current marketing situation	Analyzes events and trends in the environment that can affect the organization, its marketing, and its stakeholders:
	• Internal situation (mission, resources, offerings, previous results, business relationships)
	• External situation (demographic, economic, ecological, technological, political-legal, social-cultural, competitive forces)
	• Market situation (market definition, market share, customer needs and behavior)
	• SWOT analysis of internal strengths and weaknesses, external opportunities and threats
Target market, customer analysis, positioning	Explains the segmentation, targeting, and positioning decisions. Also discusses the segments to be targeted, with an overview of customer and prospects' needs, wants, behavior, attitudes, loyalty, and purchasing patterns.
Objectives and issues	Outlines specific objectives, in three categories, to be achieved through the plan. Identifies any issues that may affect the organization's ability to achieve them.
	• Financial objectives
	• Marketing objectives
	• Societal objectives
Marketing strategy	Summarizes the overall strategy to be used in achieving marketing-plan objectives by creating, communicating, and delivering value to the target market.
Marketing programs	Lays out the programs supporting the marketing strategy, including specific activities, schedules, and responsibilities for:
	• Product
	• Pricing
	• Place (channels and distribution)
	• Promotion (marketing communications and influence)
	• Service
	• Internal marketing
Financial and operational plans	Financial and operational requirements and results related to marketing programs:
	• Expected revenues and profits
	• Projected budgets
	• Schedules and responsibilities
	• Additional information or resources needed for planning and implementation
Metrics and implementation control	Indicates how the plan will be implemented and evaluated, including metrics for performance measurement. Shows how and when adjustments will be made to keep plan on track toward objectives. Includes contingency plans as needed.

Larger organizations such as Yum Brands frequently require a marketing plan for each unit (e.g., individual stores or divisions) as well as for each product or brand. KFC, Pizza Hut, and Taco Bell are among the well-known fast-food brands in Yum's global empire, each following a different marketing plan for profitability. Pizza Hut, for instance, appeals to health-conscious consumers with pizza and other menu items made from all-natural ingredients. The company also has a separate marketing plan for expanding in Asian markets, where it has cooked up new dishes such as dough fritters to suit local tastes.[5]

The success of a marketing plan depends on a complex web of internal and external relationships as well as on uncontrollable environmental factors such as technological break-throughs and economic pressures. Unexpected or fast-developing circumstances can alter the environment so profoundly that even the most carefully crafted marketing plan must be revamped, as you saw in the case of Tropicana. Therefore, even after implementation has begun, marketing plans should be reexamined regularly in accordance with changes in competition, customers' needs and attitudes, product or company performance, and other factors.

DEVELOPING A MARKETING PLAN

Marketing plans generally cover a full year, although some (especially those covering new-product introductions) may project activities and anticipate results farther into the future. The marketing planning process starts several months before the marketing plan is scheduled to go into operation; this allows sufficient time for thorough research and analysis, management review and revision, and coordination of resources among departments and business units. Here's a peek at the marketing plan development of Florida's Costa Farms.

Costa Farms. This $230 million nursery company begins formulating its marketing plans more than a year in advance because it must allow for the growing season as well as the selling season of its plants. The company tracks daily sales of its 1,800 plant products to identify the most popular ones and to plan growing space and stock for the following year. It also tests dozens of new flower varieties every year for color, blooming time, hardiness, and other characteristics that matter to customers—and that must be factored into the next year's marketing plan.

Costa's marketers don't hesitate to revise a marketing plan when trends suggest new opportunities or challenges. For example, during the recent economic downturn, when some customers were reluctant to buy large, expensive orchids, the company began offering smaller, lower-priced orchids. It also developed new products such as window-sill planters for families newly interested in the financial and ecological benefits of growing their own fruits and vegetables. And it has been quick to take advantage of opportunities presented by technological developments, expanding its Web site and connecting with customers through YouTube and social networking sites.[6]

For long-term success, marketers need to strengthen relationships with their customers as well as suppliers, channel members, partners, and other key **stakeholders** (people and organizations that are influenced by or can influence company performance). Traditionally, companies kept up a monologue by sending information to stakeholders through advertisements and other promotion techniques. With a dialogue, however, information flows both ways—from the firm to its stakeholders and from stakeholders to the firm. Such a dialogue provides clues to what customers and other stakeholders think, feel, need, want, expect, and value, input that marketers need to adjust current programs and launch new programs based on a creative, practical, and adaptable marketing plan.

The following sections introduce each of the six marketing planning steps shown in Exhibit 1.2, providing an overview for the remainder of this handbook.

Research and Analyze the Current Situation

The first step is to study the current situation before charting the organization's marketing course for the coming year. Externally, marketers study environmental trends to detect demographic, economic, technological, political-legal, ecological, or social-cultural changes that can affect: marketing decisions; performance opportunities and threats; and potential profits. Marketing managers also assess the company's capabilities and the strategies of competitors so they can build on internal strengths while exploiting rivals' weaknesses and making the most of emerging opportunities. In addition, they analyze how customers, competitors, suppliers, distributors, partners, and other stakeholders might influence marketing results.

PLANNING TIP

This analysis helps you identify influences on your objectives, strategies, and performance.

Look at how Netflix's situation and its marketing plans have evolved over the years. When the company was founded in 1999 to rent movies by mail, its biggest competitor was Blockbuster. Today Blockbuster is still a factor, along with newer rivals such as Redbox, a self-service kiosk that rents DVDs for $1 per night, and Hulu.com, which airs TV episodes for free.

> **Netflix.** Netflix's first marketing plan called for customers to rent DVDs by mail, one at a time, with late fees for late returns. When the plan attracted few customers, the company switched to a no-deadline subscription program, with customers paying a flat monthly fee to have one or more of Netflix's 100,000 DVDs out at one time. Customers can also click to immediately watch movies on a computer screen or, if they own a game device such as the Xbox or Sony Playstation, on TV. Now Netflix, already highly profitable, is preparing to introduce subscriptions for online-only viewing at home. It currently serves 10 million subscribers, but with economic, social, and media trends favoring in-home viewing, its longer-term goal is to have 20 million customers by 2012.[7]

Chapter 2 contains more details on gathering and analyzing data to examine the organization's current situation and the issues and opportunities it may face.

Understand Markets and Customers

The second step in marketing planning is to analyze markets and customers (whether consumers or businesses) by researching market-share trends, product demand, and customer characteristics such as buying habits, needs, wants, attitudes and behavior, and satisfaction. Among the many questions to be studied are the following: Who is doing the buying, when, why, and how? Are buying patterns changing—and why? What products and categories are or will be in demand?

PLANNING TIP

These analyses help you decide which customers to target and how to provide value by meeting their needs.

Consider how McDonald's marketers have become expert at analyzing and responding to regional differences in customers' preferences.

> **McDonald's.** Over the years, McDonald's has become adept at adapting menu items to local tastes around the world: aloo tikka in Mumbai, kosher meats in Tel Aviv, and pork burgers in Beijing. It has also changed its menu to accommodate consumer interest in healthy eating. Its UK restaurants now serve low-salt fries, reduced-sugar hamburger buns, and organic milk. When economic worries sent consumers searching for low-priced upscale coffees, McDonald's met this new demand by expanding its McCafé espresso-based coffees to all 14,000 U.S. restaurants—which, in turn, boosted U.S. revenues and profits. In China, where McDonald's has been expanding, the company responded to changes in buying patterns by cutting some prices to stimulate more frequent purchasing.[8]

With cutting-edge technology, marketing managers can examine detailed customer buying behavior based on sales by product, by time and place, and other factors. Walmart uses sophisticated software to track each item in each store, determine how quickly it is selling (or not selling), what other items it is usually purchased with, and the likely revenue and profit consequences of cutting an item's price. Carphone Warehouse Group, a 2,400-unit chain of cell phone stores in Europe, checks sales every 15 minutes, so it can react quickly to problems or shift resources to better-performing areas.[9]

See Chapter 3 for more information about analyzing markets and customers.

Plan Segmentation, Targeting, and Positioning

Because organizations can never be all things to all people, marketers have to apply their knowledge of the market and customers to select groups within the market, known as **segments,** for marketing attention. In the past, this meant dividing the overall market into separate groupings of customers, based on characteristics such as age, gender, geography, needs, behavior, or other variables. With today's technology, however, some companies can now identify and serve segments as small as a single customer, based on what they know (or can find out) about that consumer or business.

PLANNING TIP

Use segmentation and targeting to focus on opportunities, then use positioning for competitive advantage.

The purpose of segmentation is to group customers with similar needs, wants, behavior, attitudes, or other characteristics that affect their demand for or usage of the good or service being marketed. Here's how Bank of the West uses segmentation.

> **Bank of the West.** This California-based bank, which operates in 19 states, identified a small but growing consumer segment in Kansas not being served by traditional banks: time-pressured factory workers, mainly immigrants, who need access to basic services like check-cashing. Therefore, the bank built a special ATM inside a local meatpacking plant so employees could cash checks and handle banking transactions in their free time. In California, the bank targets Asian Americans with a "Pacific Rim Banking" program offering services in English, Chinese, Japanese, and Korean. In addition, the bank has special programs to serve the banking and borrowing needs of small businesses and religious institutions in every market where it does business.[10]

Once the market has been segmented, the next set of decisions centers on **targeting,** including whether to market to one segment, several segments, or the entire market, and how to cover these segments. As the Bank of the West example shows, segmentation and targeting are vital in both consumer markets and **business-to-business (B2B) marketing**.

Next, the organization formulates suitable **positioning,** using marketing to create a competitively distinctive place (position) for the brand or product in the mind of targeted customers. This positioning sets the product apart from competing products in a way that is meaningful to customers. For example, Flip uses ease of use to differentiate its tiny camcorders; the European discount airline EasyJet promotes cheap fares to communicate its differentiation. To be effective in creating a particular image among targeted customers, companies must convey the positioning through every aspect of marketing. This is why Flip's Web site and packaging highlight the simplicity of product use, and EasyJet's Web site emphasizes ticket price rather than in-flight service. Chapter 4 discusses segmentation, targeting, and positioning in further detail.

Plan Direction, Objectives, and Marketing Support

Marketing managers are responsible for setting the direction of the organization's marketing activities, based on goals and objectives. **Goals** are long-term performance targets, whereas **objectives** are short-term targets that support the achievement of the goals. Setting and achieving shorter-term marketing, financial, and societal objectives will, over time, move the organization forward toward its overall goals, whatever they may be and however they may be expressed. Your marketing plan should include specific profit objectives, projected sales and revenues, expected expenses, and expected income. See the sample plans in *Marketing Plan Pro* for examples of how these financials are presented for different types of organizations.

PLANNING TIP

Be sure your objectives fit with the organization's overall mission and goals.

Most businesses use their marketing plans to support growth strategies, especially during economic expansions. As shown in Exhibit 1.4, growth can be achieved in six ways; in practice, some companies pursue growth through two or more of these methods.[11] For example, Boeing has developed new products (like the 787 Dreamliner jet) for its existing market of air carriers; in addition, it develops new configurations of current products (like the 737 jet) for new and existing markets. Note, however, that marketing an existing product (or variations on that product) is not as risky as marketing a new

Product Offers

Markets			
	Penetrate existing markets with current product offers	Modify current product offers for existing markets	Innovate product offers for existing markets
	Market current product offers in expanded geographic areas	Modify current product offers for dispersed markets	Innovate product offers geographically
	Expand current product offers to entirely new markets	Modify current product offers for entirely new markets	Diversify by innovating product offers for entirely new markets

EXHIBIT 1.4 Six Approaches to Growth

product or diversifying into other offerings.[12] Also, the chosen direction and objectives require marketing support, as discussed in later chapters.

Many organizations are adopting **sustainable marketing,** "the establishment, maintenance, and enhancement of customer relationships so that the objectives of the parties involved are met without compromising the ability of future generations to achieve their own objectives."[13] This requires balancing long-term goals with the short-term realities of current objectives and budgets. For example, PepsiCo recently stream-lined its production process to reduce the carbon footprint of making Walkers crackers. The idea was to make the process more eco-friendly without passing the cost along to consumers in the form of higher prices. In the long run, the change will actually save PepsiCo hundreds of thousands of dollars—as well as making the planet greener.[14] See Chapter 5 for more about planning direction and objectives.

Develop Marketing Strategies and Programs

The next step is to formulate strategies for providing value using the basic marketing-mix tools of product, place, price, and promotion, enhanced by service, to build stronger customer relationships and internal marketing to bolster support within the organization. Note that some companies can profit by developing a marketing mix for segments of one. Both Boeing and Airbus do this by adjusting the configuration of their jets, their product pricing, their delivery schedules, and their sales approach to the needs and buying cycle of each airline customer.

PLANNING TIP

Check that your strategies fit with segmentation, targeting, and positioning decisions.

Multinational firms often implement different marketing and media mixes for different countries and products, the way Honda does.

Honda. When Honda introduced the most recent redesign of its Insight gasoline–electric hybrid, it marketed the car differently in its home country of Japan and in the United States. In Japan, where the fuel-efficient Insight was first launched, it was positioned as an affordable, environmentally friendly compact car for city driving. Advance promotion built anticipation, and by the time the Insight was available, it was a hit. Instead of selling 5,000 units in the first month, Honda sold 15,000. This very positive reaction put momentum behind the Insight's entry into other markets.

In the United States, the new Insight made its debut on Earth Day to emphasize the car's environmental benefits. Knowing that Toyota's Prius has received considerable U.S. media attention, Honda supplemented conventional advertising with its first-ever product blog "to set the record straight" about the differences between the Insight and its closest competitor. Comments and questions posted on the blog helped Honda better understand U.S. consumers' attitudes and feelings, so it could adjust its marketing for this important market. Honda also continued a long-running campaign to communicate what the brand stands for through a series of short online films that focus "on our values as a company, the people who make up what Honda is about," according to the manager for corporate advertising.[15]

External marketing strategies are used to build relationships with suppliers, partners, and channel partners. Increasingly, marketers are leveraging three screens (TV, cell phone, and computer) in their marketing communications. Honda has done this with campaigns that combine text messaging, television ads, and online communications. Honda and other companies also develop an internal marketing strategy to build support among employees and managers, demonstrate marketing's value and importance to the organization, ensure proper staffing to carry out marketing programs, and motivate the proper level of customer service.

Chapter 5 contains a section on internal marketing and customer service; Chapter 6 covers product and brand strategy; Chapter 7 covers pricing strategy; Chapter 8 explores channels and logistics strategy; and Chapter 9 examines strategies for marketing communications and influence.

Plan Metrics and Implementation Control

Before the marketing plan is complete, you must plan to track progress toward objectives by identifying *metrics,* numerical measures of performance-related activities and outcomes. Many companies use specific financial measures to evaluate marketing outcomes; these may include return on marketing investment, return on sales, market share, and cost per customer acquired.[16] "Metrics vary from industry to industry, but one of the most crucial is 'cost per order' or 'cost per acquisition,'" says Google's central region managing director. He adds that "savvy marketers are zeroing in on the most cost-effective means of getting their message out."[17] Metrics are also applied to nonfinancial results, such as brand performance and customer loyalty.

PLANNING TIP

Use specific, realistic metrics to measure progress toward objectives.

By planning for metrics to compare actual outcomes against yearly, quarterly, monthly, weekly, daily, and even hourly projections of expected results, you will be able to see where the company is ahead or behind and where adjustments are needed to return to the right path. The Australian retailer David Jones tracks key metrics such as revenues and profit margin to gauge marketing performance. During the recent economic downturn, when competitors were slashing prices to get rid of excess inventory, David Jones rebalanced its product mix to focus on certain fashion categories that its customers liked best. This and other marketing changes helped the retailer improve both its revenues and its profit margin.[18]

Your plan must also show how implementation will be controlled. In the **marketing control** process, marketers measure interim performance of the planned programs against metrics, diagnose the results, and then take corrective action if results fail to measure up to expectations (see Exhibit 1.5). As an example, Malaysia Airlines calculates the daily and monthly profitability of every route it flies. Its managers compare that metric to projected results every day and implement short-term adjustments as needed.[19] Chapter 10 covers in more detail the topics of establishing metrics to measure progress and planning for implementation control.

Set marketing ⟶ Set standards ⟶ Measure ⟶ Diagnose results ⟶ Take corrective action
plan objectives   performance   if needed

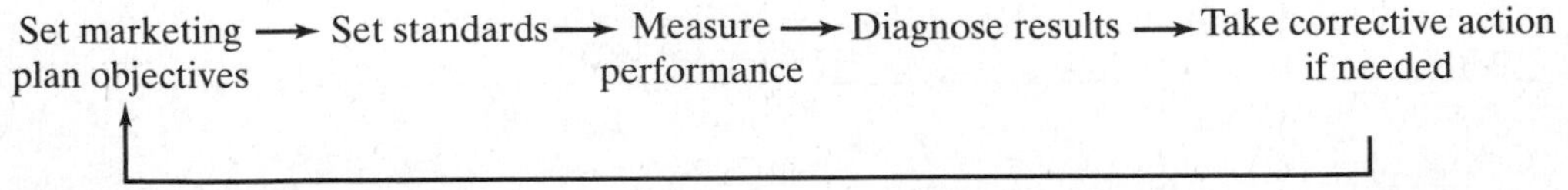

EXHIBIT 1.5 Marketing Control

PREPARING FOR MARKETING PLANNING

Considering the new urgency and the new possibilities for marketing planning, marketers need to understand and be ready to use any and all of the primary marketing tools, often called the marketing mix (or the four Ps). They must also be prepared to support the marketing mix with both service and internal marketing.

Primary Marketing Tools

Every marketing plan uses the four marketing-mix tools of product, pricing, place (channel), and promotion to create a unique blueprint for providing value, building relationships, and making a difference. Exhibit 1.6 shows some of the new and traditional marketing-mix elements that may be used in a marketing plan. Based on your marketing plan's objectives and marketing strategies, you will select specific elements and combine them to create a unique marketing mix for each product, brand, market, or customer segment.

PRODUCT OFFERING   Although the product can be either a tangible good or an intangible service, many offerings are actually a combination of tangibles and intangibles.[20] Intuit's product line shows how this works.

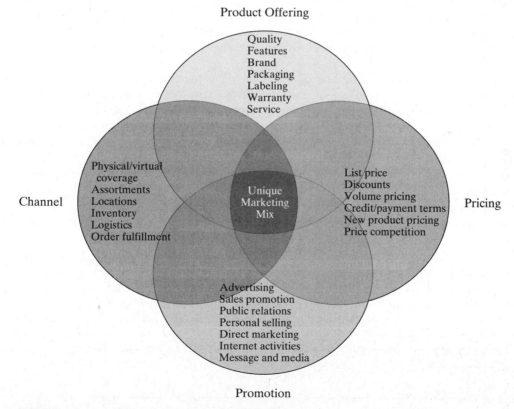

Product Offering

Quality
Features
Brand
Packaging
Labeling
Warranty
Service

Channel

Physical/virtual
  coverage
Assortments
Locations
Inventory
Logistics
Order fulfillment

Unique
Marketing
Mix

Pricing

List price
Discounts
Volume pricing
Credit/payment terms
New product pricing
Price competition

Advertising
Sales promotion
Public relations
Personal selling
Direct marketing
Internet activities
Message and media

Promotion

EXHIBIT 1.6 Combining Tools in the Marketing Mix

Intuit. Intuit offers a variety of software products for different customer segments. Its boxed versions of QuickBooks for small businesses and TurboTax for consumers, sold in stores, contain CDs for home installation. The company also offers intangible versions such as downloadable updates and online-only services. One way Intuit acquires new customers is by offering a free online-only version of TurboTax that consumers can use to calculate income taxes and file forms electronically. Many of these customers are so satisfied that they then buy the full-featured packaged version of this software. In addition, Intuit hosts online forums where customers can help each other with accounting and taxes, an intangible element that provides value as part of the product offering.[21]

In planning product strategy, think about all the components and about customers' perceptions of the offering as a whole. When ConAgra was cooking up Healthy Choice Café Steamers frozen meals, it learned that health-conscious customers were just as interested in convenience as they were in flavor. The company therefore developed an innovative package that can be microwaved to produce a healthy, tasty fresh-steamed meal. The product line was one of the most successful new food introductions of 2008 and continues to sell well.[22]

Branding is such an important aspect of the product offering that marketing plans must spell out how the company will support and evaluate brand performance.[23] In addition to manufacturers' national brands, many large retailers now market products under their own brands: Walmart has its Great Value brand, while rival Costco has its Kirkland brand.[24] In Great Britain, grocery chains Tesco and Sainsbury use their own brands to fend off competition from Aldi and other deep-discount retailers.[25]

PRICING   What should the organization charge for its product offering? Pricing decisions are based on a number of factors, including how customers perceive the value of the offering; how the organization positions the product; what the product's development, production, and distribution costs are; the competitive structure of the market; and the value that the organization expects to gain. Pricing can be so complex that companies such as General Electric and Home Depot use special software to set and change prices.[26] Technology is bringing new possibilities and new flexibility to pricing, as eBay, Orbitz, and other Web-based businesses have demonstrated.

Higher pricing can support an upscale image or better quality, but it also carries the risk that customers may perceive the price as too high relative to the product's perceived benefits. A low-price strategy can attract new customers, boost market share, and fend off rivals; however, it requires a careful balance between building relationships and building profits. At times, one competitor's pricing can upend an industry's pricing. During the economic crisis, the upscale retailer Saks Fifth Avenue suddenly slashed prices up to 70 percent on expensive designer apparel and accessories "to make sure the company survives," according to the CEO. Some competitors matched the discounts to avoid being stuck with unsold inventory; a few boutiques closed rather than sell at or below cost. Saks Fifth Avenue's CEO told *The Wall Street Journal* that one of the biggest questions being asked is this: "Will people ever buy at full price again?"[27]

CHANNEL   Channel (place) strategy involves decisions about how, when, and where to make goods and services available to customers. Many consumer products pass through one or more layers of wholesalers and retailers in the course of reaching buyers. Thus, manufacturers must check frequently with their channel partners to learn about customers' buying patterns, needs, and requests. "What happens in Ohio at Best Buy is going to be quite different [from what happens] at Dixons in Manchester [UK]," says the head of worldwide manufacturing for Cisco Systems, which makes networking equipment under the Linksys brand, among others.[28] Cisco also makes components and products for direct sale to business customers through a channel without wholesale or retail participation. Transportation, inventory management, and other logistics issues should be included in the channel strategy part of your marketing plan, as well.

PROMOTION Promotion covers all the tools used to communicate with and exert influence on the target market, including advertising, public relations, sales promotion, personal selling, and direct marketing techniques such as catalogs and e-mail. Because of media proliferation and audience fragmentation, some companies are putting less emphasis on mass media like network television and increasing their use of online marketing, mobile marketing (via cell phone), and social media such as YouTube. In fact, spending on ads displayed next to keyword search results on Google and other search sites has been growing at an annual rate of 20 percent.[29]

Of course, when using a variety of messages and media, you must carefully integrate and manage the overall content and impact of the communication campaign. Here's how the Tap Project is successfully engaging donors and raising money for UNICEF's safe water initiatives.

The Tap Project for UNICEF. Started in 2007, the Tap Project is an annual weeklong fundraiser that helps UNICEF expand activities to achieve its 2015 goal of halving the number of people worldwide with little or no access to safe drinking water. Participating restaurants ask customers to donate $1 for each glass of ordinary tap water served at the table. Restaurants receive posters, donation cards, and other marketing materials for staff and customer communication. UNICEF also engages donors through YouTube and Internet radio; free ads in national magazines; free ads on Web sites such as MapQuest.com; and free out-of-home ads in shopping malls, health clubs, and other outdoor locations. Although the media and graphics vary, the message is always the same: Donate $1 (or, in Japan, 100 yen) and give one child clean water for 40 days. Customers can even use cell phone text messages or click online to donate.[30]

Supporting the Marketing Mix

No marketing plan is complete without support strategies for customer service and internal marketing. Why is customer service so important? First, it reinforces positive perceptions of a brand, product, and company—and customers expect it (or even demand it). Second, as you know from your own experience, good service can clearly differentiate a company from competitors.

Third, poor or inconsistent customer service simply will not satisfy customers; even worse, customers are likely to tell others about their dissatisfaction, generating negative word-of-mouth communication.[31] And fourth, great service can help the organization retain current customers and bring in new ones through reputation and referral. The

PLANNING TIP

Remember that good internal relationships are a prerequisite to good customer service.

Zappos example earlier in this chapter illustrates the enormous power of high-quality customer service to strengthen customer loyalty and enhance reputation.

At the very least, your marketing plan should allow for handling customer inquiries and complaints; you may also need to cover installation (e.g., for appliances, floor coverings, or giant turbines), technical support (e.g., for computer products), and training (e.g., for software). Web-based FAQs and help indexes, e-mail, live text chat, live online telephony, and/or toll-free telephone contact are common customer service tactics. Bank of America, Dell, and UPS are a few of the growing number of firms that answer customer service questions through Twitter.[32]

The internal marketing strategy focuses all employees on serving customers and builds support for the marketing plan. Internal marketing can explain the marketing plan and its objectives, unify the organization's implementation efforts, and help employees understand their role in ensuring customer satisfaction (and service).[33]

Guiding Principles

Supplementing the marketing tools and support discussed earlier, you should apply four guiding principles for a marketing plan that will provide value, build relationships, and make a difference: (1) anticipate change, (2) engage everyone, (3) seek alliances, and (4) make marketing meaningful. These guiding principles, summarized in Exhibit 1.7, are explored in the following sections.

ANTICIPATE CHANGE The global economy is a fact of business life. With geographical distance less of an obstacle than ever before, marketers can easily enter new markets and connect with the best suppliers, partners, resellers, and deals—as can their competitors. As a result, marketers need to actively anticipate change

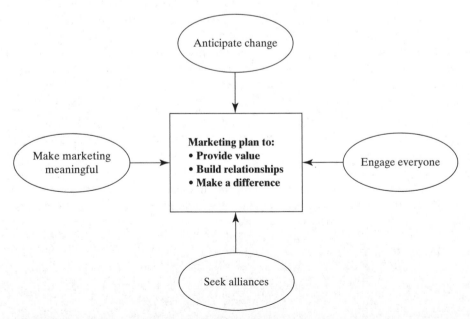

EXHIBIT 1.7 Guiding Principles of Marketing Planning

by constantly monitoring the environment for early warning signs of new trends that suggest potential opportunities and threats. They must also anticipate changes in resources and internal capabilities that will affect their ability to exploit new possibilities and effectively manage marketing plan implementation.

Learn to anticipate the short-term and long-term impact of significant environmental changes and react accordingly. Recently, when consumers worried about job security started cutting back on restaurant visits, the Cheesecake Factory chain quickly introduced a lower-priced value menu. To reinforce long-term loyalty, it also launched a reward program offering members a discount on future meals. Trio's Restaurant, in Ridgeland, Mississippi, reacted to the same economic situation by switching from formal to casual dining, revamping its menu to emphasize lower-priced entrees, and changing its name to Crab's Seafood Shack. Although the average customer check is lower, the restaurant will profit in the long run because it now serves three times as many customers as before.[34]

ENGAGE EVERYONE   At one time, marketing and sales personnel were the only people responsible for an organization's marketing functions. Now all employees must be engaged in marketing, and all contact points must be seen as opportunities to add value and strengthen customer relationships. Everything about the company sends a signal, so companies must project the right impression and meet customers' expectations through more than marketing. To keep employees actively engaged, they must be informed about products, promotions, and whatever else they need to satisfy customers. Many firms circulate printed or electronic newsletters, post news on internal Web sites or blogs, or send updates via e-mail or text messaging to keep employees informed. Keep this in mind as you prepare your marketing plan.

Organizations of all kinds are also paying special attention to customer engagement in their marketing plans. The online retailer Amazon.com was a pioneer in allowing customers to post product reviews, both good and bad. Now all kinds of marketers engage consumers and business customers by inviting product reviews and ratings. Many, such as Dell, Honda, and Marriott, engage customers through blogs where company bloggers post messages and respond to comments left by visitors. Dell aggressively seeks out online conversations that mention its brands (which number about 5,000 every day) and responds to as many comments as possible. It also started IdeaStorm.com to engage customers in conversations about new marketing ideas—conversations that often result in Dell tweaking its marketing plans.[35]

SEEK ALLIANCES   Successful marketers work through a network of alliances with carefully chosen suppliers, channel members, partners, customers, and community leaders (see Exhibit 1.8). The purpose is to provide the mutual support, capabilities, and innovations that participants need to satisfy their customers, meet their objectives, and be competitive. In essence, the company's network of alliances is in competition with the networks that rival companies have assembled.[36] Think about the value of making alliances as you get ready for your marketing plan.

PLANNING TIP

Seek out creative ideas and insights from customers, suppliers, and channel members.

- *Suppliers* not only provide raw materials, parts, and other inputs; they can offer insights regarding the external environment. Increasingly, companies are connecting with suppliers to lower costs and exchange data for mutual profitability. These alliances are critical because the quality of a product depends, in large part, on the quality of suppliers' materials. Walmart, for instance, holds regular supplier meetings to exchange information and coordinate marketing plans for specific products, geographic areas, and buying periods.

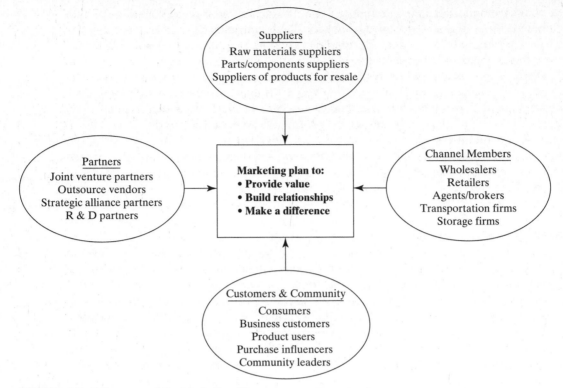

EXHIBIT 1.8 Alliances and the Marketing Plan

- *Channel members* such as wholesalers and retailers have daily contact with customers and can provide vital feedback about buying patterns and preferences. Channel choices are critical because customers associate the firm's brand and value with the quality and convenience of their shopping experience. Consumer products giant Procter & Gamble (P&G) stays in touch with channel members to learn about new consumer buying trends, solve distribution problems, and brainstorm product and packaging variations for mutual profit.
- *Partners* in joint ventures, outsourcing, or other arrangements contribute their core competencies and market knowledge. Linking with a partner that has complementary capabilities and strengths gives both more marketing power. For example, Hulu.com, a joint venture of several media companies, is a fast-growing video site where visitors can view episodes of TV shows that have appeared on partners' networks as well as entertainment from other sources. The joint venture will profit from moves such as selling commercial time at the start of videos.[37]
- *Customers* can be excellent partners because they are eager for products that solve their problems or, in the case of businesses, want to better serve their own customers. Procter & Gamble is an advertising customer of the online search engine Google. Not long ago, the two companies exchanged employees to spark new thinking on both sides. P&G personnel learned about social media and came away with ideas about Internet marketing. Google personnel learned about P&G's product management system and came away with insights to apply to their company's marketing strategy.[38]

- *Community* leaders from civic groups, charities, school groups, and other parts of the community can contribute feedback about the organization's image and activities and inform management thinking about social issues, local concerns, and sustainable marketing ideas. One example is Home Depot, which donates materials for community projects like playground construction and encourages employees to volunteer locally. Why is community involvement so important? "Things have become a lot more interdependent," says Home Depot's CEO. "There are a broader range of constituents." He also believes that community involvement is "just the right thing to do."[39]

MAKE MARKETING MEANINGFUL By definition, marketing has meaning because it satisfies customer needs. Yet certain types of advertising, among other marketing activities, are sometimes perceived as excessive, intrusive, or frivolous. Knowing that today's customers have so many choices, companies are increasingly formulating marketing plans that reflect their organizational values

PLANNING TIP

Think carefully about how your marketing plan can make a difference.

and that use marketing to make a difference to society. By serving a larger purpose—such as protecting the environment, helping the community, or saving endangered habitats—companies can counter negative perceptions, build a positive reputation, and earn the admiration of customers and other stakeholders.

Walmart has taken up this challenge and become a leader in eco-friendly marketing and operations. Although critics still disapprove of the retailer's labor practices and approach to competition, Walmart's aggressive strategy for going green has won praise and made a difference to the environment. The company has redesigned its stores for energy conservation; reduced its carbon footprint by streamlining its supply chain, revamping its transportation procedures, and reducing packaging; kept tons of waste out of landfills by recycling materials and slashing its use of plastic bags; and put a big marketing push on environmentally safe products. It's also adding sustainability labels to indicate the ecological impact of each product.[40]

Other companies are making marketing meaningful in their own ways, by aligning themselves with worthy causes such as raising awareness of health threats, providing volunteers for community cleanups, or donating products and money to fight world hunger. The search company Google promotes science and math education; the cosmetics firm Avon fights domestic violence. Whatever the cause, Michael Porter and his colleague Mark Kramer observe that the decision should be based on "whether it presents an opportunity to create shared value—that is, a meaningful benefit for society that is also valuable to the business."[41] As you prepare your marketing plan, think about how you can make marketing more meaningful for others as well as for your organization.

Summary

Marketing planning is the structured process of determining how to provide value to customers, the organization, and key stakeholders by researching and analyzing the current situation; developing and documenting marketing's objectives, strategies, and programs; and then implementing, evaluating, and controlling marketing activities to achieve the objectives. The purpose of marketing planning is to provide a disciplined yet flexible framework for guiding the company toward its value and relationship objectives.

The marketing plan documents the results of the marketing planning process and explains strategies and programs for providing value, building relationships, and making a difference. It also serves an important coordination function and allows for accountability by showing how results will be measured and adjustments made if needed. The marketing plan provides direction for employees and managers; encourages collaboration; outlines resource allocation; and delineates the tasks, schedules, and responsibilities planned to accomplish objectives.

The six broad steps in marketing planning are (1) research and analyze the current situation; (2) understand markets and customers; (3) plan segmentation, targeting, and positioning; (4) plan direction, objectives, and marketing support; (5) develop marketing strategies and programs; and (6) plan metrics and implementation control. Every marketing plan uses the four marketing-mix tools of product, pricing, place (channel), and promotion, supported by customer service and internal marketing, to create a unique blueprint for providing value, building relationships, and making a difference. Four guiding principles for marketing planning are to anticipate change, engage everyone, seek alliances, and make marketing meaningful.

Your Marketing Plan, Step by Step

Answer the following questions to take the first steps in preparing your marketing plan.

1. What good or service will you focus on in your marketing plan? If you are preparing a plan based on a real offering, choose one specific brand and product, such as the Toyota Prius car or Starbucks restaurants. Another option is to focus on a real company that offers one type of good or service, such as Netflix (movie rentals). If you are working on a marketing plan for your business or for a local business—or preparing a plan based on a hypothetical product—make your offer concrete by briefly describing the good or service, benefits, competition, and intended customers.

2. What background information is publicly available about your chosen product or product category? Refer to Exhibit 1.3 as you consider whether you will be able to gather sufficient research about competitors, customers, communications, pricing, and other details that a good marketing plan should cover. If a business has asked you to do a marketing plan for one or more products, ask to see historical data on sales, profit margin, pricing, distribution, results of promotions, and other relevant marketing details. (Bear in mind that some information may not be made available because the firm considers it proprietary.)

3. What sources will you use to gather information about your chosen product or category? List publications, associations, Web sites, and blogs that cover this industry; add any experts you might consult; and include your personal experience with this or similar goods or services. Watch for news stories, ad campaigns, and anything else that might spark interesting ideas as you begin formulating your marketing plan. Conduct an Internet search and bookmark sites with reliable sources of up-to-date facts and figures about the marketing situation for this product or company.

4. For idea starters, review several of the sample plans in the *Marketing Plan Pro* software bundled with this book. Read the executive summary, and note what kind of information is included in the situation analysis sections of each plan. Also browse the SonicSuperphone sample plan in this book's appendix before you dive into writing your own marketing plan.

Endnotes

1. Alissa Walker, "Zappos' Tony Hsieh on Twitter, Phone Calls, and the Pursuit of Happiness," *Fast Company,* March 16, 2009, http://www.fastcompany.com/blog/alissa-walker/member-blog/tony-hsiehs-zapposcom; Sharon Gaudin, "Web 2.0 Tools Like Twitter, Facebook Can Foster Growth in Hard Times," *Computerworld,* March 13, 2009, www.computerworld.com; Jeffrey M. O'Brien, "Zappos Knows How to Kick It," *Fortune,* February 2, 2009, pp. 54+.

2. "Sound Long-Term Strategy Is Key, Particularly in a Crisis: Harvard's Michael Porter," *INSEAD Knowledge,* October 2008, http://knowledge.insead.edu.

3. Natalie Zmuda, "Tropicana Line's Sales Plunge 20% Post-Rebranding," *Advertising Age,* April 2, 2009, http://adage.com/article?article_id=135735; Stuart Elliott, "Q & A with Stuart Elliott," *New York Times,* March 2, 2009, http://www.nytimes.com/2009/03/02/business/media/02adnewsletter2.html; Stuart Elliott, "Tropicana Discovers Some Buyers Are Passionate About Packaging," *New York Times,* February 22, 2009, www.nytimes.com; Kenneth Hein, "Tropicana Squeezes Out Fresh Design with a Peel," *Brandweek,* January 19, 2009, p. S30.

4. Kenneth Hein, "Why Best Buy's CMO Sicced His Blue Shirts on Twitter," *Brandweek,* October 31, 2009, www.brandweek.com; Miguel Bustillo, "Best Buy Confronts Newer Nemesis," *Wall Street Journal,* March 16, 2009, p. B1; Miguel Bustillo, "Big-Box Retailer Goes Little," *Wall Street Journal,* February 12, 2009, p. B8; Arundhati Parmar, "General Mills, Best Buy Among Companies Using 'Crowdsourcing' Sites to Foster Innovation," *Finance and Commerce Daily Newspaper,* March 10, 2009, n.p.

5. Karen Cho, "KFC China's Recipe for Success," *INSEAD Knowledge,* March 2009, http://knowledge.insead.edu; Elaine Wong, "'The Hut' Gives Pizza a Healthier Spin: Q&A Dialogue with Brian Niccol," *Brandweek,* March 9, 2009, p. 8.

6. George Tasker, "Costa Nursery Farms Expands Marketing Plan," *Miami Herald,* March 2, 2009, www.herald.com.

7. Alex Pham, "Coming Soon to a Playstation 3 Near You," *Los Angeles Times,* October 26, 2009, http://latimesblogs.latimes.com/technology/2009; "Netflix to Offer Streaming-Only Movie Service," *InformationWeek,* February 26, 2009, www.informationweek.com; Ken Belson, "As DVD Sales Slow, the Hunt Is On for a New Cash Cow," *New York Times,* June 13, 2006, p. C1+; Christopher Null, "How Netflix Is Fixing Hollywood," *Business 2.0,* July 2003, pp. 41–43.

8. Paul Ziobro, "McDonald's Profit Rises 5.9%," *Wall Street Journal,* October 22, 2009, www.wsj.com; Tom Sellen, "Coffee Connoisseurs Sniff Out Cheaper, No-Frills Fix," *Wall Street Journal,* March 16, 2009, p. C6; Dominic Walsh, "British Beef, Reduced Salt, Lower Sugar, Free Range Eggs, Roast Coffee—Is This Really McDonald's?" *The Times (London),* March 9,

2009, http://business.timesonline.co.uk; Martin Fackler, "Will Ratatouille Bring Japanese to McDonald's?" *Wall Street Journal,* August 14, 2003, pp. B1, B5.

9. Maureen Tkacik, "Markdown-onomics," *New York,* January 23, 2006, pp. 38+; Jeanette Borzo, "Get the Picture," *Wall Street Journal Europe,* January 16, 2004, pp. R2+; George Anders, "Why Real-Time Business Takes Real Time," *Fast Company,* July 2001, pp. 158–161.

10. Rachel Zoll, "Boom-years Borrowing Hits Churches," *Associated Press,* March 14, 2009, n.p.; Garance Burke, "Banks Tailor Products for Latino Immigrants," *Marketing News,* April 1, 2006, p. 37; www.bankofthewest.com.

11. See Philip Kotler and Kevin Lane Keller, *Marketing Management,* 13th ed. (Upper Saddle River, NJ: Pearson Prentice Hall, 2009), Chapter 2; and Alan R. Andreasen and Philip Kotler, *Strategic Marketing for Non-Profit Organizations,* 6th ed. (Upper Saddle River, NJ: Prentice Hall, 2003), pp. 80–82.

12. George S. Day, "Feeding the Growth Strategy," *Marketing Management,* November–December 2003, pp. 15+.

13. Frances Brassington and Stephen Pettitt, *Principles of Marketing,* 3rd ed. (Harlow, Essex, UK: Financial Times Prentice Hall, 2003), p. 19.

14. Jo Roberts, "Sustainability: It Need Not Cost the Earth," *Marketing Week,* February 19, 2009, p. 16.

15. Philip Nussel, "Ford, Honda Vie for 2nd Place in US Hybrid Sales," *Automotive News,* October 15, 2009, www.autonews.com; Ian Rowley, "Toyota, Honda Heat Up the Hybrid War," *BusinessWeek,* March 27, 2009, www.businessweek.com; Ian Rowley, "Honda CEO Fukui Steps Aside," *BusinessWeek Online,* February 24, 2009, www.businessweek.com; Hans Greimel, "As Losses Mount, No Bold Plan at Toyota," *Automotive News,* March 2, 2009, p. 1; Stuart Elliott, "For the Honda Brand, a Cinematic Stroke," *New York Times,* January 12, 2009, www.nytimes.com.

16. See Paul W. Farris, Neil T. Bendle, Phillip E. Pfeifer, and David J. Reibstein, *Marketing Metrics: 50+ Metrics Every Executive Should Master* (Upper Saddle River, NJ: Wharton School Publishing, 2006), Chapter 1.

17. Michael Krauss, "Which Metrics Matter Most?" *Marketing News,* February 28, 2009, p. 20.

18. Terry McCrann, "Mark McInnes Ensures There's No Other Store Like David Jones," *Herald Sun*

(Australia), March 19, 2009, www.news.com.au/heraldsun.

19. Alex Dichter, Fredrik Lind, and Seelan Singham, "Turning Around a Struggling Airline," *McKinsey Quarterly,* November 2008, www.mckinseyquarterly.com.

20. See "Model of Exchange Shifts Towards Services," *Marketing News,* January 15, 2004, p. 25.

21. Janet Paskin, "Can Intuit Handle Taxing Times?" *Smart Money,* February 12, 2009, www.smartmoney.com.

22. Elaine Wong, "New Products Boost ConAgra's Sales," *Brandweek,* March 26, 2009, www.brandweek.com; Elaine Wong, "After Much R&D, ConAgra Gets Totally Steamed Up," *Brandweek,* November 3, 2008, p. 15.

23. For brand metrics, see Donald R. Lehmann, Kevin Lane Keller, and John U. Farley, "The Structure of Survey-Based Brand Metrics," *Journal of International Marketing,* vol. 16, no. 4, 2008, pp. 19–56.

24. Ann Zimmerman, "Walmart Boosts Private Label to Court Thriftier Consumers," *Wall Street Journal,* March 17, 2009, www.wsj.com.

25. Ruki Sayid, "Be a Canny Consumer and Make Big Savings with Supermarket Own Brands," *Mirror (London),* January 4, 2009, www.mirror.co.uk.

26. Julie Schlosser, "Markdown Lowdown," *Fortune,* January 12, 2004, p. 40; "Zilliant," *Fortune,* November 24, 2003, p. 210.

27. Vanessa O'Connell and Rachel Dodes, "Saks Upends Luxury Market with Strategy to Slash Prices," *Wall Street Journal,* February 9, 2009, www.wsj.com.

28. "Manufacturing Complexity," *The Economist,* June 17, 2006, pp. 6–9.

29. Emily Steel, "Spending on Internet Advertising Starts to Cool," *Wall Street Journal,* March 30, 2009, www.wsj.com.

30. Louis Llovio, "Richmond Restaurants Participate in UNICEF's Tap Project," *Richmond Times-Dispatch,* March 21, 2009, www.timesdispatch.

com; Mariko Kato, "Tokyo-Area Restaurants Join Africa Water Drive," *Japan Times,* March 19, 2009, www.japantimes.co.jp; Stephanie Green, "Diners Fund Safe Water," *Washington Times,* March 25, 2009, p. B10, www.tapproject.org.

31. Jane Spencer, "Cases of 'Customer Rage' Mount as Bad Service Prompts Venting," *Wall Street Journal,* September 17, 2003, pp. D4+.

32. "Better Living Through Twitter," *Wall Street Journal Wallet Blog,* February 23, 2009, http://blogs.wsj.com/wallet/2009/02/23/better-living-through-twitter.

33. Chris Checco, Larry Mosiman, and Scott Radcliff, "Ending Internal Marketing Conflict," *DM News,* September 3, 2008, www.dmnews.com.

34. Megan Rowe, "Trendspotting: What's Hot for '09," *Restaurant Hospitality,* January 2009, p. 24.

35. David Greenfield, "From Idea to Innovation," *Network Computing,* April 9, 2009, http://networkcomputing.in/From-Idea-To-Innovation-001Apr009.aspx; Erin Nelson, "Online: An Essential Path to Igniting Brand Passion," *Forbes,* March 26, 2009, www.forbes.com.

36. See Philip Kotler and Kevin Keller, *Marketing Management,* 13th ed. (Upper Saddle River, NJ: Pearson Prentice Hall, 2009), Chapter 2.

37. Brad Stone and Brian Stelter, "ABC to Add Its Shows to Videos on Hulu," *New York Times,* May 1, 2009, www.nytimes.com; Douglas MacMillan, "Hulu Attracts Crowds but Not Ads," *BusinessWeek,* March 31, 2009, www.businessweek.com.

38. Ellen Byron, "A New Odd Couple," *Wall Street Journal,* November 19, 2008, www.wsj.com.

39. Brian Grow, "The Debate Over Doing Good," *BusinessWeek,* August 15, 2006, pp. 76+.

40. "Can Walmart Be Sustainable?" *New York Times,* August 7, 2009, p. A18; "From Bad to Great," *The Economist,* November 29, 2008, p. 70.

41. Michael E. Porter and Mark R. Kramer, "Strategy & Society," *Harvard Business Review*, December 2006, p. 6.

2   Analyzing the Current Situation

In this chapter:

PREVIEW

Rapid and sometimes profound change is the norm in today's marketing environment. As a marketer, you have to constantly scan the environment to identify, monitor, and interpret the forces and trends that affect your marketing and your markets. Only by analyzing your current situation—the first step in the marketing planning process—can you set the stage for a marketing plan that will provide value, build relationships, and make a difference. Over time, you'll gain the experience and knowledge to recognize early signs of changes in the marketing environment and think through the consequences for your planned marketing activities.

In this chapter, you'll learn about scanning the internal environment, including the organization's mission, resources, product offerings, previous results, business relationships, keys to success, and warning signs. You'll also learn about examining the external environment, including demographic, economic, ecological, technological, political-legal, and social-cultural trends, as well as competitor analysis. The results of your internal and external monitoring come together in a SWOT (strength, weakness, opportunity, and threat) analysis that sets the stage for marketing decisions. Environmental scanning and analysis constitute Step 1 in the marketing planning process (see Exhibit 2.1).

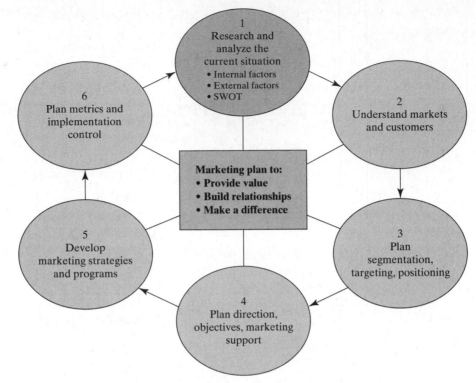

EXHIBIT 2.1 Marketing Planning: Step 1

APPLYING YOUR KNOWLEDGE

This is a good time to set up the structure of your marketing plan so you can document the outcome of your environmental scanning and analysis efforts. Use the *Marketing Plan Pro* software bundled with this book to create your plan or prepare a written plan following the outline shown in Exhibit 1.3 and the sample plan in the appendix. Answering the questions in "Your Marketing Plan, Step by Step," at the end of this chapter will help you navigate the scanning and analysis process. Also see this chapter's checklist, which includes key questions to ask as you examine your current marketing situation.

CHAPTER 2 CHECKLIST   Your Current Situation

To analyze the marketing environment for planning purposes, examine these two sets of factors:

Internal Factors

✔ What is the organization's mission, and how will my marketing plan support it?
✔ What human, financial, informational, and supply resources can I count on for my marketing plan?
✔ What company products, results, and relationships must I consider in my marketing plan?

✔ What critical elements could make the difference between good and poor marketing performance?

✔ What critical warning signs might signal potential marketing problems?

✔ What strengths and weaknesses do internal factors represent for my organization?

External Factors

✔ What are the most important demographic, ecological, technological, political-legal, and social-cultural trends affecting my brands and my customers?

✔ How are local, regional, national, and global economic trends likely to affect my marketing plan?

✔ What are the latest competitive trends, and which ones require immediate marketing attention?

✔ Which industries and companies might present future competition?

✔ How quickly are changes occurring in the external environment?

✔ What opportunities and threats do external factors pose for my organization?

✔ What risks would my organization be willing to accept when dealing with these opportunities and threats?

ENVIRONMENTAL SCANNING AND ANALYSIS TODAY

To formulate a flexible and practical marketing plan, you need to monitor key factors in the **macroenvironment** that can affect the marketplace and marketing performance. These include broad demographic, economic, ecological, technological, political-legal, and social-cultural forces.

In addition, you have to examine specific groups in the **microenvironment** that more directly influence marketing activities and performance, such as customers, competitors, channel members, partners, suppliers, and employees. Because the marketing environment is more dynamic than in the past, this part of the planning process has assumed a new sense of urgency.

Some marketers watch the environment in a passive way, taking note when they find a development that seems relevant to what the company is doing or that could signal a competitor's next move. However, the best marketers actively scan for environmental developments at all times, not just when writing a market plan. This helps them envision many possibilities as well

PLANNING TIP

Scan the environment actively and constantly for new developments.

as answer specific questions that shape the implementation of the current marketing plan, such as "What emerging technology might replace our business?" and "How might changes in online buying behavior affect demand and competition for our products?"

Consider how Nintendo's marketers examine the environment, interpret emerging trends, and plan to fend off threats while exploiting profit opportunities.

Nintendo. Just a few years ago, demand for the Nintendo Wii video game console was so strong that it outstripped supply for two consecutive holiday buying seasons. The handheld Nintendo DS was also a hot item for holiday gift giving. By wooing women and older consumers, two segments not traditionally associated with video games, Nintendo fought its way to the top of the video game industry, outselling rivals Sony and Microsoft.

Then Nintendo's marketers spotted environmental changes in the works. Sony's PlayStation had begun outselling the Wii in Japan, a market that is both lucrative and viewed as a leading-edge indicator of consumer trends worldwide. Nintendo's marketers also saw that consumers were increasingly interested in playing games online and on smartphones, a change that could threaten sales of game consoles. In response, Nintendo introduced Web-enabled DS models and has been testing online interactive entertainment. Internally, the company has increased manufacturing efficiency to improve profit margins and has stepped up development of a wider range of products for the entire family.[1]

Nintendo's marketers recognize that in the fast-moving video game industry, any marketing plan can quickly become outdated. So they actively scan the environment at all times, rather than relying on a once-yearly situation analysis. Although the Wii and the DS have been big hits for Nintendo, its marketers are alert to even subtle changes in technology, consumer behavior, and competition. Will smartphones become the handheld game device of choice, displacing the DS? Will consumers want to download videos using game devices? What new consoles and games are being introduced by Microsoft and Sony? Nintendo's marketers watch the environment so they can adjust their plans for future profit.

SWOT Analysis

PLANNING TIP

Be aware that one firm's strength may be another firm's weakness.

Through *environmental scanning and analysis,* you'll collect and examine data about environmental forces to better understand your company's strengths, weaknesses, opportunities, and threats.

- *Strengths* are internal capabilities that can help the firm achieve its goals and objectives. For a cell phone manufacturer, strengths might include design and engineering expertise, a well-known brand, and production efficiency. Remember that a company need not actually possess the strengths—it must have clear *access* to the strengths, through alliances or other means.
- *Weaknesses* are internal factors that can prevent the firm from achieving its goals and objectives. For a catalog company, weaknesses might include an outdated order fulfillment system, inadequate access to credit for buying products from wholesalers, and an inexperienced management team.
- *Opportunities* are external circumstances that the organization might be able to exploit for higher performance. As an example, increased media and regulatory attention to water contamination issues might present an opportunity for a maker of water-filtering equipment. Under conditions of uncertainty, as when the economy is very unpredictable, marketers may evaluate opportunities in terms of acceptable risk, instead of looking only for the most attractive profit or market-share potential.[2]
- *Threats* are external circumstances, outside the organization's direct control, that might hurt its performance now or in the future. For a family restaurant seeking to expand, threats could include increased competition, higher food costs, and high borrowing costs. Threats may be countered, but because they are not under the company's direct control, they can't be entirely eliminated.

EXHIBIT 2.2 Hypothetical SWOT Analysis for Southwest Airlines

Strengths	*Weaknesses*
(Internal capabilities that can help firm achieve marketing plan objectives)	*(Internal factors that might prevent firm from achieving objectives)*
1. Financial control and stability 2. Experienced, enthusiastic employees	1. Service limited to U.S. destinations 2. Offerings not diversified
Opportunities	*Threats*
(External circumstances that can be exploited to achieve objectives)	*(External circumstances that might prevent firm from achieving marketing plan objectives)*
1. Competitors cutting flights and services 2. Airport expansion plans	1. Rapid rise in fuel costs 2. Severe economic downturn

A **SWOT analysis** shows the strengths, weaknesses, opportunities, and threats of your organization. This helps you understand your company's strengths, which you can exploit through marketing, and prepare to defend against vulnerabilities that competitors might use against you. It's also a good way to analyze external factors that might pose opportunities for profit and threats that might prevent your marketing plan from being successful.

PLANNING TIP

See how strengths fit with opportunities for providing value, building relationships, and making a difference.

The outcome should be a grid like Exhibit 2.2, which will become an important part of your marketing plan. This exhibit shows a brief hypothetical SWOT for Southwest Airlines. Also see the sample SWOT analysis in the appendix for another view of how this grid looks. Ideally, you should conduct a SWOT analysis of each major competitor (and key would-be competitors) to examine the possible influence on your marketing situation, the overall industry, and the overall market.

Evaluating Strengths and Weaknesses

How do you know what is a significant strength and what is a significant weakness? Exhibit 2.3 shows four criteria to be used in making this determination as you sift through the results of your environmental scans and create a SWOT analysis grid.

EXHIBIT 2.3 Judging Organizational Strengths and Weaknesses

Consider the strengths of Google, which have had a significant effect on the company's marketing plans over the years.

Google. One of Google's main strengths is its organizational bias toward quickly developing and launching many new products—and just as quickly dropping those that don't live up to preset criteria. The company encourages its engineers to spend up to 20 percent of their time on projects of their own choosing. This is how Google Earth and Gmail got their start. On the other hand, Google let Lively (a virtual world similar to Second Life) live only four months because it attracted relatively few users. Google's top managers recognize that speed and decisiveness are competitive strengths in the fast-moving digital world.[3]

ANALYZING THE INTERNAL ENVIRONMENT

PLANNING TIP

This analysis gives you the background to set objectives, target customers, and create appropriate strategies for providing value.

Given the new urgency of marketing planning, it's more important than ever to conduct a scan of the internal environment. Look at your organization's overall mission, which provides direction for marketing planning efforts. Also review the organization's resources, offerings, previous results, business relationships, keys to success, and warning signs that may point to significant changes ahead (see Exhibit 2.4).

Mission

The **mission** states the fundamental purpose of a company, nonprofit organization, or governmental agency—its core ideology, in the terminology of Collins and Porras—defining its focus, indicating how it will provide value, and outlining its envisioned future. A statement of mission is important because it helps align strategy, resources, and activities as managers and employees work toward the organization's future.[4] The mission is also "a promise the company makes to its employees," says Jeffrey Abrahams, author of *The Mission Statement Book.* "That promise becomes an integral part of the branding of the company."[5]

Whether long or short, a mission statement should be specific enough to give direction to those involved in marketing planning and implementation throughout the organization. It also suggests how the organization will make a difference. Exhibit 2.5 shows the mission statements of several different types of organizations. Notice how the Target mission, for instance, mentions outstanding value, continuous innovation, and exceptional guest (shopper) experience. The retail chain's marketers understand that their plans must

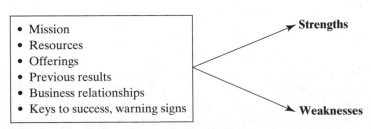

EXHIBIT 2.4 Analyzing the Internal Environment

EXHIBIT 2.5 Mission Statements

Organization	Type of Business	Mission
Target	Retailer	To make Target the preferred shopping destination for guests by delivering outstanding value, continuous innovation, and an exceptional guest experience by consistently fulfilling our "Expect More, Pay Less" brand promise.
Southwest Airlines	Airline	Dedication to the highest quality of customer service delivered with a sense of warmth, friendliness, individual pride, and company spirit.
Terex	Heavy equipment manufacturer	To delight our current and future construction, infrastructure, mining, and other customers with value added offerings that exceed their current and future needs.
Brooklyn Public Library	Municipal library	To ensure the preservation and transmission of society's knowledge, history and culture, and to provide the people of Brooklyn with free and open access to information for education, recreation, and reference.
Guggenheim Foundation	Nonprofit cultural organization	To promote the understanding and appreciation of art, architecture, and other manifestations of visual culture, primarily of the modern and contemporary periods, and to collect, conserve, and study the art of our time.

Sources: www.target.com; www.southwest.com; www.terex.com; www.brooklynpubliclibrary.org; www.guggenheim.org.

support and bring this mission to life in the stores and on the company's Web site. Through its value, innovation, and guest experience, Target aims to make a difference in the lives of its customers.

Resources

Next, look at the resources the organization has available to it or has the ability to obtain, including human, financial, informational, and supply resources. No company has access to unlimited resources; therefore, management must carefully balance resource allocation to ensure successful performance. Some questions to ask in examining internal resources include the following:

- *Human resources:* Does the workforce have the needed education, skills, and training? Do managers have the initiative and entrepreneurial drive to support the mission? Is the company using recruitment and training to prepare itself for the future? Is morale high or low? Is turnover high or low? If applicable, what is the state of relations with unionized workers and their leaders?
- *Financial resources:* Does the company have the capital (or access to capital) to support marketing and achieve its objectives? What funding issues must be addressed over the period covered by the marketing plan? Will the company or nonprofit organization have the financial strength to implement all planned activities, or should activities be phased in as financing becomes available?

PLANNING TIP

Check that you'll have sufficient resources to implement onetime and multiyear marketing programs.

- *Informational resources:* Does the company have the data needed to understand its customers and the marketplace? What informational sources are available to support marketing planning, implementation, and control? Who in the organization is responsible for ensuring that informational resources are in place when needed?
- *Supply resources:* Does the company have (or can it obtain) steady and affordable supplies of parts, components, materials, and services needed for operations and production? Are its suppliers stable and committed to the organization? What new suppliers are emerging, and what new capabilities do they offer that will benefit the organization?

Resource availability is critical for performance in every industry. Sometimes companies can arrange external sources or supplement existing resources through new strategic alliances, new supply-chain relationships, or short-term substitutions. Shortages force marketers to change their plans, as happened during a recent period of maple syrup shortage.

Maple Syrup Shortage. Vermont restaurants count on a stable and affordable local supply of maple syrup, because customers know the state's reputation for high-quality syrup. When unfavorable weather hurt production not long ago, restaurants faced limited supplies and sky-high prices for good syrup. In response, one family restaurant drastically reduced the amount of syrup it serves, rather than switch to a substitute or drop syrup from the menu. IHOP's first Vermont restaurant took a different approach. Although IHOP offers customers a choice of four flavored corn-syrup toppings without charge, the Vermont restaurant is the only unit in the chain to serve real maple syrup on request. However, because the shortage has driven wholesale prices up, this IHOP will charge 99 cents per packet for its maple syrup.[6]

Offerings

This part of the analysis examines what the organization is currently offering in the way of goods and services. If information is available, look at the product mix and the lines within that mix, asking questions such as the following: What products are being offered, at what price points, and for what customer segments? What value does each product provide by solving a customer's problem or fulfilling a need? What is the age of each product, and what are its sales, profit, and share trends over time? How does each product support sales of the line—are some sold only as supplements or add-ons to others? How does each product contribute to the company's overall performance? Does one product account for a large portion of sales and profits?

Also determine whether the company's products are keeping up with movement in the category. That's critical, as Palm found out.

Palm. In 1996, the Palm Pilot was a breakthrough product in the personal digital assistant (PDA) product category. However, a growing number of customers are replacing their PDAs with smartphones—cell phones that double as handheld computing and

Web access devices. Unfortunately, Palm failed to anticipate the speed with which the iPhone and other smartphones would overtake PDAs. Its development of an advanced smartphone product, the Pre, lagged on for two years after the iPhone debuted—even as sales of Palm's other products trended downward. Can Palm refresh its product offerings and regain strength before competitors take over the product category?[7]

Marketers should also determine how their organization's offerings relate to its mission and to its resources. Do the products use the firm's resources most effectively and efficiently while following the mission? Are other offerings needed to restore the focus or fulfill the long-term purpose described in the mission? Answering these questions helps you assess internal strengths and weaknesses in preparation for future marketing activities.

Previous Results

The company's previous results also offer important clues to internal factors and trends that can affect results. By analyzing the previous year's sales, profits, and other financial results—and comparing these results with trends over several years—you can get a big picture of overall performance. Analyze the results of the previous years' marketing programs to see what worked and what did not. If exact figures aren't readily available, look at percentage increases and decreases to understand the trends in the business.

Among the questions to ask are the following: Which products did well over the past year, and which did not? Which communications drew the best response? Which channels were responsible for the most sales? How did price changes affect results? What are the most recent trends in results? The point is to separate effective from ineffective activities and to understand how well marketing has performed in the past as a prelude to planning marketing programs for the future.

PLANNING TIP

Put results into context by examining how environmental factors influenced the firm's performance.

Business Relationships

A closer look at relationships with suppliers, distributors, and partners can help determine whether changes should be made in the coming year. Although cost is always a critical factor, companies must also ask whether their suppliers and distributors (1) have the capacity to increase volume if needed, (2) maintain a suitable quality level, and (3) can be true partners in providing value to satisfy customers. How has the roster of suppliers and dealers changed over time? Is the company overly dependent on one supplier, channel member, or partner? Does the company expect its partners to provide special expertise or services?

Business relationships can be a vital strength for a young organization's marketing plan, as Michael Welch found out when he founded Blackcircles:

Blackcircles. Founder Michael Welch studied the market and worked in the industry before starting Blackcircles, based in Edinburgh, Scotland, to market car and truck tires online for less. Although he had many contacts with tire suppliers, he needed a roster of local garages to mount the tires for his buyers. "I wanted to give customers an online proposition, so they could choose the tires, choose the garage, choose the time and date, pay, and just turn up and get the tires fitted," Welch remembers. One by one, the entrepreneur forged relationships with 900 garages across the United Kingdom and began promoting Blackcircles through relationships with the Tesco grocery chain and other large firms. This emphasis on business relationships has helped Blackcircles grow annual sales to more than $20 million.[8]

Keys to Success and Warning Signs

Not everything in a marketing plan is equally important. Marketers should identify, in just a few sentences, the special factors that most influence the firm's movement toward fulfilling its mission and achieving superior performance. Pinpointing these keys to success can put the focus on the right priorities in planning the year's marketing strategies and programs. For example, Apple's keys to success are (1) design savvy, (2) technological innovation, and (3) brand image. The combination of these three elements has propelled the company to success in smartphones, computers, and digital entertainment players.

Every organization should scan for the major warning signs that indicate potential problems with leveraging the keys to success and performing as planned. For Apple, one such issue might be a technological advance that could make its iPhone or iPod obsolete. Other possible warning signs for Apple might be government regulations that affect technology standards and quality problems that could tarnish the brand image. Paying close attention to these issues will help Apple's marketers plan to reach their objectives.

ANALYZING THE EXTERNAL ENVIRONMENT

Within the external environment, marketers need to examine broad demographic, economic, ecological, technological, political-legal, and social-cultural trends (see Exhibit 2.6). They must also pay special attention to strategies and movements of competitors. Whereas scans of the internal environment are designed to uncover strengths and weaknesses, scans of the external environment are designed to uncover opportunities and threats that can be effectively addressed in the marketing plan.

PLANNING TIP

Use this analysis to identify opportunities and threats that must be factored into your marketing decisions.

As you examine your competitive situation, analyze substitute products and potential entrants to help identify current and future threats that you can try to counter through marketing. Both suppliers and buyers can affect what you and your rivals market, how, when, and at what price—all critical elements to

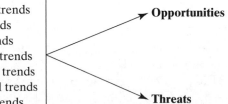

- Demographic trends
- Economic trends
- Ecological trends
- Technological trends
- Political-Legal trends
- Social-Cultural trends
- Competitive trends

Opportunities

Threats

EXHIBIT 2.6   Analyzing the External Environment

consider in your marketing plan. Finally, remember that every competitive analysis represents a point in time, because the forces are constantly shifting and evolving.

Exhibit 2.7 shows an example of how the external environment might affect marketing planning at Southwest Airlines. Notice that there are marketing implications—including possible changes in marketing—that result from a careful study of these external forces. As you learn about the following factors in the external environment, think about how they might impact your product or brand and your competitors.

Demographic Trends

Consumer and business markets are moving targets—never static, always changing, which is why every marketing plan must be flexible enough to be changed as markets change. For marketers of consumer products, population trends and characteristics suggest the size of the market and strength of demand. For marketers of business products, indicators of

EXHIBIT 2.7   The External Environment of Southwest Airlines

Element and Potential Impact	Possible Changes in Marketing
Economic trends: Economic recovery can boost demand for business and leisure travel; tight credit conditions can restrict Southwest's ability to pay for new jets and facilities.	As demand rises, manage pricing to encourage buying and maintain profitability; if credit is difficult to obtain, implement expansion plans more slowly.
Demographic trends: Population shifts and changes in centers of business activity affect demand for travel to and from certain areas.	Plan to add flights to areas experiencing population growth; research brand attitudes and buying behavior of businesspeople who travel to meet with businesses in industrial centers.
Technological trends: Higher consumer usage of smartphones and other mobile devices; availability of new technology for promotions and customer service.	Offer multiple communication alternatives for travelers who want to research flights and fares, be notified of flight delays, and more; engage customers in conversation on Twitter, YouTube, and other interactive sites.
Ecological trends: Concerns about environmental safety can affect attitudes toward air travel.	Publicize efforts to reduce engine emissions and protect ecological balance in and near airports; research customer attitudes toward specific issues directly affecting Southwest.
Social-cultural trends: Public interest in social responsibility can affect company reputation.	Publicize Southwest's involvement with Ronald McDonald House, local volunteer groups, and educational programs.
Political-legal trends: Changes in passenger screening and airport security mean changes in check-in and boarding procedures.	Communicate with customers to manage their expectations about checking in for their flights, alert them to airport delays, and reassure them about flight safety.
Competitive trends: Consolidation in the airline industry is creating larger, more powerful competitors; price wars can affect revenue and profits.	Differentiate Southwest on the basis of service quality; maintain competitive pricing to retain customer loyalty.

market size and strength include trends in business formation and certain organizational characteristics. However, these point-in-time examinations of demographic trends must be routinely updated to reflect any changes.

CONSUMER DEMOGRAPHICS   Population growth is creating and expanding markets around the world, whether through higher birth rates, longer life spans, or immigration. Yet the population is actually shrinking in some areas as people move elsewhere, such as from urban to suburban or rural markets or from one state or country to another. For this reason, marketers need to follow the population trends in the markets where they currently do business or are considering doing business, using U.S. Census data and other research. They must also explore the composition of the consumer population: age, gender, ethnic and religious makeup, education, occupation, and household size and income, as well as trends over time.

Marketers at Tata Motors believe that India's demographic trends present a sizable opportunity for the company.

Tata Motors. The largest automaker in India, Tata Motors has been eyeing the buying power of the country's 350 million middle-class consumers. Its marketers know that many of these families get around on motorcycles and scooters because they can't afford cars. With these demographics in mind, Tata designed the world's cheapest car, named the Nano, which it introduced in 2009. As part of its marketing plan, the company partnered with the State Bank of India to offer financing for Nano purchasers. By Tata's estimate, the low base price (just over $2,000) means an increase of 65 percent in the number of families in India who will be able to afford a car—quite a sizable market.[9]

BUSINESS DEMOGRAPHICS   Companies that operate in business markets need to scan the environment for information about the size and growth of the industries that they sell to, as measured by number of companies, number of locations or branches, number of employees, and sales revenues. They should also pay attention to trends in new business formation, which can signal emerging opportunities to market products such as office furniture, computers, accounting services, telecommunications services, and cleaning supplies. Palo Alto Software, which makes the *Marketing Plan Pro* software packaged with this text, is particularly interested in new-business formation as an indicator of demand for its marketing-planning software as well as its *Business Plan Pro* business-planning software.

Just as consumer marketers examine population trends in different geographic markets where they are selling or want to sell, business marketers must look at business population trends. For instance, B2B marketers might determine which cities and states host the most new start-ups as a factor in identifying promising markets for B2B products such as business loans, computers, and insurance.

Economic Trends

In today's interconnected global economy, deepening recession (or rapid recovery) in one part of the world can affect consumer and business buying patterns thousands of miles away. For Goodyear Tire & Rubber, unfavorable economic conditions in Asia would likely slow the pace of development, which will affect sales of oversized tires for construction vehicles. Thus, marketers have to keep a close eye on local, regional, national, and even global economic trends, watching for signs of change.

To better understand the buying power of consumers (or business customers), marketers should analyze buyer income, debt, and credit usage. When personal income is rising, consumers have more buying power; lower debt and more available credit also fuel consumer buying. The reverse is also true: When consumers are losing their jobs, facing wage cuts, or worried about their debt, they stop spending. That's why companies known for luxury items, such as France's Louis Vuitton Moët Hennessy and Germany's BMW, saw profits drop due to much lower demand and sales during the recent recession.[10] Similarly, businesses with higher debt may not buy as much or as often as businesses with lower debt and more available credit. For planning purposes, consider how specific trends may affect the company's industry, its products, its competitors, and targeted geographic markets.

Ecological Trends

The natural environment can influence companies in a variety of ways. Shortages of raw materials such as water, timber, oil, minerals, and other essentials for production can cause major headaches for companies, just as the shortage of maple syrup affected restaurants in Vermont. Marketers also have to examine the various environmental issues that affect their organizations because of government regulation or social attitudes. What pollution or environmental problems directly and indirectly affect the business? Manufacturers of furniture and wine corks, for instance, are increasingly concerned about the source of the wood they use. Clorox knows that consumers worry about how chemicals in household cleaning products might affect the environment.

Today, more marketers are applying for green certification labels such as the Green Good Housekeeping Seal and the EcoLogo to demonstrate that their goods and services are eco-friendly.[11] Even businesses that don't position their products as green must watch ecological trends and anticipate movements or regulations that can influence marketing performance. Pressure from customers, environmental advocates, and other stakeholders can influence how marketers deal with ecological issues.

Technological Trends

Technology reaches into every aspect of the marketing mix, from digitally enhanced advertisements to new packaging materials and methods and beyond. Key trends include the ongoing global penetration of smartphones, smaller computers, digital media, and the incorporation of electronic capabilities into a wider range of products. How will technology affect your product, customers, competitors, and marketing mix?

The Internet alone has spawned countless marketing opportunities, from online retailing and wholesaling to security solutions for viruses, stolen data, and other problems. Consider how Bank of America is using technology to enhance its customer service.

Bank of America. One of the world's largest financial institutions, Bank of America harnesses technology to serve its customers in numerous ways. Nearly 30 million customers use its online banking services to check account balances, transfer funds between accounts, and pay bills. Another 2 million customers use their cell phones to access its mobile banking services. The bank also offers talking ATMs for visually-impaired customers and answers customers' questions via e-mail and Twitter. Not only do these technological developments improve customer service—an important element in customer retention—they also improve Bank of America's internal efficiency.[12]

Broad questions about technological trends include the following: What cutting-edge innovations are being introduced, and how do they affect the organization's customers, suppliers, distributors, marketing, and processes? How are these technologies affected by, or generating, industrywide standards and government regulations? What substitutes or innovations are becoming available because of new technology, and how are these changes likely to affect suppliers, customers, and competitors? Understanding such trends can reveal threats (such as inventions or changes in standards that will make existing technology obsolete) and opportunities (such as quickly adopting a new technological standard).

Political-Legal Trends

As part of the external scanning process, marketers need to examine the legal and regulatory guidelines that govern diverse business and marketing practices. Numerous state and federal laws cover competitive behavior, pricing, taxation, promotion, distribution, product liability, labeling, and product purity, among other elements, in the United States. Moreover, U.S. government agencies such as the Federal Trade Commission and the Department of Justice watch for questionable business practices.

Businesses have to be aware of political and regulatory trends in every country where they operate. Microsoft, for instance, has had high-profile regulatory encounters over the years. The European Union challenged Microsoft's bundling of an Internet browser with its Windows operating system on antitrust grounds; Germany fined Microsoft for unduly influencing retail pricing of a software product; Russia cited antitrust laws as the reason for scrutinizing Microsoft's market share; and the U.S. FTC examined potential privacy issues raised by Microsoft's newest Web browser.[13] U.S.-based Intel is currently fighting a $1.4 billion fine levied by the European Union for monopoly abuse, a regulatory situation that will affect the firm's marketing of its computer chips throughout that region.[14]

Social-Cultural Trends

Increased diversity in markets—and in the workforce—is a key social-cultural trend affecting today's marketing. Using U.S. Census data and other sources, marketers can learn more about the cultural diversity of specific geographic markets. These include nation of origin, primary language, and other details that can help in tailoring the offer and the message to specific groups. Wider exposure to other societies also creates new business opportunities. For example, the U.S. custom of making a big fuss over the high school prom has spread to Great Britain, thanks to TV and movies. Building on this trend, the UK depart-ment store John Lewis now features an expanded spring line of fancy prom dresses.[15]

As a marketer, you should remain alert to the unexpected opportunities and threats created by popular culture. Also remember that fad products tend to experience meteoric sales increases followed by sharp sales declines when another craze takes the spotlight (remember Power Rangers and Pokemon?). Yet the core beliefs and values that pervade a society or subculture, which change only slowly over time, also create opportunities and threats. And note that attitudes toward ethical and social responsibility issues, influenced by core beliefs and values, can have an impact on marketing plans and corporate image.

Competitor Analysis

Analyzing competitors and the competitive climate can help marketers better understand market dynamics, anticipate what rivals will do, and create more practical marketing plans. Start by identifying current competitors and possi-ble sources of competition in the near future, to avoid being blindsided by a new entrant (the way Palm was surprised by Apple's iPhone). Also look at trends in market share to get a sense of which competitors are becoming more powerful. And be aware of opportunities to do business where there are many potential customers but few competitors, as Burger King does.

PLANNING TIP

Look for new ideas by probing customers' reactions to competitors' strengths and weaknesses.

Burger King. Burger King has been profiting by opening outlets in busy locations where competition is less fierce. As an example, it likes airport locations because of the number of passengers and crew members who pass by—and because competi-tion is limited. Burger King operates more than 200 airport restaurants, including several in China's Beijing and Shanghai airports. The company also developed a smaller version of its restaurant, known as the Whopper Bar, for cruise ships, sports stadiums, and other locations where space is at a premium. Not only are Whopper Bars cheaper to operate, they're well suited to niches that competitors might view as too small.[16]

Michael Porter's model of the competitive forces affecting industry profitability and attractiveness shows that competition in a particular segment is affected by the number of potential entrants, the power of suppliers and buyers, and the potential threat presented by substitute products (see Exhibit 2.8). Burger King's marketers know that airport termi-nals have a limited amount of space to rent to restaurant and retail tenants. This poses a barrier to entry that allows restaurants in the terminal (such as Burger King) to face less competitive pressure than they would in most other situations. Because buyers have fewer choices inside the terminal, the threat of substitutes is lower than in most other situation. This also lessens the competitive pressure felt by Burger King's airport locations.

During this competitive analysis, you will learn about the unique competitive advantages of each rival. Yet customers ultimately determine the value of a firm's compet-itive advantage, which means that any organization can build advantage by discovering what customers need or desire and delivering it more effectively and efficiently (and perhaps more distinctively) than competitors. That's how Starbucks originally turned a

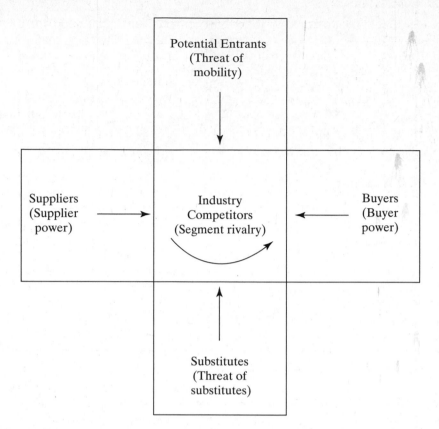

EXHIBIT 2.8 Competitive Forces Affecting Industry Profitability and Attractiveness

run-of-the-mill product, coffee, into an everyday luxury and an experience for which millions of customers pay handsomely.

On the other hand, Starbucks also knows that no competitive advantage is forever. For a long time, any new entrants to the upscale coffee market had to contend with Starbucks's established brand and leadership position. However, once McDonald's challenged Starbucks by introducing its McCafé line of popularly priced specialty coffees, Starbucks adjusted its marketing plan to showcase its premium quality and remind loyal customers of other competitive advantages.[17]

Competitive analysis helps marketers determine which of Porter's generic competitive strategies is most appropriate for the company's unique situation.[18] With a **cost leadership strategy,** the company seeks to become the lowest-cost producer in its industry (Trader Joe's private-label grocery products are an example). With a **differentiation strategy,** the company creates a unique differentiation for itself or its product based on some factor valued by the target market (such as iPod's stylish design). With a **focus strategy,** the company narrows its competitive scope to achieve a competitive advantage in its chosen segments. Which strategy a company chooses depends, in part, on its analysis of internal strengths and weaknesses and external opportunities and threats.

Summary

Environmental scanning and analysis is the process of gathering data about the environment and analyzing the findings to understand the company's strengths, weaknesses, opportunities, and threats in preparation for marketing planning. The macroenvironment consists of broad demographic, economic, ecological, technological, political-legal, and social-cultural forces. The microenvironment consists of groups that more directly influence performance, such as customers, competitors, channel members, partners, suppliers, and employees.

In scanning the internal environment, marketers examine the organization's mission, resources, offerings, previous results, business relationships, keys to success, and warning signs. In scanning the external environment, they examine demographic, economic, ecological, technological, political-legal, and social-cultural trends, as well as the competitive situation. Using the data gathered during these environmental scanning steps, marketers conduct a SWOT analysis so they can plan to take advantage of strengths and opportunities while defending against weaknesses and threats.

Your Marketing Plan, Step by Step

Answer the following questions as you scan the environment, and prepare a SWOT analysis for your marketing plan.

1. If your plan focuses on a real product or company, how will you research its internal and external environment? In addition to examining the product or company's Web site and literature, look for online, printed, video, and audio content from the following sources. If you're focusing on a hypothetical product or brand—or creating a marketing plan for an entirely new business or product—you can use publicly available information from the following sources to research close competitors and the industry as background for creating specific details for your plan.
   a. industry groups, analysts, conferences, and research
   b. business and news media
   c. academic and professional groups
   d. advocacy and community groups
   e. government agencies and publications
   f. professional and customer product reviews
   g. social media sources such as Facebook and Twitter
2. Summarize what you learn about each internal and external factor named in Exhibits 2.4 and 2.6.
3. To get more information about competitors, start with their Web sites. Also check stores or distributors for written materials and details about products, and other marketing particulars. Look at which distributors and retailers carry competing products and how those products are displayed, promoted, and priced. Do an Internet search for customer and distributor comments, both positive and negative, to identify

competitors' weaknesses and strengths. Finally, check news sources for the latest developments about competitors' resources, results, and business relationships. Summarize the main points you learn about your current and emerging competitors.

4. What are your chosen product or company's strengths and weaknesses? To find out, classify each bit of information you've collected about your product into one of four categories:
   a. "positive internal" (potential strengths from factors in the internal environment)
   b. "negative internal" (potential weaknesses from factors in the internal environment)
   c. "positive external" (potential opportunities from factors in the external environment)
   d. "negative external" (potential threats from factors in the external environment)

Do the same with the information you've collected about competitors. Next, compare your product's positive and negative internal information with competitors' positive and negative internal information. Using your judgment and these comparisons, determine which of your product's "positive internal" items represent significant strengths and which of your product's "negative internal" items represent significant weaknesses. Summarize your conclusions as part of the SWOT analysis in your marketing plan, using a grid similar to the one in Exhibit 2.2. Also check the sample plan in the appendix to see SWOT analysis in action.

5. Review the information you've gathered about your product's external environment and classified as either "external positive" or "external negative." Thinking about your organization's mission and internal situation, as well as the competitive information you've gathered, which items on your list represent significant opportunities—and why? Which represent significant threats—and why? Document your conclusions to complete the SWOT analysis in your marketing plan. Be ready to review your SWOT as you continue your marketing planning and move ahead to Chapter 3.

Endnotes

1. Kenji Hall, "Can Nintendo Rebuild?" *Business Week Online,* November 2, 2009, www.business-week.com; Daisuke Wakabayashi and Yukari Iwatani Kane, "Nintendo Loses Some of Its Luster," *Wall Street Journal,* April 8, 2009, www.wsj.com; A. Yoskowitz, "Wii Now Costs 45 Percent Less to Manufacture," *After Dawn.com,* April 7, 2009, http://www.afterdawn.com/news/archive/17482.cfm; Yukari Iwatani Kane, "Q&A with Nintendo's President," *Wall Street Journal,* April 7, 2009, www.wsj.com; Matt Richtel, "Video Game Makers Challenged by Next Wave of Media," *New York Times,* March 30, 2009, www.nytimes.com/2009/03/30/technology/30game.html.

2. Stuart Read, Nicholas Dew, Saras D. Sarasvathy, Michael Song, and Robert Wiltbank, "Marketing Under Uncertainty: The Logic of an Effectual Approach," *Journal of Marketing,* vol. 73, no. 3, May 2009, pp. 1–18.

3. Robert D. Hof, "The Geekdom of Google," *BusinessWeek,* November 5, 2009, www.businessweek.com; Vindu Goel, "Why Google Pulls the Plug," *New York Times,* February 15, 2009, p. BU-4; Jessica E. Vascellaro and Scott Morrison, "Google Gears Down for Tougher Times," *Wall Street Journal,* December 3, 2008, p. A1.

4. James C. Collins and Jerry I. Porras, *Built to Last* (New York: HarperBusiness, 1994), pp. 220–221.

5. Quoted in Maureen Jenkins, "What's Our Business? Why Every Employee Needs to Know the Company's Mission Statement," *Black Enterprise,* October 2005, p. 71; Jeffrey Abrahams, *The Mission Statement Book* (Berkeley, CA: Ten Speed Press, 1999).

6. Martha T. Moore, "Maple Syrup-Makers Strike Gold," *USA Today,* March 30, 2009, www.usatoday.com; Lauren Ober, "Local IHOP Taps into the 'Real Stuff,' " *Burlington Free Press,* March 25, 2009, http://www.burlingtonfreepress.com/article/20090325/BUSINESS/90325011.

7. Jeffrey Bartash, "AT&T's Rivals Still Seek Answer to IPhone," *Wall Street Journal,* November 6, 2009, www.wsj.com; Kit Eaton, "Could Palm Survive a Failed Pre Smartphone?" *Fast Company,* March 23, 2009, www.fastcompany.com; Randall Stross, "For Palm, Some Tough Acts to Follow," *New York Times,* March 22, 2009, www.nytimes.com.

8. Andrew Bolger, "Tyre Seller Pursues Latest Spin-off," *Financial Times,* April 8, 2009, www.ft.com; Rachel Bridge, "How I Made It: Founder of Black Circles.com, Michael Welch," *Sunday Times (London),* April 5, 2009, http://business.timesonline.co.uk.

9. Arun Jayan, "Tata Revs Up to Take on Premium SUV Contenders," *Indian Express,* October 21, 2009, n.p.; Gal Luft, "The Micro-Car: Tata Nano Could Change How the Masses Get Around," *Chicago Tribune,* April 5, 2009, www.chicagotribune.com; Santanu Choudhury, "Tata Nano Goes on Sale," *Wall Street Journal,* April 9, 2009, www.wsj.com.

10. "The Lapse of Luxury," *The Economist,* February 24, 2009, www.economist.com

11. Caryn Rousseau, "Iconic Good Housekeeping Seal Goes Green," *Marketing News,* April 15, 2009, p. 29.

12. Ben Worthen, "Branching Out: Mobile Banking Finds New Users," *Wall Street Journal,* February 3, 2009, www.wsj.com; "Better Living Through Twitter," *Wall Street Journal Wallet Blog,* February 23, 2009, http://blogs.wsj.com/wallet/2009/02/23/better-living-through-twitter.

13. Ina Fried, "Russia May Increase Oversight of Microsoft," *CNET News,* April 2, 2009, http://news.cnet.com; Ina Fried, "Microsoft Fined Over Office Pricing in Germany," *CNET News,* April 9, 2009, http://news.cnet.com; Jessica Hodgson and Scott Morrison, "Microsoft IE8 Browser Seeks Compromise On Privacy, Ad Growth," *Wall Street Journal,* March 23, 2009, www.wsj.com.

14. Charles Forelle, "EU Levies $1.45 Billion Fine on Intel," *Wall Street Journal,* May 13, 2009, www.wsj.com.

15. Jemima Lewis, "America's Most Pernicious Export: The Prom," *The Telegraph (U.K.),* March 21, 2009, www.telegraph.co.uk; Jeanne Whalen and Isabella Lisk, "Alien Invasion: High-School Prom Lands in England, Causes a Bother," *Wall Street Journal,* June 17, 2008, p. A1.

16. "BK Whopper Bar Continues Global Spread," *QSRMagazine.com*, October 20, 2009, www.qsr magazine.com/articles/news/story.phtml?id=9520; Ron Ruggless, "BK Debuts Whopper Bar Concept," *Nation's Restaurant News,* March 23, 2009, p. 6; "Here Comes a Whopper," *The Economist,* October 25, 2008, p. 78.

17. Sean Gregory, "Latte with Fries? McDonald's Takes Aim at Starbucks," *Time,* May 7, 2009, www.time.com.

18. Discussion is based on Michael Porter, *Competitive Advantage* (New York: Free Press, 1985), pp. 11–26.

3 Understanding Markets and Customers

In this chapter:

PREVIEW

No two markets are exactly the same, no two markets stay the same forever, and no company can afford to sell to or satisfy every customer in every market on earth. Even well-heeled giants like Hormel, Honda, and Hewlett-Packard must make informed decisions about which local, regional, national, and international markets to serve and about the specific customer groups they can develop marketing plans to satisfy most profitably.

This chapter discusses how to research and analyze markets and customers, Step 2 in the marketing planning process (see Exhibit 3.1). First you'll learn how to define your market, examine overall characteristics, and calculate market share, a prelude to selecting markets and segments to target. Next, you'll learn more about understanding the needs and behavior of consumers and business customers in light of the constant change that affects marketing activities. Finally, you'll see how primary research and secondary research are used during the preparation of a marketing plan.

APPLYING YOUR KNOWLEDGE

As you read this chapter and move ahead with marketing planning, continue to record your conclusions and decisions using *Marketing Plan Pro* software or in a written marketing plan. Look at the sample plans in *Marketing Plan Pro* and the sample in this book's appendix to see how companies present this part of the plan. Also use this chapter's checklist when preparing to analyze your markets and customers.

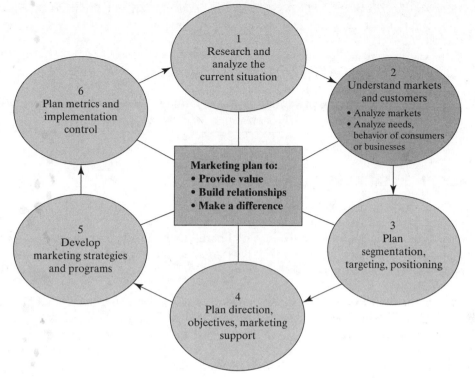

EXHIBIT 3.1   Marketing Planning: Step 2

CHAPTER 3 CHECKLIST   Analyzing Markets and Customers

Understanding the Market and Market Share

✔ How can the market be described in terms of product, customer need, and geography?

✔ What general demographics, characteristics, needs, behavior, and preferences pertain to this product and category in this market? How are these changing?

✔ What are the current and projected sales of or demand for your product in this market?

✔ What is the market share of your company, brand, or product?

✔ What is the market share of each competitor, and how is each share changing over time?

✔ How can you use your marketing plan to make the most of opportunities and minimize threats stemming from your market's characteristics and your market share?

Understanding Consumers and Business Customers

✔ What customer needs can your offering profitably satisfy?

✔ How do customers perceive the value of competing offerings that could satisfy their needs?

✔ Who are the customers in each market, and what are their buying patterns?

✔ How are the needs and behavior of consumers as customers influenced by cultural considerations, social connections, and personal factors?

✔ For business customers, who is involved in the buying decision, what is each participant's role, and what does each need to know during the buying process?

✔ How are the needs and behavior of business customers influenced by organizational connections and considerations?

✔ How can your marketing plan build on these influences to provide value and strengthen relationships with consumers or business customers?

ANALYZING MARKETS TODAY

Just as the marketing environment is highly changeable, so too is a **market,** all the potential buyers for a particular product. In a **consumer market,** people are buying for themselves or their families; in a **business market,** people are buying for their companies, nonprofit groups, or other organizations. When you think about a "market," think "people"—because ultimately it's people who make the buying decisions for themselves, their households, or their businesses.

Also remember that people's preferences, behavior, and attitudes can shift at any time, creating new consumer or business markets and changing existing markets (even to the point of markets disappearing). As Exhibit 3.2 indicates, market analysis is a vital backdrop for understanding the dynamic needs and behavior of consumers and business customers you want to reach through your marketing plan.

Nike has successfully dealt with different market situations by studying each market and understanding the needs and concerns of consumers, locally and globally.

Consumer Analysis
- Needs
- Cultural considerations
- Social connections
- Personal factors

Market Analysis
- Market and needs definition
- Market changes
- Market share

Business Customer Analysis
- Needs
- Organizational connections
- Organizational considerations

EXHIBIT 3.2 Market and Customer Analysis

Nike. Nearing its 50th birthday, Nike still rings up $18 billion in revenues year after year because it knows how to research, analyze, define, and target its markets. In meeting the needs of its customers, Nike applies its knowledge of innovation, performance, and style to provide value. For example, it makes fashion-forward Mercurial boots to meet the functional needs and style expectations of European men who play soccer. It also makes comfortable, supportive Musique shoes to meet the fitness needs of U.S. women who participate in aerobic dance. Even during difficult economic times, the company has been able to sprint ahead of competitors and increase market share because it knows its markets and customers so well.

Digital initiatives are an integral part of Nike's marketing strategy, says a marketing executive, because "consumers are spending their time online, so that's where we need to be." A good example is the Nike+ program, which helps consumers work toward their fitness goals: A computer chip embedded in the wearer's Nike running shoes sends speed and distance data to his or her iPod during every run. Users can upload their statistics to the Nike+ site, chart their progress over time, and race against runners in other cities or nations. Looking beyond profits, Nike promotes sustainability and works with local groups to make sports the focal point of wellness and social-change initiatives in communities worldwide.[1]

As Nike knows, every market is different, which affects planning for the marketing mix of products, channel choices, communications, and pricing for each market. The first step for Nike, as for other marketers, is to broadly define the market and its needs.

Broad Definition of Market and Needs

A market can be defined at five basic levels: (1) potential market, (2) available market, (3) qualified available market, (4) served or target market, and (5) penetrated market.[2] Exhibit 3.3 shows these definitions with a rental car example. The potential market contains the maximum number of customers that exists for a company's product (recognizing, of course, that no one product can appeal to every possible customer). Note that if the product already exists, the penetrated market consists of people who are already buying it.

The remainder of the market consists of nonbuyers (potential customers) who are aware of the offering or value its benefits, have access to it, are of the proper age or have the skill to buy or use it, and can afford it. Marketers, therefore, want to narrow their focus by gaining a thorough understanding of the potential, available, and qualified available markets.

PLANNING TIP

When formulating your marketing plan, research and analyze the broad market for your product.

For planning purposes, markets may be described in terms of geography as well as by product or customer definition. "The U.S. smartphone market" is a broad description of one target market that Apple seeks to serve with its iPhone. Because of international telecommunication standards, Apple must define each target market geographically: "The U.S. smartphone market" and "the London smartphone market" are two examples.

Another way to define the market is in terms of customer need: "The Cleveland market for weed killer" is an overall description of the group of customers and prospects who want a product that will wipe out weeds. Within that market may be subsets of consumers and business customers who want to get rid of specific weeds, such as poison ivy, for aesthetic or health reasons. Also within that market may be subsets of customers who want to get rid

Type of Market	Definition	Rental Car Example
Potential market (*broadest definition*)	All customers who may be interested in a particular offering	Any driver who needs temporary transportation
Available market (*subset of the potential market*)	Customers who are interested, possess sufficient income, and have access to the offering	Any driver who can afford the rental fees and is in the area served by rental-car services
Qualified available market (*subset of the available market*)	Customers who are qualified to buy based on age (for products that cannot be sold to underage consumers) or other criteria	Drivers in the available market who have valid licenses and meet minimum or maximum age restrictions
Target market (*subset of the qualified available market to be served*)	Customers that the company intends to target for a particular offer	Drivers in the qualified available market who need to travel from airports to final destinations in the area
Penetrated market (*subset of the target market*)	Customers who are already buying the type of product sold by the company	Drivers in the target market who have previously rented cars

EXHIBIT 3.3 Defining the Market

of weeds in an eco-friendly way. Another way to define markets more precisely is to describe them in terms of broad consumer or business categories, such as "the Cleveland residential market for weed killer" or "the Cleveland residential market for environmentally safe weed killer."

Next, the company conducts research into the broad needs of the available market. Here, the emphasis is on identifying general needs prior to a more in-depth investigation of each segment's particular needs. This research also helps the company identify what customers value and how its image, products, services, and other attributes can be positioned for competitive differentiation. Consider the situation of Kiva Systems.

Kiva Systems. Kiva Systems wants robots to become as commonplace in warehouses and distribution centers as they are in automated manufacturing facilities. The potential market for its robots and similar technology is estimated at $38 billion. Customers are looking for speed, accuracy, and efficiency. In most warehouses, employees sort goods received from manufacturers, store them in designated locations, and then fulfill orders by plucking items from storage and assembling each customer's order individually. But with goods stored far and wide within huge warehouses, fulfilling an order can take time and cost money.

Now Walgreen's, Staples, Zappos, and other retailers have hundreds of Kiva's robots, linked through wireless communications, fetching goods ordered by customers from far-flung sections of their huge warehouses. The robots quickly bring all items to packing stations where employees stand ready with boxes labeled for each order. One early customer, Staples, found that using Kiva's robots doubled the productivity of its human employees and eliminated the need for extensive, expensive conveyor belts. Kiva Systems does face competition, however, from automated equipment that can move much larger, much heavier loads than its robots can handle.[3]

Along with a broad understanding of needs, marketers look at general demographics to get a rough sense of what each market is like (in the aggregate). As an example, U.S. Census information shows the number of people and households in specific areas of the country. Then marketers look beyond sheer numbers, researching gender, age, education, marital status, income, home ownership, and other characteristics that relate to their products.

In the business market, marketers can use the **North American Industry Classification System (NAICS)** to classify industries and investigate industry size; the main source for such data is the U.S. Census Bureau. Additional research about industries, products, and geographic markets is available from a wide variety of sources, including international trade organizations, global banks, foreign consulates, universities, and business publications. As with consumer markets, the next step is to obtain meaningful characteristics that relate to the product, such as the annual sales, number of employees, or industries served by the businesses in the market.

Kiva Systems, for example, knows that some companies in particular NAICS classifications make or distribute products that are too large or heavy for its warehouse robots to handle. Because only some businesses are potential buyers, the company must identify and research the industries that would have a need for its robots, such as wholesalers and retailers of books, household items, and other general merchandise. Then Kiva's marketers can examine each market in more detail to ascertain needs and buying behavior.

Markets as Moving Targets

Markets are always in flux: Consumers move in or out, are born or die, start or stop buying a good or service; businesses change location, go into or out of business, expand or divest units, start or stop buying a product. Thus, at this stage of the market analysis, marketers need to locate projections of demographic changes in the markets and forecast future demand for (or sales of) their type of product, as a way of sizing the overall market over time. (Forecasting is discussed in Chapter 10.)

PLANNING TIP

Consider the markets of today and tomorrow when developing objectives and strategies.

Is the population expected to grow or shrink, and by how much? How many new businesses are projected to enter or leave the market? What are the projections for total industry sales of the product over the coming years? Do these projections suggest a sizable market, a stagnant market, or a shrinking market? The answers to these questions influence what you say in your marketing plan regarding targeting and objectives.

PC Market. During economic downturns, sales of many products plateau or decline, and the personal computer (PC) market is no exception. Within the broad market, however, sales of different types of products are projected to grow at different rates. In China, where the PC market has been rising steadily, laptop sales are growing at an annual rate of 20 percent even as desktop PC sales are falling by 6 percent annually. In the U.S. market, sales of netbooks—smaller than notebook computers—are growing especially quickly.

Manufacturers that have a sizable presence in smaller computers, such as Acer, are profiting from these trends. Companies that have stayed out of PCs, such as Nokia, are carefully studying market trends to determine whether to start offering smaller computers. PC sales trends also figure in the marketing plans of computer chip makers, where Intel and AMD are battling for market share and profits.[4]

Much research is publicly available for major markets and for products, but marketers of groundbreaking products often must conduct their own research to project demand and sales. This part of the marketing planning process also feeds into the SWOT analysis discussed in Chapter 2, because it can reveal new opportunities or threats that must be addressed.

Market Share as a Vital Sign

PLANNING TIP

Keep market share in mind to set realistic objectives and suitable metrics for assessing results.

Market share is the percentage of sales in a given market held by a particular company, brand, or product, calculated in dollars or units (ideally, both). Market share usually changes over time as companies and their competitors court customers, the market grows or shrinks, and competitors enter or exit. You can use market share information as a baseline for understanding historical market dynamics and a standard for setting and measuring marketing plan objectives. In simple terms, market share is calculated according to this formula:

$$\frac{\text{One company's product sales in the market (units or dollars)}}{\text{Overall sales of such products in the market (units or dollars)}}$$

Thus, if Firm A sells 2 million units in the 50 states, and overall market sales for all competitors selling that kind of product are 10 million units, A's U.S. market share would be calculated as:

$$\frac{2,000,000}{10,000,000} = .20 = 20\%$$

Units are frequently used for market-share calculations because differences in company pricing policies can distort share comparisons. However, companies don't always report unit sales publicly. As a result, if a company wants to calculate its market share and those of its competitors, it may have to use dollar sales. Suppose Firm A sells $15 million worth of a product in the U.S. market, where overall industry sales of such products are $100 million. Its nearest competitor, Firm B, sells $12 million worth of products in the U.S. market. Then A's share would be 15 percent and B's share would be 12 percent.

As noted earlier, market share is a point-in-time snapshot showing the relative positions of competitors during a particular period—positions that can and do constantly change. The PC market shares of Hewlett-Packard, Dell, Acer, and Apple in the United States change month by month, with Dell and HP vying for the lead most recently. In early 2008, Dell's U.S. market share (calculated by units) was 30 percent. By late 2009, Dell's market share had fallen, leaving it barely ahead of HP, which increased its U.S. share to nearly 26 percent. Acer was in third place, with a share of 14 percent, and Apple was in fourth place, with a share of 9 percent. More than bragging rights are involved: These fierce competitors are always watching market-share changes and remain ready to tweak marketing plans for better unit sales.[5]

Clearly, market share is one of the vital signs of a business, to be monitored over time as a way of spotting potential problems as well as potential opportunities in the marketplace. Companies should develop share information for each product in each market, regularly update share numbers to track shifts, and examine shifts as possible triggers for control measures (discussed in detail in Chapter 10).

In addition, market share directly affects segmentation and targeting, because a company with marketing strategies to capture a larger and larger share of a shrinking market segment could end up with nearly 100 percent of a market too small to be profitable. Palm, for instance, has shifted most of its resources to smartphones, which are rapidly overtaking sales of stand-alone personal digital assistants, the company's original product. On the other hand, most companies take special notice of markets in which demand is projected to skyrocket, using share over time to identify opportunities, understand competitive dynamics, and set and measure progress toward objectives. This is why Dell, known for its PCs, is entering the smartphone market in countries where demand is soaring.

ANALYZING CUSTOMER NEEDS AND BEHAVIOR

With the market analysis as backdrop, marketers use research to examine the needs, buying behavior, and attitudes of the customers in their markets. This research forms the foundation for decisions about which segments to target, the most effective way to position the product in each market, and what marketing strategies and tactics are most appropriate for profitably satisfying customers. The chapter-ending section on marketing research briefly discusses how marketers can study and understand customers' behavior and buying decisions.

Forces in the external environment can play a key role in affecting the who, what, when, where, why, and how of consumer and business buying behavior. This is one of the reasons for studying the current situation, as discussed in Chapter 2. For example, when the economy is in recession, many consumers and business customers change their buying patterns—sometimes purchasing less or less often, sometimes seeking out lower-priced alternatives, as Kroger's marketers know.

PLANNING TIP

Analyze market needs in the context of competing offers.

Kroger. With $76 billion in annual sales and 2,400 stores across the country, Kroger is the second-largest U.S. retailer of groceries. Since 2006, Kroger's marketing plan has included a heavier emphasis on store-branded foods and household products. Now its expanded offerings include a wider range of store-branded products in three quality levels, all priced lower than the national brands. Price isn't the only differentiating feature; depending on consumer needs and preferences—and on the competition—Kroger differentiates some of its store brands on the basis of innovative packaging, natural ingredients, and convenient usage.

During the recent recession, many economically squeezed consumers sought to lower their grocery bills by buying store brands instead of national brands. As a result, Kroger's sales of store brands increased to a record 35 percent of the chain's overall sales. Moreover, the increase in sales volume helped Kroger gain market share, even in areas where it competes with Walmart, the nation's largest grocery retailer.[6]

The attitudes and habits of consumers and business customers are clearly affected by the marketing-mix programs implemented by different companies competing for their attention, loyalty, and buying power. From the customer's perspective, no marketing tactic stands in isolation: It is only one tactic used by the company and one of many stimuli in the market (some of which are noticed and acted upon, most of which are not). As a result, marketers must not only understand their markets and the environmental forces shaping customer actions, but also learn to see the totality of their marketing activities and the actions of competing firms through their customers' eyes.

Remember that stated needs are generally the tip of the iceberg; customers also have unstated needs (e.g., a good or service) and sometimes secret needs (e.g., relating to their self-concept or other internal needs). Thus, it is vital to understand the problem each customer seeks to solve and what that customer really wants from the solution. Remember that the needs, wants, attitudes, behavior, and decision-making processes of consumers differ, in general, from those of business customers. The next sections highlight important influences to understand when preparing plans for consumer and business markets (see Exhibit 3.4).

Consumer Markets

Who is buying or using the product? When, where, how, and why? What is the consumer's decision-making process for buying that product, and how are the process and the decisions changing over time? Look at both internal and external sources of data for this analysis of consumer needs, decision making, and behavior.

When making decisions about more complex purchases, such as a PC, consumers generally take more time, gather more information about alternatives, weigh the decision

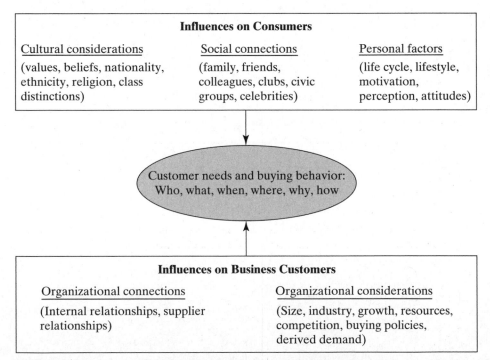

EXHIBIT 3.4 Analyzing Customer Needs, Behavior, and Influences

more carefully, and have strong feelings in the aftermath of the purchase. Inexpensive items bought on impulse, such as candy, are not usually subjected to as much scrutiny before or after the purchase. By investigating the entire process consumers follow to buy, use, and evaluate their products, marketers can determine how, when, and where to initiate suitable marketing activities.

PLANNING TIP

Do more than ask about needs, because many consumers are unaware of what influences their behavior.

Early in the buying process, for example, marketers may need to emphasize benefits that solve consumer problems. Later in the process, marketers may need to communicate where the product can be purchased; still later, marketers may want to reassure consumers that they made the right buying decision. The exact nature and timing of the marketing activities will depend on what the marketer learns about consumer decision making (as well as on the marketer's strategy and resources, of course).

Although the level of influence varies from individual to individual, consumer needs, wants, and behaviors are affected by cultural considerations, social connections, and personal factors.

CULTURAL CONSIDERATIONS As buyers, consumers feel the influence of the culture of the nation or region in which they were raised as well as the culture in which they currently live. This means that consumers in different countries often approach buying situations from different perspectives because of differing values, beliefs, and preferences. Without research, marketers can't know exactly what those differences are or how to address them. For example, Coca-Cola tailors a marketing plan to the culture(s) of each of the 200 nations where it sells beverages.

Coca-Cola. More than 75 percent of Coca-Cola's profit comes from marketing beverages outside North America, which is why the company pays close attention to cultural differences and similarities. "Asians have different languages, cultures, religions," says a marketing executive in its Pacific Group. "But in most cases, consumer motivations are very, very similar." This allows Coca-Cola to develop products for one market and then expand them to other markets, with slightly different distribution and promotional support. In China, Coca-Cola developed and launched Minute Maid Pulpy, a fruit beverage with added pulp. The product was so successful that the company formulated plans for marketing it in the Philippines, Indonesia, Vietnam, and Thailand.

As a sponsor of the Billboard Latin Music Awards, the company has created event-related advertising and promotions to reach consumers throughout Latin America. As a sponsor of the FIFA World Cup, the company has created special events such as taking the trophy on a tour of 50 African nations. With soft-drink sales declining in the United States, Coca-Cola knows that its future growth will be based, to a large extent, on its ability to market effectively to consumers in many cultures.[7]

Subcultures are distinct groups within a larger culture that exhibit and preserve distinct cultural identities through a common religion, nationality, ethnic background, or lifestyle. A variety of subcultures drive U.S. consumers' decisions and behavior. Cuban Americans frequently have different food preferences than, say, Chinese Americans. Teenagers—an age subculture—have different food preferences than seniors.

Class distinctions, even when subtle, also influence consumer behavior. The members of each class generally buy and use products in a similar way; in addition, people who aspire to a different class may emulate the buying or usage patterns of that class. Savvy marketers learn how such distinctions operate and then apply this knowledge to decisions about products, marketing communications, distribution arrangements, price levels, and service strategies.

SOCIAL CONNECTIONS Consumers have a web of social connections that influence how they buy—connections such as family ties, friendships, work groups, and civic organizations. Family members, for example, directly or indirectly control household spending for many goods and services. Children ask parents to buy products advertised on television; parents buy things to keep children healthy or safe; families make group decisions about vacations. Social connections include friends and fans on Facebook, Twitter, and other social media networks. For instance, Walt Disney Pictures maintains a Facebook page for adults (and children) who are interested in its movies and DVDs.

PLANNING TIP

Monitor social media sites to see what consumers say about your brand.

Understanding how social connections affect the buying decision is critical for marketers creating plans for products intended for specific family members, usage, or occasions, as the online toy retailer ebeanstalk found out.

Ebeanstalk. Although the founders of ebeanstalk.com started out marketing toys to new parents, they were surprised to learn that 40 percent of their customers are grandparents buying gifts for grandchildren. Why? Because ebeanstalk tests toys and games and sorts them into age categories so grandparents can easily select appropriate gifts for the children in their lives. Now the company targets grandparents as well as its original segment of new parents, in particular young mothers. The retailer maintains an advisory group of 700 mothers (the "Mother Board") for feedback and comments about age-appropriate toys. It also partners with "mommy bloggers" who influence the toy-buying decisions of readers. And to introduce the brand to parents-to-be, ebeanstalk offers a special selection of baby shower gifts.[8]

As with class distinctions, aspirations to different social connections can be a powerful influence on buying behavior. In apparel, for example, preteens want to look as grown up as possible, so they emulate teen fashions; teenagers dress like the music and movie stars they admire; and managers seeking to move up follow the clothing cues of higher-level managers. Within each social group, consumers look to certain opinion leaders for advice or guidance about buying decisions.

PERSONAL FACTORS Personal factors are another major category of influences on consumer buying, covering life cycle, lifestyle, and psychological makeup, among other factors. *Life cycle* refers to the individual's changing family situation over time—single, cohabitating, engaged, married, married with children, divorced, remarried, and so on. Each of these life-cycle phases entails different buying needs, attitudes, and preferences that, in turn, can be identified through research and addressed through marketing. Engaged couples, for instance, are targeted by marketers selling formal wear, wedding invitations, catering services, and other wedding products; new parents are targeted by marketers selling entirely different products (the way ebeanstalk markets toys).

Lifestyle is the pattern of living that a person exhibits through activities and interests—how the individual spends his or her time. To understand the complexities of lifestyle and its influence on consumer buying, marketers use sophisticated techniques to examine variables known as **psychographic characteristics,** which together form a picture of the consumer's lifestyle. Some markets are better approached through psychographics. The cruise industry, for example, relies heavily on lifestyle marketing:

> **Cruise marketing.** No matter what their hobby or interest, travelers can find a cruise for every lifestyle. Norwegian, Silversea, Cunard, and many other cruise lines offer theme cruises that cater to consumers who love chocolate or photography; want to meet famous authors or athletes; or seek to improve their physical fitness or financial savvy. Another marketing trend is toward shorter voyages to accommodate today's busier lifestyles. Carnival Cruise Lines now specializes in trips of five days or less, and Lindblad Expeditions—famous for its lengthy adventure cruises to Antarctica—is marketing four-night cruises for North American travelers who prefer to stay closer to home.[9]

Internal elements such as motivation, perception, and attitudes—all part of the consumer's psychological makeup—can strongly influence consumer behavior. **Motivation** stems from the consumer's drive to satisfy needs and wants. For example, the popular search engine Google is constantly testing new features from its Google Labs (http://labs.google.com) and adding the best to motivate users to return to the site again and again. The more people who click on Google, the bigger its audience for advertising, which fuels profitability.

Perception is how the individual organizes environmental inputs (such as ads, conversation, and media) and derives meaning from them. When marketers talk about "cutting through clutter," they are discussing how to make the marketing message stand out among many messages bombarding consumers throughout the day—not just to capture attention but to motivate consumers to respond.

Attitudes are the individual's lasting evaluations of and feelings toward something, such as a product or a person. Especially after an event that puts an entire product category in a negative light, marketers need to plan for encouraging positive attitudes and perceptions. After reports of peanut butter being recalled due to possible contamination, J. M. Smucker launched a campaign to reassure consumers that its Jif and Smucker's peanut butters were safe and not involved in the recall.[10]

Business Markets

Like consumer markets, business markets are made up of people—individuals who buy on behalf of their company, government agency, institution, or not-for-profit organization. In the context of business buying, however, these people are generally influenced by a different set of factors. Marketers therefore need to examine organizational considerations and connections when analyzing business buying decisions and behavior.

PLANNING TIP

Dig deeper to understand underlying needs and internal concerns of business customers.

ORGANIZATIONAL CONNECTIONS   Although exactly who does the buying differs from company to company, officially designated purchasing agents are not the only people involved with the buying decision. Buyers are usually connected with other internal players. For instance, another employee or manager may initiate the buying process by suggesting a purchase; those who actually use the product may play a role, by providing specifications, testing alternatives, or evaluating purchases; and buyers may need connections to the managers who are authorized to approve a purchase.

In a business that buys express delivery services, as an example, a manager in one department may make the actual decision but managers in other departments may have a say or request assistance. Knowing this, FedEx has a laboratory to test customers' packaging and develop devices to improve the safe arrival of shipped items. One recent innovation for monitoring fragile and perishable items is a small chip that checks the temperature, light, location, and humidity inside a FedEx package. This wins FedEx support among a number of internal players and helps business customers satisfy their own customers.[11]

Depending on the organization and its structure, other internal players may wield some type of influence, such as insisting on compatibility with existing goods or services or controlling access to buyers. Not every player will participate in every purchase, so marketers must understand the decision process that takes place inside key customer organizations and plan appropriate marketing activities to reach the right players at the right time with the right message.

Finally, learn about the organization's current relations with competing suppliers, including long-term contracts, evaluations, requirements, and other elements. Many firms have long-term buying relationships with suppliers who meet preset quality and performance standards. Companies that outsource certain key functions, the way Japan's Daishi Bank outsources its back-office IT operations to IBM, generally sign multiyear agreements with the chosen supplier; other suppliers have a long wait before they can even try to bid for the business.[12] Researching a business customer's supplier connections and requirements is a good first step toward getting on the short list of approved suppliers and making the sale.

ORGANIZATIONAL CONSIDERATIONS Organizational considerations include the company's size and industry, share and growth, competitive situation, buying policies and procedures, financial constraints, and the timing of purchases. In researching these factors, marketers need to find out, for example, whether a corporation buys centrally or allows each unit to buy on its own; whether companies participate in online marketplaces; and what funding and scheduling issues affect the purchase. Internal priorities are another organizational consideration.

Business buying is also affected by **derived demand,** the principle that demand for business products in an industry is based on demand for related consumer products. As an example, a surge in demand for motorcycles, cars, and small trucks in Southeast Asia has prompted BASF, a chemical company based in Germany, to expand the production and distribution of its automotive paint coating materials in Thailand, Vietnam, Indonesia, and the Philippines.[13]

Derived demand requires that B2B marketers be aware of emerging trends and needs in consumer markets and be ready to help customers serve *their* customers. If suppliers are unprepared to deliver on time and within budget, marketers that serve consumers will have difficulty providing the value that their customers demand when and where needed. On the other hand, derived demand can also mean slower orders and sales for B2B marketers. During the recent economic downturn, low demand for air travel prompted many airlines to reduce flight schedules and find ways to slash expenses, which affected suppliers such as Boeing. Cathay Pacific Airways delayed delivery of new Boeing aircraft for a year, while other airlines cancelled their Boeing orders.[14]

PLANNING MARKETING RESEARCH

This chapter has covered a wide range of issues that should be researched to give organizations a better understanding of markets and customers during the marketing-planning process. Often the best way to start is with **secondary research**—information already collected for another purpose. Secondary research is more readily available and less expensive than **primary research,** research conducted to address a specific marketing question or situation. Exhibit 3.5 shows a few ways in which research can be used to support the marketing plan.

Secondary Research

Secondary research is often the starting point for a situation analysis, and it can be quite valuable—if you understand its limitations. Check the dates and the sources. Some sources offer new or updated statistics and profiles on a regular basis; others provide a snapshot covering a specific period, which can be useful but may be quickly outdated. Also consider the source's credibility to be sure the information is from an unbiased and reputable source. If a source reports data but did not actually conduct the research, find out where the information came from and whether it was changed from the original. If you don't know anything about the source, try to verify the information's accuracy before you rely on it for marketing purposes.

EXHIBIT 3.5   How Research Supports a Marketing Plan

Type of research	Definition	Examples of support for a marketing plan
Secondary	Research using data already collected for another purpose	• As part of situational analysis, to gain a broad overview of demographic trends in a certain market by examining U.S. Census data. • As part of metrics, to compare actual response to company communications with typical response rate within the industry.
Primary	Research conducted to address a specific marketing question or situation	• As part of product strategy, to investigate the benefits and attributes that customers want when buying this type of product. • As part of channel strategy, to determine what kind of in-store display will capture shopper's attention and result in the highest sales. • As part of pricing strategy, to understand how customers value the offering and competing offerings. • As part of communication strategy, to see whether customers receive, understand, and respond to a particular message or campaign.

Plan to use multiple sources of secondary research so you can get the benefit of different viewpoints and so you can check each source's details against what the other sources say. Look for the details you need in each source, taking note of how current the information is and extracting the specifics to be included in various sections of your marketing plan. Be prepared to explain and interpret the information in the context of your brand's situation.

Often secondary research is too general to answer detailed questions about particular markets and types of customers. That's where primary marketing research comes in. Marketers who are qualified to do so can conduct primary research to support the planning process. Some companies have specialists on staff to conduct primary research or prefer to hire outside specialists to do so.

Primary Research

Primary research starts with a definition of what you need to know about a specific market and how that knowledge will help you create a more effective marketing plan. For example, a carpet manufacturer might want to know more about the buying process families use to determine when to buy new carpeting for an existing home. This knowledge can help its marketers better plan the timing and content of communications to trigger interest in the brand and in specific carpet products. The manufacturer can also gain insight into stated and unstated needs that carpeting can satisfy, such as making a room more comfortable (stated) and communicating social status (unstated).

The next step is to plan for collecting data through observation, surveys (online, by phone, or by mail), experiments, and other research methods. Marketers are increasingly interested in ethnographic research, online research, and neuromarketing.

ETHNOGRAPHIC RESEARCH   When marketers use *ethnographic research*, they observe how customers behave in actual product purchase or usage situations and ask questions to clarify the reasons for their behavior. Researchers at Intel, which makes computer chips, know that customers can't always articulate what they want in a product. Therefore, the researchers observe customers to detect subtle differences in usage and expectations, such as how teenagers and baby boomers think about and use smartphones. These insights help guide Intel's long-term strategy and product development plans.[15]

Walt Disney uses ethnographic research to better understand the attitudes and behavior of an important target market for cable TV programming, tween boys (ages 6–14). Trained researchers observe tween boys as they shop; visit them at home to learn what they choose and use and why; and watch what they do in their free time. Based on this research, Disney now has tween actors in its TV shows carry skateboards with the bottoms facing outward (to show off the personalization, which tweens like to do) and creates characters who work hard to improve their skills (which tweens admire).[16]

ONLINE RESEARCH   Many marketers employ *online research*—research conducted via the Internet—because the cost is relatively low, it can be implemented and fine-tuned on fairly short notice, and the results are available in short order. On the other hand, the results will not be entirely representative of a product's market because not all consumers and business customers use online media or participate in online surveys. Nonetheless, many companies use formal online surveys or informally study consumer comments in online communities such as Facebook for clues to attitudes and purchase intentions. Cadbury, the

UK candy manufacturer, noticed that 20,000 people had become fans of Facebook pages devoted to bringing back Wispa, a chocolate bar it had discontinued four years earlier. The company decided to reintroduce Wispa—and sales have been strong ever since.[17]

Companies that use *behavioral tracking* want to research what customers do when they visit certain Web sites or click on certain ads. Google, for instance, tracks users' online activities so it can examine behavior patterns and serve up ads based on interests revealed by these patterns.[18] Other firms find behavioral tracking helpful for marketing purposes, as well.

Staples. The office-supply retailer Staples owns Corporate Express, which recently used behavioral tracking to analyze which products customers viewed, which they purchased from its site, and in what combination. Based on this research, the company's next marketing plan called for changes to its Web site. Now when customers click to view one product, they see suggestions for related products that other customers normally purchase at the same time. This change helped increase revenues and customer retention. Staples has also used online research to understand consumer attitudes toward and usage of paper shredders and other products it sells.[19]

NEUROMARKETING   One of the newest areas of marketing research is *neuromarketing*, using brain science to investigate and understand consumer reactions to marketing activities. Procter & Gamble and other companies are budgeting more for neuromarketing because they want to dig deeper into what happens inside consumers as they see products in stores, view or hear advertising messages, buy and use goods and services, and evaluate their buying decisions.[20] And neuromarketing can help nonprofit marketers plan for better communication. For example, a researcher at Yale University is using neuromarketing to determine how to improve the effectiveness of public service advertising aimed at cutting obesity rates.[21]

Using Marketing Research

If marketing research is not available or must be carried out, you should indicate this in your marketing plan and include the research as part of your plan's budgets and schedules. Also plan ongoing marketing research to help measure results during implementation. For instance, you might use advertising research to test messages and media as well as to study customer response; you might use test marketing to gauge reaction to new products. Research studies of customer satisfaction, market share changes, and customer attitudes and buying patterns are also valuable for spotting and analyzing clues to the company's effect on the market and customers (as well as seeing how competitors are doing).

PLANNING TIP

Summarize research findings, identify key needs and influences, and plan for new research.

At times, you may be forced to make decisions based on incomplete data; given the fast pace of the global marketplace, you'll rarely have enough time or money to conduct exhaustive research covering every contingency. Therefore, you'll have to assess the risk of waiting for more research compared with the risk of seizing an opportunity before it slips away or before competitors gain an edge.

Finally, privacy is a major issue in marketing research. Although marketers can do a better job of targeting segments and planning marketing activities by gathering and analyzing vast amounts of data, research also raises some privacy concerns. Most people are aware that supermarket purchases, Web-surfing habits, and other behavior can be easily tracked. This raises questions such as the following: What information is being collected and how is it used? Can individuals be personally identified? How are individuals protected by privacy laws, industry self-regulation, and companies' privacy policies? The Federal Trade Commission, for instance, is taking a closer look at companies' use of *behavioral tracking* research for targeting consumers online.[22] If your marketing plan calls for marketing research, don't ignore privacy concerns that your stakeholders may have.

Summary

When analyzing markets, companies start by broadly defining the general market and the needs of customers in that market. Markets are always changing, as consumers or business customers enter or leave and start or stop buying a product. For this reason, marketers should project market changes and analyze demand in detail prior to selecting a specific segment to target. Many companies track their market share over time, compared with that of competitors, to understand market dynamics and establish a standard for measuring marketing results.

Research is important for analyzing consumers and business customers. In consumer markets, cultural considerations, social connections, and personal factors help shape needs, wants, and behavior patterns. Marketers also research how consumers think and act in each stage of the buying decision process. Business buyers are influenced by both organizational considerations and organizational connections. Companies can use secondary research and primary research to gain a better understanding of their markets and customers. However, marketers may be forced to plan marketing activities based on incomplete data to keep up with fast-moving market opportunities or to counter competitors.

Your Marketing Plan, Step by Step

Continuing your analysis of the current marketing situation, use the following questions as starting points for learning more about both markets and customers. Document your answers in your marketing plan.

1. Where will you find secondary research about consumer markets? Try to locate at least three solid sources. In addition to searching specific key words, try:
   a. Population data from U.S. Census (www.census.gov)
   b. Demographic data from U.S. government (www.business.gov/expand/business-data/demographics.html)
   c. International demographic data from U.N. (http://unstats.un.org/unsd/demographic/products/vitstats/)
   d. The American Customer Satisfaction Index (http://www.theacsi.org/)
   e. Google Insights for Search (http://www.google.com/insights/search/#)
   f. College and university library sources (such as http://www.lib.umich.edu/govdocs/)

2. Where will you find secondary research about business markets? In addition to searching specific key words, try the following as you locate three or more good sources:
   a. U.S. government statistics about production and sales (www.business.gov/expand/business-data/sales-statistics.html)
   b. NAICS industry data (www.census.gov/eos/www/naics/)
   c. *Industry Week* magazine (www.industryweek.com/)
   d. *BusinessWeek* magazine (www.businessweek.com)
   e. *E-Commerce Times* (http://www.ecommercetimes.com/)
   f. College and university library sources (check your school's resources)

3. From the information you've collected, extract details to define the market for your product, including the

potential available, qualified available, and target markets. Summarize your findings in a grid similar to that in Exhibit 3.3. Be as specific as possible in your definitions, recognizing that you may have to adjust these definitions later (after you complete your research and plan your targeting strategy). If your marketing plan is for a product already in existence, also define the penetrated market. For a marketing plan that focuses on business customers, include NAICS codes in your definitions.

4. If your marketing plan focuses on a real product, research and estimate its current market share (in unit or financial terms). Whether your plan focuses on a new, real, or made-up product, estimate the market shares of the major competitors in the industry, based on your research. How have share trends in this product category changed over time? What

environmental factors seem to have affected these share changes? What are the implications for your marketing plan?

5. For marketing plans that focus on consumer markets, use secondary research to find data about how culture, social connections, and personal factors are likely to affect the people in your defined markets. Explain your findings in your marketing plan and include two specific ideas for how your marketing plan will make use of these insights.

6. If your plan focuses on business customers, research how organizational connections and considerations (including derived demand) are likely to affect the businesses, nonprofits, or institutions in your defined market. Explain your findings in your marketing plan, including at least two specific points about how your marketing plan will tap into these influences.

Endnotes

1. Jeff Brooks, "The Rise of 'Advertility,'" *Adweek*, November 9, 2009, www.adweek.com; Eleftheria Parpis, "Nike Plays New Game," *Adweek*, February 23, 2009, p. AM12; "Nike: Just Do Digital," *Revolution*, January 9, 2009, p. 26; www.nike.com.

2. Based on Gary L. Lilien and Arvind Rangaswamy, *Marketing Engineering*, 2nd ed. (Upper Saddle River, NJ: Prentice Hall, 2003), p. 159.

3. Carl Schramm, Robert Litan, and Dane Stangler, "New Business, Not Small Business, Is What Creates Jobs," *Wall Street Journal*, November 6, 2009, www.wsj.com; Jessie Scanlon, "Kiva Robots Invade the Warehouse," *BusinessWeek*, April 15, 2009, www.businessweek.com; Christopher Steiner, "Bot-in-Time Delivery," *Forbes*, March 16, 2009, www.forbes.com.

4. Matt Richtel, "Dell Still Struggles; HP and Acer Grow," *New York Times*, April 15, 2009, www.nytimes.com; "IDC: 2009 Toughest Year for China's PC Market," *Business Daily Update*, March 4, 2009, n.p.; "Nokia Looking to Make Laptops," *Informationweek*, February 26, 2009, www.informationweek.com; "PC Processor Sales Plunge; AMD Loses Share," *PC Magazine Online*, February 11, 2009, www.pcmag.com.

5. Rex Crum, "Gartner Says PC Sales Rose Worldwide in Third Quarter," *MarketWatch*, October 14, 2009, www.marketwatch.com; Jim Dalrymple, "Apple Market Share Rises Slightly as PC Shipments Fall," *Macworld*, April 16, 2009,

www.macworld.com; Matt Richtel, "Dell Still Struggles; HP and Acer Grow," *New York Times*, April 15, 2009, www.nytimes.com.

6. Catherine Boyle, "Tempus: Consumer Goods Hold Promise for Investors Shopping Around," *The Times Online (London)*, October 24, 2009, http://business.timesonline.co.uk; "Kroger: Private-Label Sales at a Record 35%," *MediaPost News*, March 10, 2009, www.mediapost.com; "Kroger Reports 8% Rise in Profit," *Los Angeles Times*, March 11, 2009, p. B4; Andrew Martin, "Moving Up the Food Chain," *New York Times*, December 13, 2008, p. B1.

7. Emily Fredrix, "Coca-Cola's Foreign Sales Strong in 3Q, Profit Up," *Associated Press*, October 20, 2009, www.google.com/hostednews/ap/article; Betsy McKay and Anjali Cordeiro, "Coke Warns of Challenges from Stronger Dollar," *Wall Street Journal*, February 13, 2009, p. B3; Ayala Ben-Yehuda, "Burger King, Coke to Launch Latin Awards Promo," *Billboard*, March 21, 2009, p. 18; Valerie Bauerlein, "Soda-Pop Sales Fall at Faster Rate," *Wall Street Journal*, March 31, 2009, p. B7; Normandy Madden, "Crossing Borders by Building Relationships," *Advertising Age*, October 13, 2008, p. 32.

8. Stuart Elliott, "The Older Audience Is Looking Better Than Ever," *New York Times*, April 20, 2009, www.nytimes.com; "Toy Testers to the Rescue," *WABC News*, March 24, 2009, http://abclocal.go.com/wabc/story?section=news/local&id=6725984.

9. Si Liberman, "Pursue Higher Learning on the High Seas," *New York Times,* March 15, 2009, p. L3; Amy Gunderson, "Navigating Shifting Tides and Waves of Interest," *New York Times,* February 15, 2009, p. TR7; "All Fans on Deck," *Washington Post,* January 18, 2009, p. P1.

10. Rob Duncan, "It's Not Just Peanuts," *TMCNet,* April 7, 2009, http://outbound-call-center.tmcnet.com/topics/hosted-call-center/articles/53816-its-not-just-peanuts-how-rapid-customer-response.htm.

11. Jane Roberts, "Innovators at Fedex Labs Harnessing the Future," *Memphis Commercial Appeal,* January 25, 2008, www.commercialappeal.com/news/2008/jan/25/whats-coming-next/.

12. "Daishi Bank Extends Outsourcing Contract with IBM," *Global Banking News,* April 17, 2009, n.p.

13. "BASF Expands Coatings Business in ASEAN," *Coatings World,* January 2009, p. 18.

14. Jeffrey Ng and Yvonne Lee, "Cathay Pacific Trims Capacity, Delays Aircraft Delivery," *Wall Street Journal,* April 17, 2009, www.wsj.com; Michelle Dunlop, "Boeing Delivery Cuts to Hit Everett Factory," *HeraldNet (Everett, Washington),* April 10, 2009, www.heraldnet.com/article/20090410/BIZ/704109892/1005.

15. Ken Anderson, "Ethnographic Research: A Key to Strategy," *Harvard Business Review,* March 2009, www.hbr.org.

16. Brooks Barnes, "Disney Expert Uses Science to Draw Boy Viewers," *New York Times,* April 14, 2009, www.nytimes.com.

17. "Case Study: Cadbury," *Marketing Week,* March 5, 2009, p. 28.

18. Nicholas Kolakowski, "Are Google's Behavior-Based Ads a New Privacy Concern?" *EWeek,* March 12, 2009, http://www.eweek.com/c/a/Search-Engines/Are-Googles-BehaviorBased-Ads-a-New-Privacy-Concern-241278/.

19. Karen J. Bannan, "Corporate Express Uses Behavioral Tracking to Boost Sales, Reduce Churn," *BtoB,* June 9, 2008, www.btobonline.com; "Staples Survey Reveals: A Shred a Day Keeps the Stress Away," *Reuters,* February 11, 2009, www.reuters.com.

20. Elisabeth A. Sullivan, "Pick Your Brain," *Marketing News,* March 15, 2009, p. 10; Cheryl Lu-Lien Tan, "The Neuroscience of Retailing," *Wall Street Journal,* May 15, 2008, www.wsj.com; "The Way the Brain Buys," *The Economist,* December 20, 2008, pp. 105–107.

21. Stuart Elliott, "A Neuromarketer on the Frontier of Buyology," *New York Times,* December 24, 2008, www.nytimes.com.

22. Wendy Davis, "AOL Vet Takes Helm of Privacy Group," *Online Media Daily,* April 7, 2009, www.mediapost.com/publications.

Planning Segmentation, Targeting, and Positioning

In this chapter:

PREVIEW

Instead of trying to market to a single neighborhood, city, state, nation, region, or planet—on the assumption that everyone has the same needs, behavior, and attitudes—most marketers focus on specific customer groups (*segments*) within a given market. This chapter explores the process of segmentation, targeting, and position, which is Step 3 in marketing planning (see Exhibit 4.1).

    You'll first review the overall process and then learn about the variables used to identify segments within consumer and business markets. Next, you'll see how marketers evaluate segments and choose coverage strategies for those to be targeted. Finally, you'll learn about positioning strategies for competitive advantage.

APPLYING YOUR KNOWLEDGE

After reading this chapter, continue creating your marketing plan by summarizing your decisions using *Marketing Plan Pro* software or in a written marketing plan document. Also look at the sample marketing plans in the software and in this book's appendix for ideas about how to present segmentation, targeting, and positioning decisions. See this chapter's checklist for questions about segmenting consumer and business markets.

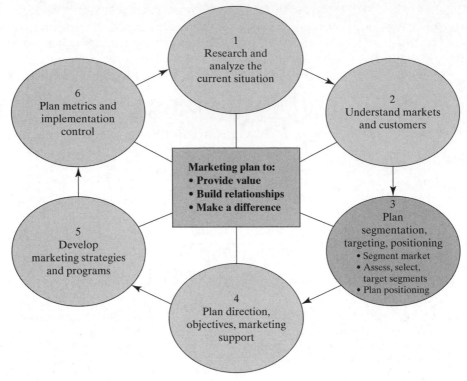

EXHIBIT 4.1 Marketing Planning: Step 3

CHAPTER 4 CHECKLIST Identifying and Evaluating Segments

Segmenting Consumer Markets

✔ Can demographics be used to group consumers according to needs or responses that differ by gender, household size, family status, income, occupation, education, religion, race, nationality, and social class?

✔ Can geographic variables be used to group consumers according to needs or responses that differ by nation, region, state, city, postal code, climate, and distance?

✔ Can psychographic variables be used to group consumers according to needs or responses that differ by lifestyle, activities, and interests?

✔ Can behavioral and attitudinal variables be used to group consumers according to needs or responses that differ by benefits expected, usage occasion, user status, loyalty status, technological orientation, attitudes, price sensitivity?

Segmenting Business Markets

✔ Can demographics be used to group business customers according to needs or responses that differ by industry, business size, business age, and ownership structure?

✔ Can geographic variables be used to group business customers according to needs or responses that differ by nation, region, state, city, climate, postal code, and distance?

✔ Can behavioral and attitudinal variables be used to group business customers according to needs or responses that differ by benefits expected, usage occasion, user status, loyalty status, technological orientation or usage, purchasing patterns, attitudes, supplier standards and evaluation?

Evaluating Segments

✔ Which segments should be eliminated for legal and ethical reasons or due to potentially negative stakeholder reaction?

✔ Which segments should be eliminated due to poor fit with company resources, capabilities, and mission?

✔ Which segments fit well with company resources, mission, goals, priorities, and offerings?

✔ How attractive is each segment in terms of market factors like growth and profitability; competitive factors like threat of substitution; economic and technological factors like required investment; and business environmental factors like regulation?

SEGMENTING CONSUMER AND BUSINESS MARKETS

As markets shift and the marketing environment evolves, what was once considered a mass market has now become fragmented and diverse. For example, marketers of widely used products such as soft drinks used to count on network TV advertising to reach millions of people during prime time. Today, network TV audiences are dwindling as a growing number of U.S. consumers time shift and media shift. Some order movies and sporting events on demand at any hour; some download episodes from Hulu or iTunes to watch immediately or later on a TV, computer or laptop, digital media player, or smartphone; some watch movies streamed live from the Internet or rent DVDs by mail; some click through hundreds of cable TV channels for a spontaneous viewing experience; and some click to search and view videos on YouTube.

Just as no two people's media habits are alike, no two people have exactly the same backgrounds, needs, attitudes, behavior, tastes, and interests. As a result, marketers are moving away from *mass marketing*—using one marketing mix to reach what was once seen as a single mass market—and toward *segment marketing*. *Segments* were defined in Chapter 1 as sizable groupings of consumers or business customers with similarities (such as similar needs, buying preferences, or attitudes) that respond to marketing efforts.

> ***PLANNING TIP***
>
> No product can be all things to all customers; segmentation and targeting focus your marketing.

Segments and Niches

Market segmentation is the process of grouping customers within a market according to similar needs, habits, or attitudes that can be addressed through marketing. If all the people in all the segments (either consumers or business customers) reacted in the same way to the same marketing mix, there would be no need for segmentation. But because no two people are exactly alike, companies can address these differences through marketing.

In the milk market, for instance, one segment consists of people who want to limit their fat intake and therefore are interested in buying low-fat milk products. Another segment consists of people who prefer flavored varieties and therefore will pay attention to ads featuring chocolate milk drinks. Yet a third segment consists of people who want to limit milk intake for health reasons and therefore browse the dairy section of local grocery stores looking for soy milk or other substitutes. The customers within each segment have similar needs or are seeking the same benefits, so they tend to react in the same way to the marketing activities geared for that segment (whether it's a product, an ad, a discount, or a store display). Yet people outside the segment are less likely to notice, let alone respond to these marketing efforts.

Within a segment, marketers can often identify **niches**—smaller segments with distinct needs or benefit requirements, such as people who buy low-fat milk in individual serving sizes at meal time. Over time, tiny niches can expand into small yet profitable segments, as two entrepreneurs in Toronto found out.

Sweetpea. Jarred food and organic food products are distinct segments within the multimillion-dollar market for commercial baby food. However, few competitors were addressing the needs of Canadian parents seeking organic frozen baby food when Tamar Wagman and Eryn Green started Sweetpea Baby Food. They got the idea when Wagman and her husband, a professional chef, experimented with cooking baby food with organic ingredients. For heat-and-serve convenience, the Wagmans froze each batch in ice-cube trays so they could pop out individual cubes to microwave when their baby was hungry.

Recognizing the commercial potential of this niche, Wagman asked her husband to create a wider range of recipes. She and Green outsourced cooking and packaging to a local food manufacturer, while they signed up wholesale and retail partners. Today Sweetpea offers 10 varieties of frozen baby food, markets its products in 350 stores throughout Canada, and rings up nearly $1 million in annual sales. Its niche has become so attractive that Sweetpea faces competition from Bobobaby, Healthy Sprouts, and other Canadian firms founded by mothers who want their babies to eat only organic foods.[1]

Reasons to Segment

Segmentation allows marketers to focus their resources on the most promising opportunities. This improves marketing efficiency and effectiveness as the organization gets to know each segment's customers and what they want and need. Such customer intimacy also enables marketers to notice changes in the segment and respond quickly. Finally, it gives marketers the choice of entering segments in which only a limited number of competitors are active or in which their most powerful or well-funded rivals are not competing.

As shown in Exhibit 4.2, segmentation lays the foundation for decisions about targeting and coverage strategy. The **target market** is the segment of the overall market that you choose to pursue. With these decisions, you're ready for positioning, giving the brand or product a distinctive and meaningful place (position) in the minds of targeted customers, as discussed later in this chapter.

Select the Market

The first step in segmentation is to select the general market(s) in which the company will target customers, based on the market definition, situational analysis, and SWOT analysis. Eliminate markets or segments that have no need for the product or are inappropriate for

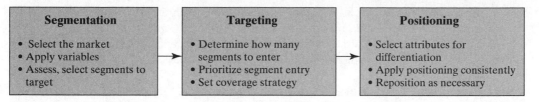

EXHIBIT 4.2 Segmentation, Targeting, and Positioning

other reasons, such as geographic distance, lack of purchasing power, ethical questions, or troubling environmental threats. Also eliminate segments that are illegal or out of bounds for other reasons beyond the company's control (i.e., tobacco companies and alcohol marketers can't legally market to underage consumers).

> *PLANNING TIP*
>
> Broadly define the market, then delete inappropriate markets or segments.

Now marketers are ready to start to identify distinct segments within the markets they have defined. People and businesses differ in many ways, but not every difference is meaningful from a marketing perspective. The purpose of segmentation is to form groups of customers that are internally similar yet sufficiently different that each group will not react in exactly the same way to the same marketing activities. If all segments were similar or responded in the same way to marketing, segmentation would not be needed—the company could simply use one marketing mix for the entire market. Therefore, marketers create segments by applying one or more variables to the chosen consumer or business market.

APPLYING SEGMENTATION VARIABLES TO CONSUMER MARKETS

Marketers can isolate groupings within consumer markets using behavioral and attitudinal, demographic, geographic, and psychographic variables (see Exhibit 4.3). Consumer markets can be segmented with just about every one of these variables; the choice depends on the company's detailed marketing research profiling customers and analyzing their buying behavior. Sophisticated marketers often apply a combination of variables to create extremely well-defined segments or niches for marketing attention.

> *PLANNING TIP*
>
> Use marketing research to profile customers and identify variables for meaningful segmentation.

Common sense also plays a role: Some variables simply don't lend themselves to certain markets. For example, the consumer market for paper towels might be segmented in terms of education, but will the resulting groupings reveal differing needs or responses

EXHIBIT 4.3 Segmentation Variables for Consumer Markets

Type of Variable	*Examples*
Behavioral and attitudinal	Benefits perceived/expected, occasion/rate of usage, user status, loyalty status, attitude toward product and usage, technological orientation, price sensitivity
Demographic	Age, gender, family status, household size, income, occupation, education, race, nationality, religion, social class
Geographic	Location (by country, region, state, city, neighborhood, postal code), distance, climate
Psychographic	Lifestyle, activities, interests

to marketing efforts? On the other hand, income and household size are likely to be better variables for segmenting this market, since either (or both) may result in groupings that have different needs or respond differently to marketing activities. The following sections take a closer look at the main consumer segmentation variables.

Behavioral and Attitudinal Variables

Behavioral and attitudinal variables are, in many cases, the best way to identify a consumer group for marketing purposes. This is because such variables help marketers analyze the specific value that a group of consumers expects from a particular offering. Note that benefits required or expected, usage occasion and status, loyalty status, technological orientation, and attitudes toward products or usage generally cross demographic and geographic lines, yielding segments based on how consumers act or feel rather than on where they live or how old they are. For example, air travelers look for different benefits: Business travelers may put more value on convenient schedules, whereas vacation travelers may put more value on affordability. Therefore, marketers will use different marketing messages for each of these segments, putting the emphasis on what people need or the benefits they seek.

PLANNING TIP

Behavioral and attitudinal variables create segments that cross demographic and geographic lines.

Segmenting by usage occasion helps marketers group consumers based on the occasion(s) when they buy or use a product. User status—whether a consumer has ever used the product, is a first-time user, or is a regular user—is particularly important when a company wants to increase sales by selling to nonusers, first-time users, or light users. Do consumers in the market tend to be brand loyal or do they constantly switch—and why? Companies often mount one marketing program to reinforce loyalty and another to court switchers from other brands.

Attitudes and behavior play an important role in Harley-Davidson's marketing.

Harley-Davidson. "We stand for freedom and independence," says Harley-Davidson's CEO. Some customers sport a Harley tattoo to express their inner outlaw; most live the brand by accessorizing their Harley motorcycles and wearing Harley-branded clothing. Company marketers know that the average age of a Harley owner is 49, most are male, and the average annual household income of its buyers tops $85,000. They also know that the brand has broader appeal than demographics alone can describe or target. "Harley brings together all walks of life," the company's chief marketing officer explains. "You'll find a neurosurgeon talking and riding with a janitor. It's a family."

To rev up U.S. sales, Harley's marketing plan includes segmentation by product usage (with special programs for teaching inexperienced riders to use a motorcycle) and by gender (with special programs targeting women who have the "Harley" attitude). The company particularly wants to encourage and reinforce brand loyalty because, the CEO notes, "half of our customers are people who have never owned a Harley."[2]

Demographic Variables

Many organizations apply demographic variables because these are common and easily identified consumer characteristics. In addition, they often point to meaningful differences in consumer needs, wants, and product consumption, as well as media usage. For instance, Dove and other skin-care marketers segment customers on the basis of gender, knowing that men and women have different needs, attitudes, and behavior patterns.

Segmenting on the basis of income can help marketers of upscale goods and services, such as luxury Silversea Cruises, identify consumer segments with the means to buy. It can also help marketers of lower-priced products focus on customers who need to stretch their dollars. An example is the retail chain Dollar General, which segments by income and geography and now rings up $10 billion in annual sales. Dollar General has also created private-label brands to appeal specifically to its targeted segments.[3] Combining demographic variables can focus marketing even further; Charles Schwab looks at household income, investment assets, and several other variables when segmenting the market for brokerage services.

Marketers must avoid stereotyping customers when using demographic variables such as race, nationality, and income. Adding behavioral and attitudinal variables linked to customers' underlying wants and needs will reveal customer motivations and benefits that can be addressed, segment by segment, through marketing. That's how Foster Bank has prospered.

Foster Bank. Foster Bank was originally founded to serve Korean-speaking consumers in "Little Seoul" on Chicago's northwest side. Knowing that recent immigrants were more comfortable banking in their own language, Foster's employees had to speak fluent Korean. Foster also adapted its banking practices to this group. For instance, because Korean American households often included multiple generations, Foster began taking extended family income into account when evaluating loan applications. Based on population growth, Foster added children's bank accounts to bring its brand to the attention of the next generation of banking customers.

Over time, many in the original customer base began migrating to other neighborhoods—and Foster followed. This opened new opportunities to serve other fast-growing immigrant populations, including consumers from Poland, Pakistan, and China. Foster again adapted by ensuring that each new branch was staffed by employees fluent in the languages of the local population. It also reached out to the adult children of its customers with electronic banking and other services for the tech savvy.[4]

Geographic Variables

Companies routinely use geography to segment consumer markets. The decision to use geographic variables may be based on a company's ability to sell and service products in certain areas or climates, its interest in entering promising new markets, or its reluctance to sell in certain areas because of environmental threats or unfavorable climate. For instance, Apple uses geography to segment the consumer market for iPhones because different regions require mobile phones geared to different telecommunications systems.

Still, companies that segment by geography must carefully note meaningful differences within each area and similarities that cross geographic boundaries.

PLANNING TIP

Geographic segmentation may cover a single neighborhood or an entire continent.

> **Waitrose.** A fast-growing grocery chain based in Southern England, Waitrose competes with Tesco and other national and local rivals by featuring organic foods and emphasizing quality and service. Because customers all over the United Kingdom are interested in organic foods, Waitrose can broaden its segmentation beyond the boundaries of current store locations. The retailer now serves a wider geographic area through online shopping. In fact, to attract customers in new geographic areas, Waitrose recently eliminated delivery charges for groceries ordered from its online store.[5]

Psychographic Variables

Segmenting on the basis of psychographic variables such as lifestyle, activities, and interests can help companies gain a deeper understanding of what and why consumers buy. Sometimes psychographic segmentation is the only way to identify a consumer group for special marketing attention, because activities and interests tend to cross demographic and geographic lines. People who share an interest in sports, for instance, may live anywhere and be of almost any age or gender. Baseball fans in Japan and in Washington state cheer when Ichiro Suzuki, a former star in Japanese baseball, steps up to the plate for the Seattle Mariners.[6]

Marketers who apply both psychographic and demographic variables may be able to create one or more segments that will respond to different marketing initiatives. The key is to identify the specific psychographic variables (and any other variables) that correspond to meaningful differences. For instance, the search engine Yahoo! applies both psychographic and demographic variables to create 140 specific consumer segments for its advertisers to target online. Users supply basic personal data when they register for Yahoo services and the site tracks what users do and where they go online to form a clearer picture of their actual interests.[7] Thanks to this segmentation, advertisers can match the content and timing of online offers to the interests and characteristics of the segments they wish to target.

APPLYING SEGMENTATION VARIABLES TO BUSINESS MARKETS

As Exhibit 4.4 shows, business marketers can segment their markets using three major categories of variables: (1) behavioral and attitudinal, (2) demographic, and (3) geographic. In many cases, marketers use a combination of variables, including industry (a demographic variable), size of business (another demographic variable), location (a geographic variable), and purchasing patterns (a behavioral variable). Again, the purpose is to create segments that are internally similar but don't have the same needs or don't respond exactly the same as other segments when exposed to the company's marketing activities.

PLANNING TIP

Think creatively about grouping customers using multiple variables, including behavior and attitude.

Behavioral and Attitudinal Variables

Segmenting by behavior or attitude (such as purchasing patterns, user status, attitude toward technology, loyalty status, price sensitivity, order size/frequency, attitudes, or benefits expected) is especially effective because it helps marketers understand what specific

EXHIBIT 4.4 Segmentation Variables for Business Markets

Type of Variable	*Examples*
Behavioral and attitudinal	Purchasing patterns and process, user status, benefits expected, supplier requirements and evaluation, attitude toward product and usage, technological orientation, loyalty status, order size/frequency, buyer/influencer/user attitudes
Demographic	Industry, business size, business age, ownership structure
Geographic	Location (by country, region, state, city, neighborhood, postal code), distance, climate

business segments want and value, as well as how and why they buy. Purchasing patterns can vary widely; for example, companies have differing buying policies and practices and buy at different times or intervals. Understanding buying cycles and policies can help marketers design and deliver the right offer at the right time. Similarly, companies that are frequent users may require a different offer or message than first-time buyers.

Demographic Variables

The main demographic variables in business markets are industry, business size, business age, and ownership structure. Industry segmentation is a good starting point, but it doesn't necessarily result in groupings that are sufficiently different to warrant different marketing approaches. Therefore, marketers typically segment further on the basis of size (as measured by annual revenues or unit sales, number of employees, or number of branches) or even rate of growth, reasoning that businesses of different sizes or growth rates have different needs. And combining demographics with behavioral and attitudinal variables allows B2B marketers to fine-tune marketing for specific segments, the way Dell is doing.

Dell. To market information technology goods and services to the business market worldwide, Dell segments by organization size, industry, usage, and other variables. One segment that gets separate marketing treatment in Dell's marketing plan is large companies, as defined by number of employees and other demographics. Another segment is that of small- and medium-sized businesses, defined by number of employees and annual revenues; a third is public-sector organizations, defined by industry (such as government agencies and educational institutions).

Dell crafts effective marketing mixes according to the combination of each segment's demographics and behavioral and attitudinal variables. For example, Dell found that small business owners worry about the people and money needed to manage IT systems while they're trying to grow their businesses; large companies worry about choosing IT components to fit their needs and serve their customers reliably and securely. For small businesses, Dell developed a Web-based system for managing IT systems, with three pricing levels based on how much support each company requires. For large businesses, Dell developed a consulting service for assessing IT needs and recommending a cost-effective, customized solution for each situation.[8]

Marketers that segment according to business age are looking for differing needs or purchasing patterns that relate to how long the business has been in existence. Businesses in the formation stage often have a higher need for office or factory space, computers and equipment, accounting and legal services, and other offerings needed for starting a new business. In contrast, older businesses may need repair services, upgraded computers and equipment, and other goods and services related to maintaining an existing business. Segmenting by ownership structure also can reveal meaningful differences. For instance, the insurance and accounting needs of sole proprietorships are not the same as those of corporations. Only by segmenting the market can marketers identify these differences for appropriate marketing attention.

Geographic Variables

Business marketers, like their consumer counterparts, can use geographic variables such as nation, region, state, city, and climate to segment their markets. This allows grouping of business customers according to concentration of outlets, location of headquarters, and geography-related needs or responses. It also enables business marketers to consider how geographic differences affect each segment.

By applying geographic as well as demographics and behavioral/attitudinal variables, marketers can get a better picture of each segment and have more information on which to evaluate the attractiveness of individual segments. Here's how John Deere uses geographic variables in its business markets:

John Deere. Agricultural and construction businesses in different areas have different needs, demographics, behavioral characteristics, and attitudes toward the equipment they use. Applying multiple segmentation variables helps Illinois-based John Deere group its customers accordingly. As one example, Deere has long exported U.S.-made agricultural equipment to India. Over time, it found some farmers in India needed more nimble tractors capable of making very tight turns. In response, Deere developed small, maneuverable tractors for this segment. Soon Deere's marketers recognized that U.S. hobby farmers had similar needs—and now Deere imports its smaller, India-made tractors to the United States.

As another example, Deere marketers know that some construction firms prefer to rent rather than buy graders and other equipment, either to save money or because their projects don't always require the use of graders. The company therefore offers graders for rent that are designed for occasional users who need to learn the controls on the fly.[9]

PLANNING TIP

Determine criteria for assessing the attractiveness of segments under consideration.

ASSESSING AND TARGETING SEGMENTS

Once you have applied segmentation variables to a market, you need to assess each segment so you can select the most promising ones for targeting and also determine your coverage strategy for these segments.

Segment Evaluation

In preparation for evaluation, screen out segments that are extremely unsuitable or unattractive, based on poor fit with the firm's resources, goals, mission, and priorities (identified during the analysis of the current situation). Also eliminate segments that require specialized skills or extraordinary resources that are beyond your organization's reach or mission.

Exhibit 4.5 shows factors used to evaluate segments and identify the most promising ones for marketing attention. As this exhibit indicates, one key measure of attractiveness is the market segment itself, including current and future opportunity for sales and profits. Large, more profitable, or faster-growing segments are generally more attractive than smaller, less profitable, or slower-growing segments. In assessing opportunity, marketers also look at how each segment would affect the company's ability to reach its overall goals, such as growth or profitability.

A second factor is the potential for competitive superiority. Can the company effectively compete or lead in the segment? How intense is the competitive pressure in each segment? How well differentiated are competing products and companies that are already targeting each segment? As you saw at the start of the chapter, Sweetpea Baby Foods was an early entry in the frozen organic baby-food segment; now other firms eyeing this segment will have to contend with established competitors and brand loyalty.

A third factor is the extent of environmental threats. Based on the environmental scanning and analysis, what macroenvironmental threats, such as more restrictive regulatory guidelines, exist now or could emerge to hamper the company's performance in the segment? Would entering a particular segment stir up controversy and hurt the company's image among stakeholders? Economic and technological factors are the fourth category; these include investment required for entry, expected profit margins, and barriers to entry/exit in the segment.

Now that you've screened out segments you will not enter, determine how many segments you will enter and rank the remaining segments in order of priority for entry.

Fit with company resources and competencies

Market factors Size; growth rate; life-cycle stage; predictability; price elasticity; bargaining power of buyers; cyclicality of demand	**Economic & technological factors** Barriers to entry and exit; bargaining power of suppliers; technology utilization; investment required; margins
Competitive factors Intensity; quality; threat of substitution; degree of differentiation	**Business environment factors** Economic fluctuations; political and legal; regulation; social; physical environment

Identify most promising segments and order of entry

EXHIBIT 4.5 Assessing Segment Attractiveness

Some marketers do this by weighing the evaluation criteria to come up with a composite score for each segment. This shows which segments are more attractive and allows comparisons based on higher profit potential, faster projected growth, lower competitive pressure, or other criteria.

Different marketers plan for different ranking systems and weighing criteria, based on their mission and objectives, resources, core competencies, and other considerations. As shown in the simplified ranking in Exhibit 4.6, some segments may score higher for competitive superiority but lower for fit with organizational resources, for instance. The overall score generally determines which segments are entered first; here, segment B has the highest overall score and will be the top priority for marketing attention. Other marketers prefer to rank segments according to similar needs or product usage. And some examine how much risk they would be willing to accept in each segment, ranking segments from most acceptable to least acceptable risk.[10]

PLANNING TIP

Summarize your ranking and targeting decisions in the marketing plan.

Concentrated, Undifferentiated, and Differentiated Marketing

What coverage strategy will you use for the segments you want to enter? Many companies use **concentrated marketing,** identifying the most attractive segment and concentrating marketing attention on only that one. The advantage is that the company can focus all its marketing activities on a single customer grouping, the way Sweetpea is doing. However, if the segment stops growing, attracts more competition, or changes in other ways, it might become unattractive almost overnight.

At the other extreme, a company may decide to target all segments with the same marketing strategy, which is **undifferentiated marketing.** This mass-marketing approach ignores any segment differences and is based on the assumption that one marketing strategy for the entire market will yield results in all segments. Although undifferentiated marketing requires less investment in product development, advertising, and other tactics, it is rarely used today because it doesn't adequately address the needs of fragmented, diverse markets.

Instead, companies that target multiple segments generally use **differentiated marketing** to create a separate marketing strategy for each segment. Colgate, which once used mass marketing to target everyone who needed toothpaste—one product for all, one benefit for all, one campaign for all—has become expert at differentiated marketing. It targets an immensely diverse group of segments with individual marketing mixes: people who want whiter teeth, people who want less tooth tartar, people who have sensitive teeth, and so on. Differentiated marketing is often used by business marketers such as Airgas.

EXHIBIT 4.6   Sample Segment Ranking

Segment	Score for segment growth, potential	Score for competitive superiority	Score for fit with resources and capabilities	Score for economic, technological factors	Score for environmental threats	Overall score
A	3	5	2	4	3	17
B	5	4	4	3	4	20
C	2	2	3	2	5	14

Scoring key: 5 = highly attractive, 4 = moderately attractive, 3 = average, 2 = moderately unattractive,
        1 = highly unattractive

Airgas. The marketing plans of Airgas, the largest U.S. distributor of industrial gases, include marketing activities geared to the unique needs and characteristics of each targeted segment. One example is its targeting of industrial users and whole-sale suppliers of refrigerant gas. Airgas's marketers learned that R-22 refrigerant gas (used in older refrigerated systems) was being phased out in the United States, due to environmental concerns. The company would not be able to manufacture new R-22, but it would be able to sell *recycled* R-22. Because 80 percent of the industrial refrigerant market was then using R-22, Airgas's marketers recognized an opportunity to reclaim used R-22 when users installed new equipment and resell recycled R-22 to users who hadn't yet upgraded their equipment.

In the past, industrial users who got rid of older refrigerated systems had to pay to return used R-22 to gas wholesalers. Airgas's marketing plan presented a fresh approach: Airgas, not the industrial user, would pay gas wholesalers for receiving used R-22 and returning it for recycling. Airgas would clean and resell the recycled R-22 to industrial users who needed new supplies of the older refrigerant. This program, which targeted wholesalers and users of R-22, was highly successful: Within a year, Airgas had signed up 250 wholesalers to collect used R-22 and increased profits from sales of recycled gas products by 15 percent.[11]

Differentiated marketing entails considerable research to understand each segment's needs and results in higher costs for different products, different advertising campaigns, and so on. These costs must be taken into account when preparing the marketing plan and related budgets. If your resources won't stretch to cover all the targeted segments, you may need a rollout strategy for entering one segment at a time, in order of priority.

Personas for Targeted Segments

A growing number of companies are gaining customer insights by developing **personas**, detailed but fictitious profiles representing how individual customers in a company's targeted segments behave, live, and buy. Instead of marketing to a faceless, anonymous group, the company uses personas to get a well-rounded picture of a typical person in each segment. Personas give marketers a deeper understanding of what shapes each segment's needs, preferences, buying behavior, and consumption patterns. "A persona is a design tool that helps [marketers] make informed decisions, and it's an archetype we use to target our client audiences," says an executive of the Avenue A/Razorfish ad agency. "We cut across traditional demographic and psychographic information and bring it to life through photos, names, and a bio."[12]

Kadiant, a B2B marketer of sales presentation software, interviewed dozens of sales-people and then developed a series of detailed personas to portray what motivates members of its targeted segments. One persona, nicknamed Anya, describes a top performer who feels confident about the strategies and messages she's created for a variety of sales situations. Anya is competitive and spends extra time preparing for meetings with cus-tomers. Another persona, nicknamed Luke, describes an enthusiastic new salesperson, an expert networker who has less experience than Anya. He hasn't yet closed a sales deal on his own, but he works hard and he plays even harder. Kadiant didn't just paint a word picture of each persona—it created cardboard cutouts that help its marketers think about connecting with the real people in the segment.[13]

POSITIONING FOR COMPETITIVE ADVANTAGE

After selecting segments for entry and determining the coverage strategy, the next step is to decide on a positioning strategy to differentiate the brand or product on the basis of attributes that customers find meaningful. Marketing research can uncover customers' views of the brand and its competitors, revealing key attributes that influence customer buying decisions. Then the marketer must determine which attribute (or combination of attributes) supports the most meaningful differentiation and conveys a competitive advantage that will lead to achieving sales, market share, or other objectives.

Meaningful Differentiation

Companies can differentiate their brands and products by physical attributes such as product features, service attributes such as convenient installation, channel attributes such as wide availability, and pricing attributes such as bargain pricing. The choice depends on what customers value and how competitors are perceived. If customers value wide availability of a product, that point of differentiation is a potentially meaningful basis for positioning. However, it won't be a powerful point of differentiation if a competitor has already used that attribute to differentiate its product or brand. Also, a positioning will not work if it conflicts with the company's mission, goals, or resources.

Here are some examples of positioning based on meaningful differentiation:

- Porsche: powerful, status-symbol sports cars
- FedEx: fast, reliable, on-time delivery
- EasyJet: affordable, no-frills air travel in Europe
- Snapfish: convenient, inexpensive online photo service

In each case, the positioning conveys the value that the brand provides and sets the brand apart from competitors in a sustainable way. FedEx's positioning on the attribute of on-time delivery—backed up by day-in, day-out performance—has given the company a distinct image and competitive edge because of the value this attribute represents to customers.

Positioning and Marketing Leverage

Positioning alone won't build competitive advantage, although it can act as the driving force for marketing strategies and programs, setting the tone for the rest of the marketing plan. Thus, to leverage the company's investment in marketing, all marketing programs should support and reinforce the differentiation expressed in the positioning.

Remember, the environment is always changing, just as customer perceptions often change over time. You must be ready to reevaluate the basis of your product's or brand's differentiation and plan for repositioning, if necessary. Consider how Hyundai's marketing plans have changed as the competitive landscape shifted and new points of differentiation were needed to make the South Korean car company stand out in a crowded marketplace.

Hyundai. When Hyundai entered the U.S. market in 1987, its positioning was based on low price, period. Within a few years, the company faced the challenge of reassuring consumers that "cheap" doesn't necessarily mean "poor quality." Hyundai's marketers met that challenge by developing a 10-year, 100,000-mile engine and power train warranty, an offer unmatched by any U.S. competitor. Sales slowly inched up, and Hyundai established itself as an aggressive contender in the low-price car category.

By 2009, Hyundai was ready to expand by introducing higher-profit luxury cars, starting with the Genesis, a high-end sedan without the high price tag. Unfortunately, the launch of the Genesis coincided with major global economic turmoil. So Hyundai's marketers tweaked the brand's differentiation with the Assurance program, which allowed buyers to return a new car in the first year after purchase if they lost their jobs, without obligation or bad credit consequences. Although several competitors instituted similar programs, Hyundai had an edge because of its unique combination of brand awareness, improved car quality, and high value. Today, Hyundai's marketing plans continue to reinforce the company's clear overall differentiation and drive sales increases that bring the company closer to its long-term goal of higher market share.[14]

Summary

Market segmentation is the process of grouping customers within a market according to similar needs, habits, or attitudes that can be addressed through marketing. The purpose is to form groupings that are internally similar yet sufficiently different so that each grouping will not react in exactly the same way to the same marketing activities. Segmentation is the basis for targeting decisions about which market segments to enter and the coverage strategy to use. Once segments have been chosen, the company creates a positioning strategy for effective differentiation on the basis of attributes that are meaningful to the targeted segments.

The market segmentation process consists of three steps: (1) select the market, (2) apply segmentation variables, and (3) assess and select segments for targeting. Consumer markets can be segmented using behavioral/attitudinal, demographic, geographic, and psychographic variables. Business markets can be segmented using behavioral/attitudinal, demographic, and geographic variables. Next, each segment is evaluated and selected segments are ranked in order of entry, then targeted through concentrated marketing, undifferentiated marketing, or differentiated marketing. For deeper understanding of segments, some marketers use personas, detailed but fictitious profiles representing how targeted customers behave, buy, and live.

Your Marketing Plan, Step by Step

Use the following questions as starting points for the segmentation, targeting, and positioning decisions you will document in the marketing plan you've been developing.

1. Review your previous market and customer research. Which overall market will you select for your brand, product, or service?

2. If your offering is for consumers, look at Exhibit 4.3. Which of these variables might help you group consumers according to similar needs or attributes

that will respond to marketing attention? You're trying to identify segments that are internally similar yet are different from other segments (for marketing purposes). For example, within the overall market for a household product, can you form segments of consumers who expect different benefits? Would consumers who expect benefit A respond in a different way to your marketing, compared with those who expect benefit B? Can you segment the overall market for your product using age, location, or lifestyle to create groups of consumers that share some similarity but are different from other segments? Remember, the test is whether segments would respond differently to a particular marketing activity. If all segments would respond in the same way, you don't need separate segments.

3. If your offering is for businesses, look at Exhibit 4.4. Which of these three types of variables might help you group businesses according to similar needs or attributes that will respond to marketing? You want to identify segments that are internally similar yet are different from other segments (for marketing purposes). For example, within the overall market for a high-tech offering, can you form segments of business customers with similar technological orientation? Can you group customers and prospects according to industry or business size or both? Will these segments respond differently to marketing efforts?

4. Now evaluate the segments you have created, as in Exhibit 4.5, bearing in mind what you learned when you scanned the internal and external environment earlier in the planning process. Can you screen out segments that don't make sense for the product or brand, or that are a poor fit with your company's mission, capabilities, resources, or priorities? Do some segments represent risks that your company will not take?

5. Of the remaining segments, which would you rank highest and lowest on market factors, competitive factors, economic/technological factors, and business environment factors? For instance, are some segments particularly attractive because they're growing quickly (market factor) or there is little threat of substitution (competitive factor)? Are some segments unattractive because of unusually restrictive regulations (business environment factor) or very low profit margins (economic factor)? Create a segment ranking similar to that of Exhibit 4.6 to support your decision process.

6. Based on your assessment of the segments, select the most promising one for targeting. Next, determine whether your marketing plan should provide for concentrated marketing (one marketing mix for one segment), undifferentiated marketing (one marketing mix for all segments), or differentiated marketing (different marketing mixes for different segments). Explain your reasoning for the targeting and coverage strategy you select when you document your marketing plan.

7. Considering what you know about each targeted segment and your customers' needs, preferences, and behavior, what handful of attributes should you emphasize for meaningful differentiation of your offering? Describe why customers in your targeted segments would find these attributes meaningful (do customers value speedy delivery, for instance?). Use this information to draft a one-sentence positioning statement for your offering for each targeted segment.

Endnotes

1. Rasha Mourtada, "Mom's the Word for Marketing Baby Food," *Globe and Mail,* April 21, 2009, www.theglobeandmail.com; Rick Spence, "Week 5: Plan Out Your Path to Success," *Financial Post,* February 4, 2008, www.financialpost.com/story.html?id=280418; www.sweetpeababyfood.com.

2. Jerry Garrett, "Harley-Davidson to Discontinue Buell Sport Bikes," *New York Times,* October 15, 2009, www.nytimes.com; Susanna Hamner, "Harley, You're Not Getting Any Younger," *New York Times,* March 22, 2009, p. BU-1; Joseph Weber, "Harley Just Keeps on Cruisin," *BusinessWeek,* November 6, 2006, p. 71; Russell Pearlman, "Getting New Riders High on the Hog," *SmartMoney,* August 2006, pp. 28–29.

3. Geert De Lombaerde, "Dollar General Moves Closer to IPO," *NashvillePost.com,* November 2, 2009, www.nashvillepost.com; James Mammarella, "Dollar General Ready to Attack Soft Goods," *Home Textiles Today,* April 6, 2009, p. 17; "Dollar General Corp.," *BusinessWeek,* April 5, 2004, p. 116.

4. Becky Yerak, "Foster Bank Sees Profits as Other Minority Banks Struggle," *Chicago Tribune,* October 11, 2009, www.chicagotribune.com/business; M. Kathryn Kelly, "Thrift Makes a Comeback," *ABA Bank Marketing,* March 2009, p. 36; Walt Albro, "Chicago's Foster Bank," *ABA Bank Marketing,* July–August 2008, p. 16.

5. "UK's Waitrose Scraps Online Delivery Charges," *Reuters,* April 12, 2009, http://www.reuters.com/article/rbssConsumerGoodsAndRetailNews/idUSLC23921120090412; Adam Leyland, "The Price Promise," *Grocer,* March 21, 2009, p. 42.

6. Ryan Divish, "Two Big Hits in Japan Gather in Seattle," *News-Tribune (Tacoma, WA),* April 23, 2009, www.thenewstribune.com/sports/story/710923.html.

7. Julian Lee, "Web Users Under the Behavioural Microscope," *Sydney Morning Herald,* April 20, 2009, www.smh.com.au.

8. Charles Babcock, "Dell Eyes Cloud Computing," *InformationWeek,* November 5, 2009, www.informationweek.com; Lauren Simonds, "Dell Announces Nationwide Managed IT Services for SMBs," *Small Business Computing,* April 15, 2009, www.smallbusinesscomputing.com; "Dell Unveils Massive Reorganization," *InformationWeek,* December 31, 2008, www.informationweek.com.

9. "John Deere European Technical Centre Set to Open," *Farmer's Guardian*, October 29, 2009, www.farmersguardian.com; Katie Eagan Ernzen, "Deere Basks Under the Phoenix Sun," *Rental Equipment Register,* April 1, 2009, n.p.; Adrienne Selko, "The Rise of Indian Manufacturing," *Industry Week,* December 2008, p. 36.

10. See Stuart Read, Nicholas Dew, Saras D. Sarasvathy, Michael Song, and Robert Wiltbank, "Marketing Under Uncertainty: The Logic of an Effectual Approach," *Journal of Marketing,* May 2009, pp. 1–18.

11. Jocelynn Drake, "Better Portfolios through Chemicals," *Forbes.com,* November 6, 2009, www.forbes.com; Christopher Hosford, "A New Market Out of Thin Air," *BtoB,* April 6, 2009, www.btobonline.com; "MLT Creative Named Finalist for MAX Award," *Design News,* February 10, 2009, www.designtaxi.com.

12. Daniel B. Honigman, "Persona-Fication," *Marketing News,* April 1, 2008, p. 8.

13. David Meerman Scott, "How Well Do You Know Your Buyer Personas?" *Web Ink Now,* July 22, 2008, www.webinknow.com/2008/07/how-well-do-you.html.

14. Jean Halliday, "Marketer of the Year: Hyundai," *Advertising Age*, November 9, 2009, www.adage.com; Janet Stilson, "Passing Lane," *Adweek,* April 6, 2009, p. A7; Moon Ihlwan and David Kiley, "Hyundai Floors It in the U.S.," *BusinessWeek,* February 23, 2009, pp. 30–31; "Five Brands Doing It Right," *Advertising Age,* April 6, 2009, p. 10.

5 Planning Direction, Objectives, and Marketing Support

In this chapter:

PREVIEW

Where do you want your marketing plan to take you? The ultimate purpose is to help your organization achieve a number of *objectives*—short-term performance targets—that will, in turn, bring you closer to achieving *goals,* long-term performance targets tied to the mission. You set objectives in Step 4 of the marketing planning process (see Exhibit 5.1).

As discussed in this chapter, you start by determining the overall direction for the marketing plan. Whether or not you chose growth, the direction should be consistent with your organization's priorities and strengths. Next, you'll learn how to set effective marketing, financial, and societal objectives for the period covered by your plan. Finally, you'll see how customer service and internal marketing provide support for marketing-mix decisions.

APPLYING YOUR KNOWLEDGE

After reading this chapter, document your chosen direction, objectives, and marketing support decisions using *Marketing Plan Pro* software or in a written plan. Refer to a few of the sample plans in *Marketing Plan Pro* and to the plan in this book's appendix for examples of goals and objectives. Also consult this chapter's checklist for questions to ask when developing objectives for your marketing plan.

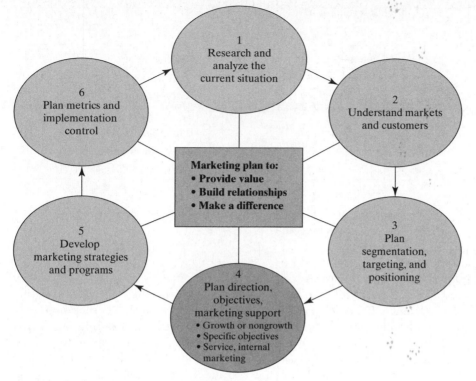

EXHIBIT 5.1   Marketing Planning: Step 4

CHAPTER 5 CHECKLIST   Do Your Objectives Measure Up?

✔ Is the objective specific, time defined, and measurable?
✔ Is the objective realistic yet challenging?
✔ Is the objective consistent with the organization's mission, goals, and priorities?
✔ Does the objective support the strategic direction of the marketing plan?
✔ Is the objective consistent with the organization's resources, strengths, and capabilities?
✔ Is the objective appropriate, given environmental opportunities and threats?
✔ Does the objective conflict with other objectives?

DETERMINING MARKETING PLAN DIRECTION

The DVD rental business Netflix wants to expand within the United States; the soft drink giant Coca-Cola wants to expand globally. These firms, like many businesses and nonprofit organizations, have marketing plans for growth. Growth is not always an appropriate direction, however; to deal with constant and inevitable change, some companies may strive to maintain current sales or revenue levels during certain years, while others may choose retrenchment (see Exhibit 5.2).

PLANNING TIP

Be guided by the mission, goals, and situational analysis when planning your direction.

Higher-level objectives and strategies

Growth
- Market penetration
- Market development
- Product development
- Diversification

Maintenance
- Sustain current revenues or market share
- Wring short-term profits from products, markets
- Prepare for future growth

Retrenchment
- Exit markets
- Drop products
- Downsize all marketing
- Limit distribution
- Close down in orderly fashion

Marketing plan objectives, strategies, and programs

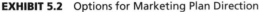

EXHIBIT 5.2   Options for Marketing Plan Direction

Although economic downturns can be difficult for businesses in the short term, they can also present good opportunities for long-term growth through careful marketing planning. David Neubacher, owner of Navakai, a technology services company in Colorado Springs, decided to postpone his aggressive growth plans during the recent recession. Instead, he got ready for future growth by revamping operations for higher efficiency and making marketing changes such as eliminating start-up fees for new clients and expanding the services he offers. When a couple of competitors went out of business, Neubacher targeted their clients and, thanks to the marketing changes he had made, he won a lot of new business. Even though the economic outlook was still gloomy, Navakai was back on track toward Neubacher's objective of generating $1.5 million in annual sales before the end of that year.[1]

What are your choices for growth strategies and nongrowth strategies? The next two sections explain what each entails and the implications for marketing planning.

Growth Strategies

If an organization wants to pursue growth, marketers can develop plans for one of these four broad strategies:[2]

Market penetration is a growth strategy in which the company sells more of its existing products to customers in existing markets or segments. It is especially viable for companies that can build on established customer relationships and positive value perceptions. Banks and retailers often use this strategy when they encourage loyal customers to buy additional offerings.

Market development involves identifying and reaching new segments or markets for existing products. Japan's Kikkoman does this with its soy sauce products. By expanding far beyond Japan into the global marketplace, Kikkoman has increased sales of its soy sauce by 10 percent a year for the past 25 years. To grow even faster, it is now modifying its soy sauce condiments for South American and European taste preferences.[3]

Product development is a growth strategy in which the company sells new products to customers in existing markets or segments. Nestlé, which markets Nescafé coffee, Nestlé chocolates, Perrier waters, and other products, is a master at using this growth strategy.

Nestlé. Based in Switzerland, Nestlé knows how to increase sales and profits by creating new products for its many markets worldwide. The fastest-growing brand in its portfolio is Nespresso, premium espresso coffee packaged in one-serving capsules for easy, foolproof brewing. Nestlé markets the capsules and special capsule coffee machines to espresso lovers through department stores, gourmet food retailers, and a chain of Nespresso boutiques in upscale city neighborhoods worldwide. Because Nestlé knows the needs and preferences of customers in its targeted segments, the company has been able to build Nespresso into a $2 billion brand and contribute to higher corporate sales even during a global recession.[4]

Diversification is a growth strategy of offering new products in new markets to take advantage of new opportunities, through internal product-development capabilities or by starting or buying a business for diversification purposes. Diversification can help an organization avoid overreliance on a small number of products and markets; on the other hand, too much diversification can dilute available resources and open the organization to competitive attacks on multiple fronts. Cisco, which makes networking equipment, diversified by acquiring Pure Digital, maker of the Flip digital video recorder. Although most of Cisco's revenues come from business markets, the company is edging into consumer markets with home networking equipment, the Flip acquisition, and new consumer products on the way.[5]

Nongrowth Strategies

Growth is not always desirable or even possible. In tough economic times, for instance, organizations often marshal their resources and strive to simply maintain current sales or market share. Another maintenance strategy is to seek the highest possible profits from current products and current customers without trying for growth. Sometimes companies are forced into a period of retrenchment because of rising costs, slower sales, lower profits, or a combination of these three.

With sufficient time, management attention, and selected investments, the most drastic change of direction—bankruptcy—sometimes leads to successful turnarounds. Less drastic decisions include withdrawing from certain markets, deleting particular products, cutting back on marketing, limiting distribution, or closing a division.

Sometimes companies limit or halt growth during a certain period. MinuteClinic, a chain of walk-in medical facilities owned by CVS Caremark, did this when it experienced slower-than-expected business during spring and summer months. During fall and winter, consumers flocked to the clinics—most housed inside selected CVS drug stores—for flu shots and treatment of other cold-weather ailments. Therefore, the company decided to temporarily close 16 percent of its clinics from March to September. It then had to modify its marketing plan, referring consumers to MinuteClinics near the closed locations during warmer weather and promoting the reopened clinics at the start of flu season.[6] Clearly, strategies for slow or no growth call for different marketing plans than those used for more aggressive growth.

SETTING MARKETING PLAN OBJECTIVES

After choosing a direction for the marketing plan, you'll set objectives as short-term destinations along the path toward longer-term organizational goals. The exact objectives set will depend on your current situation, the environmental issues and keys to success you have identified, the customers you will target, your organization's mission and goals, and your chosen positioning.

As summarized in this chapter's checklist, objectives will be effective for guiding marketing progress only if they are:

- *Specific, time-defined, and measurable.* Objectives must be specific and include both deadlines and quantitative measures so that marketers can plan the timing of activities and evaluate interim results. Marketers also should be able to measure progress by looking at sales figures, customer counts, satisfaction surveys, or other indicators. USAA, a Texas-based insurance and financial services firm, makes customer relationships its highest priority and monitors results by counting how many customers defect during each period. Its marketers carefully analyze customer data to identify new needs and provide information and offers timed to life-stage changes. Not surprisingly, USAA has one of the best records for customer retention of any firm in its industry.[7]

- *Realistic but challenging.* Marketing plan objectives should be rooted in reality yet be sufficiently challenging to inspire high performance. You need to consider the current situation to decide whether an objective is achievable or out of reach. For instance, one of Hershey's ongoing financial objectives is to achieve annual profit growth of 6–8 percent. In good economic times, this objective is realistic; in bad economic times, it can be quite a challenge. During 2009, with a price increase to offset the higher cost of cocoa, and an increase in U.S. market share, Hershey was able to meet this challenge.[8]

- *Consistent with the mission and overall goals.* Objectives set for the marketing plan should support the organization in fulfilling its mission and advancing toward its long-range goals. During the years when Ford was losing money and struggling to survive, it set short-term sales and market-share objectives to support its long-term goal of returning to profitability. It also set year-by-year objectives to support longer-term goals, such as sharpening brand focus by reducing the number of Ford-family brands to 40 by 2013.[9]

- *Consistent with internal environmental analysis.* Challenging objectives are empty words unless the organization has the appropriate resources, capabilities, and strengths to follow through. For instance, China Mobile, the world's largest wireless telecomm firm, has tens of thousands of suppliers in its network and a considerable cash position to back up its objectives of continuing to increase market share and revenues in Asia. Another source of strength is its sizable customer base: In China, the company already services more than 470 million customers and adds nearly 20 million new customers every quarter.[10]

- *Appropriate in light of opportunities and threats.* Objectives must make sense in the face of marketplace realities, opportunities, and threats. Newman's Own, which donates all profits to charity, researched the U.S. market for premium salad dressing and found it to be a $1.4 billion opportunity. Despite competition, seeking higher market share is a reasonable objective, given the size of the opportunity. Packaged fresh organic salad is another good opportunity, because this product's market has grown by 75 percent in just three years. Using marketing to increase share and revenues will help Newman's Own boost its donations beyond the $250 million already given to charities.[11]

Marketers usually set three types of objectives in their marketing plans (see Exhibit 5.3). **Marketing objectives** are targets for managing specific marketing relationships and activities; **financial objectives** are targets for managing certain financial results; and **societal objectives** are targets for achieving particular results in social responsibility. These objectives help you build relationships, provide value, and make a difference through your marketing plan. The next sections explain and show examples of each type of objective.

PLANNING TIP

Carefully coordinate service objectives with internal marketing objectives.

Marketing Objectives

Marketing objectives should include targets for managing customer relationships because these are so critical to company success. E-marketing expert Judy Strauss advises: "Objectives to raise profit, increase market share, or change stakeholder attitudes and behaviors are meaningless unless companies make effective plans to manage their most valuable asset: customer relationships."[12] Depending on the industry, direction, mission, and available resources, marketers may set targets for acquiring new customers, retaining customers, increasing customer loyalty, and increasing customer satisfaction. Customer acquisition and retention are especially vital in mature markets such as wireless telecommunications, which is why Verizon Wireless and its competitors use marketing for such objectives.[13]

PLANNING TIP

Check that achieving one objective doesn't prevent you from achieving another objective.

Some firms set additional objectives for managing relationships with other stakeholders, such as channel partners. Not-for-profit organizations usually set objectives for managing relations with members and contributors, as well as for attracting donations, grants, and corporate sponsorship. Other objectives in this category might cover marketing activities related to market share, new product development, and other vital areas.

EXHIBIT 5.3 Marketing Plan Objectives

Type of Objective	Purpose	Samples
Marketing	To use marketing to manage key relationships and activities	• Customer relationships • Channel relationships • Product development • Market share • Order fulfillment • Brand awareness
Financial	To use marketing to attain certain financial results	• Sales revenue by product • Sales revenue by channel • Break-even by product • Return on investment • Profitability
Societal	To use marketing to achieve results in social responsibility	• Greener/cleaner operations • Community involvement • Energy conservation • Charitable activities

Some sample marketing objectives might include the following:

- *Customer acquisition.* Expand the customer base by adding 200 new customers each month for the next year.
- *Customer retention.* Reduce the annual customer defection rate to 10 percent by the end of the year.
- *Customer satisfaction.* Score 96 percent or higher on the next four customer satisfaction surveys.
- *Channel relationships.* Expand distribution by placing products in four additional supermarket chains within six months.
- *Unit sales.* Sell 500 units in each targeted segment during every month next year.
- *Market share.* Capture 2 percent of the U.S. market by March 31.
- *Product development.* Develop and introduce five new products by December 31.
- *Order fulfillment.* Cut the time for fulfillment of orders from 48 to 24 hours by May 15.

All marketing objectives must lead the company toward its long-term goals. Simit Sarayi, a fast-food restaurant chain based in Turkey, sets yearly marketing objectives for the number of new outlets to open so it can progress toward its goal of having 500 restaurants around Europe by 2018.[14] As another example, Procter & Gamble's marketers are guided by corporate goals in setting their marketing objectives.

Procter & Gamble. This $80 billion giant of the consumer packaged goods industry set a companywide goal of growing to $175 billion in annual sales within 15 years. To achieve that goal, P&G sets detailed yearly marketing plan objectives for the corporation, each product category and line, and each brand (Pampers, Tide, and so on). In addition to setting global and country-by-country objectives for unit sales and market share, P&G also sets objectives for building channel relationships over time, such as getting its products into three million additional stores within three years.

Because P&G is especially focused on expanding in developing nations, it has set objectives for developing products and packaging that fit the needs and lifestyles of local buyers in each market. Yet objectives for market share and unit sales must be balanced against P&G's overall financial objectives, which include higher profitability. So when a recent economic downturn caused many consumers to cut spending or switch to cheaper brands, P&G decided to raise prices in spite of the risk to its marketing objectives. "While painful, pricing to protect the structural economics of our business is the right thing to do," the chief financial officer explained.[15]

Financial Objectives

Although the exact financial objectives will vary from organization to organization, businesses generally quantify sales volume and product targets, profitability targets such as margin or pretax profit, return on investment (ROI) targets for marketing, and break-even targets (see the discussion of pricing in Chapter 7). Not-for-profit organizations might set targets for fund-raising, among other financial objectives.

PLANNING TIP

Be sure objectives are achievable, given your resources and marketing tools.

To be effective in guiding marketing activities, financial and marketing objectives should be consistent. However, sometimes a marketing objective has to be modified or set aside to achieve an overriding financial objective (as in the case of P&G), or a financial objective may have to be postponed or changed if a particularly important marketing objective (such as launching a major new product) is to be achieved.

Some sample financial objectives might be the following:

- *Sales revenue.* Achieve $150,000 yearly sales revenue by December 31.
- *Product sales revenue.* Sell $3,000 worth of Product A every month.
- *Channel sales revenue.* Increase monthly Internet sales to $50,000 by end of year.
- *Profitability.* Increase the gross profit margin to 25 percent by end of year.
- *Return on investment.* Achieve 17 percent ROI on funds invested in direct marketing activities.
- *Break-even.* Reach the break-even point on the new service offering by June 30.

Ericsson, the Swedish telecommunications equipment firm, builds multiyear financial objectives for profit margins and break-even targets into its marketing plans.

Ericsson. When Ericsson set up a multimedia unit to provide Internet-based television service, mobile messaging, and mobile billing, it set relatively modest financial objectives in the early years. By the end of the second year, the unit was breaking even, sales were 25 percent higher than in the first year, and the profit margin had reached 2 percent. This showed some progress toward Ericsson's longer-term goals of growing the unit more quickly than the overall market and bringing profit margins up to the corporate level of 10 percent. Like most companies, Ericsson expects less profit at the start of new projects, such as the introduction of its 3G wireless network in China. "Any such new roll-out will always have lower margins in the beginning," the CEO says.[16]

Societal Objectives

These days, customers, suppliers, employees, civic leaders, and other stakeholders are looking more closely at what companies do for society—part of the push for more transparency. As a result, more organizations are including societal objectives in their marketing plans to make a difference. As shown in Exhibit 5.3, some societal objectives may call for cleaner operations or "greener" (more ecologically friendly) products, charitable donations, volunteerism or other involvement with community projects, energy conservation, and other socially responsible actions. For example, Hilton Hotels has a corporate goal of reducing water use at its properties worldwide by 10 percent before 2014. Its European hotels are already meeting short-term water savings objectives with low-flow showerheads and faucets, helping Hilton promote its green side to customers and other stakeholders.[17]

Fulfilling societal objectives polishes company or brand image and shows that the organization is doing something constructive about important issues. Setting objectives is not enough; stakeholders often follow the company's progress. So a growing number of small and large businesses, including Starbucks and IBM, post social responsibility reports on their Web sites. As an example, P&G sets both short-term and long-term societal objectives, such as developing and marketing $50 billion worth of sustainable, low-carbon-footprint new products within five years.[18] Find out more on the Business for Social Responsibility site (www.bsr.org) and the Corporate Social Responsibility Newswire site (www.csrwire.com).

Cause-related marketing falls under the umbrella of social responsibility because it links the marketing of a brand, good, or service to a particular charitable cause. Although the charity benefits, this is not outright philanthropy because of the explicit marketing connection. Cause-related marketing can be very effective in motivating consumer buying: In one study, 75 percent of the respondents said they were more likely to buy a good or service when a percentage of the price is donated to a designated cause.[19]

As a small business example, Dancing Deer, which makes cookies and cakes in its inner-city Boston bakery, donates 35 percent of the sales generated by one product line to fund scholarships for homeless mothers in Massachusetts.[20] As a big business example, P&G has a long-running cause-related marketing program in which it donates to UNICEF the cost of vaccinating one newborn against tetanus for every purchase of Pampers in Europe and the United States. It has donated the cost of more than 135 million vaccinations since the program started, bringing P&G closer to its ultimate goal of wiping out this disease before 2020.[21]

PLANNING TIP

Choose a cause that makes sense for your organization, customers, and employees.

Some sample societal objectives might include the following:

- *Conservation.* Reduce each store's use of electricity by at least 5 percent annually.
- *Reduce waste.* Increase the proportion of recyclable product parts to 50 percent by the end of next year.
- *Issue awareness.* Build awareness about breast cancer screening by attracting 15,000 visitors to a special page on the company's Web site.
- *Community involvement.* Encourage employees to volunteer for local projects on company time, receiving pay for up to 40 hours of volunteerism per year.

Social business enterprises, founded for the purpose of benefiting society in some way, place a higher priority on social objectives than on financial or marketing objectives. However, even these organizations must set and meet appropriate financial and marketing objectives to have the resources and strength to achieve their social objectives.[22] The nonprofit Ad Council also uses societal objectives to guide marketing decisions about campaigns to build awareness of or encourage action on issues such as preventing drunk driving and preventing cyberbullying (see Exhibit 5.4).

PLANNING MARKETING SUPPORT

Before you plunge into the details of planning your marketing mix, you need to set objectives for two aspects of marketing support: customer service and internal marketing (see Exhibit 5.5). Customer service is important in any business because it offers opportunities to reinforce competitive differentiation and start or strengthen customer relationships.

PLANNING TIP

Carefully coordinate service objectives with internal marketing objectives.

Internal marketing—marketing to managers and employees inside the organization—is equally important for building internal relationships as a foundation for implementing the marketing plan and satisfying customers. Setting objectives for these two areas of marketing support are discussed in the following sections.

Customer Service

From the customer's perspective, service is part of the product or brand experience, and thus has a major influence on customers' perceptions and responses. When setting

EXHIBIT 5.4 The Ad Council pretests its campaigns and measures results after the campaign to determine whether objectives have been achieved.

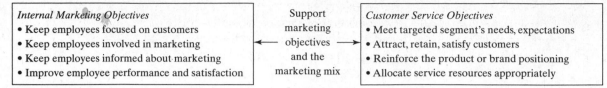

Internal Marketing Objectives	Support marketing objectives and the marketing mix	Customer Service Objectives
• Keep employees focused on customers • Keep employees involved in marketing • Keep employees informed about marketing • Improve employee performance and satisfaction	← →	• Meet targeted segment's needs, expectations • Attract, retain, satisfy customers • Reinforce the product or brand positioning • Allocate service resources appropriately

EXHIBIT 5.5 Objectives for Customer Service and Internal Marketing

customer service objectives, then, you must understand what your customers need and expect, what they consider satisfactory, and how service reflects on the brand or product. Although good customer service cannot make up for a bad product or spotty distribution, it can enhance the brand's image and may even allow a company to raise prices despite competitive pressure or other challenges.

In general, customers have different customer service needs and expectations at different points in the buying process:

- ***Customer service before the sale.*** Before they buy, customers often need assistance obtaining information about the product and its usage, features, benefits, and warranty; matching the right product to the right situation or need; researching add-ons like availability and pricing of replacement parts; and understanding how installation, training, or other postsale services operate.
- ***Customer service at the moment or point of sale.*** When they are about to buy, customers may need help choosing a specific model; scheduling delivery, pickup, or use; choosing among payment options or preparing purchase orders; arranging trade-ins or taking advantage of promotional offers; completing paperwork for warranty registration; or handling other sale-related issues.
- ***Customer service after the sale.*** After the purchase has been completed, customers sometimes need assistance installing a product; ordering refills or spare parts; scheduling maintenance or repair services; training users; or dealing with other postsale needs. Bank of America calls new customers a few weeks after they open accounts to answer questions and follow up on problems or needs. "It's low-tech, but it can have a tremendous impact on the quality of new customer relationships," says a marketing official.[23]

The marketing plan should set objectives for allocating service resources to deliver the appropriate level of customer service for each segment. It should also provide for improving self-service options when appropriate. Verizon, like many companies, maintains online community forums where customers help each other with tips and advice about trouble-shooting services such as Internet access. Recently the company set objectives for encouraging more customers to answer each other's service questions through the forums, which are also good sources of ideas for new features and products.[24]

Knowing that customer service is rarely perfect every time, marketers should include objectives for **service recovery,** how the organization will recover from a service lapse and satisfy its customers. Research shows that if customers are satisfied with the way their complaints are resolved, 70 percent will continue the relationship. In fact, those who are pleased will be more likely to tell others about their experience, bringing the company new customers through positive word of mouth.[25]

In setting service recovery objectives, companies should think about the process (such as what customers must do to register a complaint and what employees are supposed to do in response) and the results (such as measuring satisfaction with customer service). For service on the fly, some companies are planning for a Twitter presence. They designate employees to watch for tweets about customer problems and post timely responses. Marketers at Wells Fargo Bank, for example, initiated a Twitter customer service process to "stay close to our customers."[26]

Internal Marketing

Internal marketing objectives are used to focus the entire organization on the customer and generate support for the marketing plan. At the very least, internal marketing should ensure the proper staffing levels across functions and within the organization structure to carry out the marketing plan. It should also help marketers secure cooperation and involvement from other departments engaged in implementation, such as research and development, and keep employees informed about marketing activities so they can communicate knowledgeably with customers and each other. Another objective is to increase employee performance and satisfaction in a job well done.

Depending on the company's resources and priorities, internal marketing communication can take place through internal newsletters and Web pages; training and marketing or sales meetings; and other techniques. Here's how the UK electronics and appliance retailer Comet, owned by KESA Electricals, targets its 10,000 employees with internal marketing.

Comet. Through its "Comet Vision" internal marketing project, this 250-store chain has reinforced four employee behaviors that support better customer service: product knowledge, detail orientation, passion for service, and positive attitude. In addition to training sessions and ongoing communications, Comet Vision includes a recognition program in which employees nominate coworkers who have achieved excellence in one of the four behaviors. The retailer also changed its logo and employee uniforms to communicate the new customer service orientation to shoppers. Thanks to Comet Vision, customer complaints have plummeted, employee turnover has dropped, and both sales and market share have gone up.[27]

Upward communication is also vital, because it gives senior managers a feel for what the market wants and how marketing is meeting customers' needs. Executives of Walt Disney, for example, periodically suit up as Mickey or another Disney character and walk through Disney World or Disneyland to see what is happening firsthand. The company stresses internal cooperation and commitment to delivering quality service at every contact point. "Our goal is to treat one another the way we treat our guests," says the manager of performance and training. Disney is so well known for its internal marketing and customer service that it has created a division to offer training services to other companies and organizations.[28]

SHAPING THE MARKETING MIX

As shown in Exhibit 5.6, the organization's mission, direction, goals, and objectives (at the top of the pyramid) are the guiding force behind decisions about the marketing mix, marketing support, and specific marketing programs. Look to the priorities reflected at the top of the pyramid as you determine action

PLANNING TIP

The strategy pyramid shows how marketing programs are driven by strategic decisions.

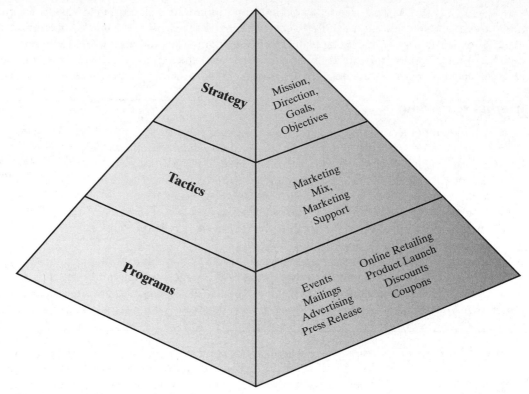

EXHIBIT 5.6 Strategy Pyramid

steps and allocate resources. All the programs you develop must not only be consistent with the mission, direction, goals, and objectives in the marketing plan, they must actually support them.

By properly implementing the programs in the marketing plan and using metrics to gauge the results, you should be able to move in the chosen direction and progress toward accomplishing your financial, marketing, and societal objectives. Understanding this essential link between strategy, goals, objectives, tactics, and programs can help you make appropriate, effective, and productive marketing-mix decisions.

Summary

A marketing plan may point the way toward growth (including market penetration, market development, product development, and diversification), maintenance of current sales levels, or retrenchment. Once the direction is set, marketers establish objectives for the marketing plan that are specific, time defined, and measurable; realistic but challenging; consistent with the organization's mission and goals; consistent with resources and core competencies; and appropriate for the external environment. Marketing objectives are short-term targets for managing marketing relationships and activities; financial objectives are short-term targets for managing financial results; and societal objectives are short-term targets for managing social responsibility results.

For marketing support, marketers need to set objectives for customer service and for internal marketing. Customer service can be provided before, during, and after the sale, with service geared to customer segments and marketing plan objectives and with appropriate objectives for service recovery. Internal marketing involves marketing to people inside the organization, necessary for building external relationships and implementing the marketing plan. The strategy pyramid illustrates the principle that marketing tactics and programs must support the mission, direction, goals, and objectives.

Your Marketing Plan, Step by Step

These questions will get you started on deciding on your direction and objectives for the marketing plan you've been developing. To see how objectives, customer service, and internal marketing are addressed in a marketing plan, review the SonicSuperphone sample in this book's appendix. Remember to document what you decide in your written plan or using Marketing Plan Pro.

1. Based on your product or organization's current situation, SWOT analysis, and long-term goals, will you use your marketing plan to pursue a growth or nongrowth strategy? Of the specific options shown in Exhibit 5.2, which will you choose for your plan—and why?

2. Now that you know the direction you will follow, create a table with three columns. The first column will contain marketing objectives; the second, financial objectives; and the third, societal objectives. Think about the marketing objectives you need to achieve to move in the direction you've chosen. Will you need to set objectives for market share, unit sales volume, number of distributors, or brand awareness? For a new business, is customer acquisition a priority? For an existing business, is customer retention a priority? List at least three marketing objectives for your plan.

3. Next, consider the financial objectives you need to set. Will you be seeking to achieve a particular level of sales revenue or profit by product or channel or market? For a new product, what break-even objective will you set? Does your organization require a minimum return on investment for

marketing? List at least three financial objectives for your plan, bearing in mind the interrelationship with your marketing objectives.

4. Think about the societal objectives to be specified in your plan. Are environmental issues important to your organization? What about philanthropic activities and community involvement? Is there a particular issue that you want to connect with your brand or product? List at least three societal objectives you will include in your plan.

5. Check your objectives against this chapter's checklist. Are the objectives relevant, consistent, realistic, measurable, and time defined? Are your targets specific enough to guide your marketing activities in the short term?

6. What type of internal marketing and customer service support is necessary to move the organization in the direction you've chosen? Review Exhibit 5.5 as you define objectives for internal marketing, such as communicating with employees. What, when, and how will you do this? Who will be responsible, and how will results be measured? Also define customer service objectives, including targets for service recovery, if appropriate.

Endnotes

1. Debbie Kelley, "Businesses Getting Creative to Survive," *Morning Call (Allentown, PA)*, May 10, 2009, www.mcall.com.
2. H. Igor Ansoff, "Strategies for Diversification," *Harvard Business Review*, September–October 1957, pp. 113–124; Philip Kotler, *Kotler on Marketing* (New York: The Free Press, 1999), pp. 46–48.
3. "Kikkoman Introduces New Flavors," *QSR Magazine.com*, July 21, 2009, www.qsrmagazine.com; "Sauce of Success: How Yuzabouro Mogi of Kikkoman Helped Turn Soy Sauce into a Global Product," *The Economist*, April 11, 2009, p. 68.
4. "Nespresso opens up in WBJ: AUS," *Food Week*, October 19, 2009, www.foodweek.com.au; Carolyn Cui, "At-Home Brewing Boosts Coffee," *Wall Street Journal*, May 5, 2009, www.wsj.com; Matthew Saltmarsh, "A Cup of Coffee, Enriched by Lifestyle," *New York Times*, February 20, 2009, www.nytimes.com.

5. Matt Hamblen, "Cisco Doubles Down on Collaboration with 61 New Products," *ComputerWorld,* November 9, 2009, www.computerworld.com; Ashlee Vance, "Cisco Flips Over Pure Digital," *New York Times,* March 19, 2009, www.nytimes.com.

6. Ted Nesi, "CVS Will Move MinuteClinic HQ to R.I.," *Providence Business News*, November 4, 2009, www.pbn.com; "CVS Fine-Tunes Clinic Strategy," *Chain Drug Review,* April 6, 2009, p. 4; Pamela Lewis Dolan, "Seasonal Slump Shutters 89 MinuteClinic Locations," *American Medical News,* March 30, 2009, n.p.

7. Andrew Parker, "A Value Focus for Enterprise IT," *Computing,* April 30, 2009, www.computing.co.uk; Scott Hornstein, "Use Care with That Database," *Sales and Marketing Management,* May 2006, p. 22; "New Metrics for Tracking a CRM Program's Success," *Report on Customer Relationship Management,* February 2002, p. 1.

8. Brad Dorfman, "Hershey's Profit Beats Estimates, Price Hikes Help," *Reuters,* April 23, 2009, www.reuters.com.

9. Alex Taylor III, "Fixing Up Ford," *Fortune,* May 11, 2009, http://money.cnn.com/2009/05/11/news/companies/mulally_ford.fortune/?postversion=2009051110.

10. Andrew Peaple, "China Mobile to Stay Close to Home," *Wall Street Journal,* October 23, 2009, www.wsj.com; Mark Lee, "China Mobile's Profit Growth Slows," *Bloomberg,* April 20, 2009, www.bloomberg.com; "Chinese Business: Time to Change the Act," *The Economist,* February 21, 2009, pp. 69–71.

11. M. Dowd, "Cool Hand Paul," *New York Times,* September 30, 2008, www.nytimes.com; Diane Toops, "Rising Stars," *Food Processing,* March 2006, pp. 26+; Jon Gertner, "Newman's Own," *New York Times,* November 16, 2003, Sec. 3, p. 4.

12. Personal communication with Judy Strauss.

13. Saul Hansell, "Signs Your Wireless Carrier Loves You," *New York Times,* May 11, 2009, www.nytimes.com.

14. Aysegul Sakarya, "Domestic Brand Aims to Be the Next McDonald's," *Hurriyet Daily News,* May 4, 2009, www.hurriyet.com.

15. Anjali Cordeiro, "Procter & Gamble, Colgate Report Better-Than-Expected Profits," *Wall Street Journal*, October 29, 2009, www.wsj.com; David Holthaus, "P&G Reaches Out to Poorer Nations," *Cincinnati Enquirer,* May 9, 2009, www.cincinnati.com; Ellen Byron, "P&G, Colgate Hit by Consumer Thrift," *Wall Street Journal,* May 1, 2009, www.wsj.com; Steve Lohr, "How Crisis Shapes the Corporate Model," *New York Times,* March 29, 2009, p. BU-4.

16. David Jolly, "Ericsson Posts Sharp Decline in Profit," *New York Times,* October 22, 2009, www.nytimes.com; Simon Johnson, "Ericsson Multimedia Head Sees Better Margins Ahead," *Reuters,* May 12, 2009, www.reuters.com; Lionel Laurent, "Weak Connection at Ericsson," *Forbes,* April 30, 2009, www.forbes.com.

17. Brad Tuttle, "Have a Green Stay," *Budget Travel,* April 2009, pp. 31–32.

18. "Procter & Gamble Deepens Corporate Commitment to Sustainability," Procter & Gamble news release, March 26, 2009, www.pg.com/news.

19. Elaine Wong, "When the Going Gets Tough, P&G Gets Philanthropic," *Brandweek,* March 7, 2009, www.brandweek.com.

20. Ben Smith, "Former Atlanta Undertaking Bike Trek to Benefit Homeless," *Atlanta Journal-Constitution,* April 27, 2009, www.ajc.com.

21. David Holthaus, "P&G Doing Good Is Good Business," *Cincinnati Inquirer,* April 24, 2009, http://news.cincinnati.com.

22. See John Markoff, "When Tech Innovation Has a Social Mission," *New York Times,* April 13, 2008, p. BU-4.

23. Charles Keenan, "Translating Customer Service to the Front Lines," *American Banker,* May 7, 2001, pp. 18A+.

24. Steve Lohr, "Customer Service? Ask a Volunteer," *New York Times,* April 26, 2009, p. BU-4.

25. Rod Stiefbold, "Dissatisfied Customers Require Recovery Plans," *Marketing News,* October 27, 2003, pp. 44–46.

26. Kathy Chu and Kim Thai, "Banks Try Social Networking," *USA Today,* May 12, 2009, www.usatoday.com.

27. "Kesa Charges for Store Displays at Comet," *Reuters,* January 27, 2009, www.reuters.com; "Awards for Excellence: Internal Marketing," *Marketing,* June 21, 2006, p. 17.

28. Rhonda Bodfield, "TUSD Staffers to Get Disney Training," *Arizona Daily Star,* October 19, 2008, www.azstarnet.com; Bruce Orwall and Emily Nelson, "Small World: Hidden Wall Shields Disney's Kingdom," *Wall Street Journal,* February 13, 2004, p. A1; "Working Their Magic: Disney Culture Molds Happy Employees," *Employee Benefit News,* September 1, 2003, www.benefitnews.com.

6 Developing Product and Brand Strategy

In this chapter:

PREVIEW

What's a good marketing investment for a company with $33 billion to spend? Cisco Systems has decided to spend much of its cash on new tech-related goods and services, introducing everything from digital billboards and videoconferencing services to home entertainment networking components and video surveillance systems. Not all of its new products will succeed, but Cisco is confident of its decision to seek new possibilities because customers "are telling us they want us to move faster" into the future.[1]

Successful new products can help your company and its customers move into the future, despite the risks. Formulating product and brand strategy is part of Step 5 of the marketing planning process (see Exhibit 6.1). In this chapter, you'll learn about the various elements to be considered in product strategy, including the value you provide to customers and the management of a product throughout its life cycle. You'll also explore key branding decisions to be made as you write your marketing plan.

APPLYING YOUR KNOWLEDGE

After studying this chapter, review the sample plan in this book's appendix and browse some of the samples in *Marketing Plan Pro* software for ideas about planning for product and brand strategy. Then continue your project by answering the questions in "Your Marketing Plan, Step by Step," at the end of this chapter. Finally, document your decisions using *Marketing Plan Pro* software or in your written plan, using this chapter's checklist as a guide to analyzing offerings and developing product strategy.

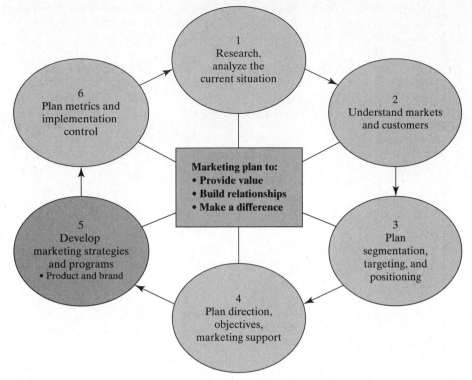

EXHIBIT 6.1 Marketing Planning: Step 5

CHAPTER 6 CHECKLIST   Analyzing and Planning Product Strategy

Current Offerings

✔ What products are being offered, at what price points, and for what customer segments?
✔ What are the unit sales, revenues, and profit trends of each product over the years?
✔ How are newer products faring in relation to older products?
✔ What is the market share of each product or line, and how does each support line sales?
✔ How does each product contribute to the company's performance and goals?
✔ Which product accounts for the largest proportion of sales and profits?
✔ How do product sales vary according to geography and channel?

Product Plans

✔ How does each product support the organization's objectives and strategic direction?
✔ What opportunities for adding value through product modifications or introductions exist?
✔ How do each product's features and benefits, quality, packaging, services, and branding provide value for customers? What enhancements would add value and help the company achieve its goals?
✔ How do each product's features and benefits, quality, packaging, services, and branding compare with competitive offerings?

✔ Where is each product in t...
✔ How can product introduct...
✔ What changes to product lin...
goals?

PLANNING PRODUCT STRATEGY

Given today's fiercely competitive global m...
ever before about the value they expect fr...
provided by the benefits delivered by its feat...
design, packaging and labeling, and branding...
shows, your strategy must be based on a th...
customers, your organization's current situation...
forces. Of course, any offering must help achieve...
tives, whether you're aiming for higher profit, mark...
especially since resources are limited and marketers ...

Goods, Services, and Other Products

What will your product be? It can consist of any of the fo...

- *Tangible goods* such as ice cream sandwiches and fil...   ...which customers can buy, lease, rent, or use.
- *Services* such as Internet search engines or cell phone services, which are primarily intangible but may involve physical items (computer or cell phone).
- *Places* such as geographic regions courting tourists, states vying for business investment, or cities seeking to host activities such as the Olympic Games.
- *Ideas* such as eating healthy or supporting human rights, with the objective of shaping the targeted segment's attitudes and behavior.

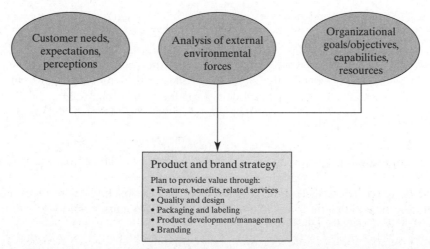

EXHIBIT 6.2 Product and Brand Strategy

or a government agency, with the objective of ...attitudes and behavior.

...d Pitt or the pop star Miley Cyrus, with the objective of ...gment's attitudes and behavior.

...a marketing plan for a service, think about how customers and ...al with the characteristics of intangibility, variability, inseparability, and ...ou can use marketing to emphasize the positive aspects of these character-...minimize the potential downsides of these characteristics, as Exhibit 6.3 suggests. ...Entertainments Group knows how to market the best qualities of Legoland, the ...ondon Eye, and its other attractions.

> **Merlin Entertainment.** Based in Poole, England, Merlin owns the Legoland theme parks, Sea Life Aquarium, the London Eye wheel, and dozens of other family attractions in 12 countries. To add to the tangible aspect of the service experience, Merlin is always opening new rides, shows, and hands-on features for adults and children alike. It doubled the number of rides in its Legoland California park from 1999 to 2009, for instance, and is currently upgrading the London Eye compartments by adding TV screens and improving wireless Internet access for riders. Because service production and consumption are inseparable, Merlin's 13,000 employees are trained to help visitors get the most out of every visit.[2]

Features, Benefits, and Services

Features are specific attributes that enable a product to perform its function. In physical goods such as backpacks, features include padded shoulder straps and strong zippers; in intangible services such as online banking, features include integrated display of all account information and one-click funds transfer. Features deliver **benefits,** the need-satisfaction outcomes that customers want from a product. For example, customers who buy cordless

EXHIBIT 6.3 Planning for Services

Intangibility	Variability
• Services have no physical existence, can't be experienced before being produced	• Service quality can vary from one experience to the next, depending on provider, facility, time of day, etc.
• Plan to market tangible aspects of a service, such as expert personnel or new equipment	• Plan to market staff's training and experience, standardized processes for quality management

Inseparability	Perishability
• Service production and delivery can't be separated from consumption	• Services can't be held in storage for future sale or consumption.
• Plan to market efficiency, effectiveness, emotional benefits of customers interacting with service employees	• Plan marketing to increase usage during slow periods, shift usage from peak periods to slower periods

EXHIBIT 6.4   Sample Needs, Features, and Benefits

Product	*Targeted Segment*	*Need*	*Feature*	*Benefit*
Cordless drill (tangible)	Do-it-yourselfers (behavioral description)	Drill holes without electricity	Extra battery pack included	Drill can be used for long periods
Theme park (intangible)	Families with young children (demographic description)	Entertain children	Supervised wading pool	Toddlers can play safely

drills are seeking the benefit of creating holes for nails and screws, although some may seek additional benefits such as convenience or status. Thus, consumers and business customers buy products not for the features alone but for the value in providing benefits that fulfill needs or solve problems (which you can uncover through your market and customer analysis).

PLANNING TIP

Seek to add value while achieving marketing, financial, *and* societal objectives.

Exhibit 6.4 shows sample needs, features, and benefits for a product and a service. Each product targets a different consumer or business segment that is described according to behavior (do-it-yourselfers) or demographics (family with young children). In each case, note how the benefit interprets the feature in relation to each segment's specific need. If you analyze each feature of your product in this way, you'll get a better understanding of the value delivered to satisfy customer needs. As you plan, keep an eye on how needs, environmental influences, and competitive offerings are evolving because these can change at any point, possibly forcing you to change your marketing plan.

Beware of "feature bloat," adding so many features that customers become confused, frustrated, or dissatisfied. Before you plan for extra features, be sure they will help you achieve specific marketing plan objectives—and not at the expense of the bottom line, if financial goals are particularly critical. Understanding your targeted segment is the key. The many features of an iPhone or a BlackBerry are designed to appeal to heavy users of wireless services, for instance, but not to value-conscious or tech-wary consumers who use their cell phones only to make or receive calls.

More companies are building customer loyalty and profits through a product strategy calling for **mass customization,** creating products, on a large scale, with features or attributes tailored to the needs of individual customers. Through mass customization, M&M candies are now available with individual sayings, photos, and even corporate logos.

> **My M&Ms.** Although Mars offers multiple variations of its M&M chocolates (flavors, package sizes, seasonal colors) in local stores, it also has moved into personalized M&Ms in a big way. At the MyMMs.com site, consumers and business customers can design their own M&M candies, choosing one color or a mix of colors, writing a message for each candy, and selecting packaging appropriate for the occasion. Sports fans can choose M&Ms printed with a favorite team's logo; a business can upload its name and logo; and proud parents can upload a new baby's photo. In addition, through a branding arrangement with Disney, Mars invites orders for M&Ms printed with popular Disney characters. A few clicks and the order is complete—to be produced and shipped within days.[3]

In your marketing plan, consider how the supplementary services related to a product can deliver valued benefits to satisfy customer needs, now and in the future. Some supplementary services may supply information for better use of the product, as in training; some services may offer consultation for problem solving or customization of the product; some services may involve safety or security, as in storage of products or data.

Quality and Design

Often defined in terms of performance capabilities, the most important definition of **quality** is how well the product satisfies customers. By this definition, a high-quality product (good or service) is one that does a competitively superior job of fulfilling customer needs. Savvy marketers know that the basic functionality of acceptable quality is the price of entry in the contemporary global marketplace. Word of mouth (or online, word of mouse) can quickly sink a product with inferior quality—and just as quickly generate interest in a product with excellent quality. Good quality is no guarantee of success, but it can help you attract new customers, retain current customers, capture market share, charge higher prices, earn higher profits, or meet other objectives.

PLANNING TIP

Determine how customers perceive your product's quality compared with that of competing products.

Your marketing plan should take into account customers' tendency to switch to a competing product if they believe its quality is superior (meeting their needs more consistently or more quickly). According to a recent worldwide study, poor service quality is the top reason for customer defections (price is a distant second).[4] Quality is a major concern among cell phone users, for example, which is part of the reason for the higher **customer churn** (turnover in customers) at some phone service carriers. For many months after Sprint merged with Nextel, unexpected service glitches caused higher churn as frustrated customers switched to other carriers. Sprint has been working to reverse the churn problem and restore its reputation with a series of new service-quality initiatives.[5]

Another focus of product strategy is design, inextricably linked to quality. A good design means more than style; it means that the product can perform as it should, can be repaired easily, is aesthetically pleasing, and meets other needs. Services are affected by design as well: New York's Long Island College Hospital has redone its emergency room design to add efficiency as well as comfort, cutting in half the waiting time for medical attention.[6]

Design is at the forefront of many product categories, from computers and entertainment electronics to home appliances and workshop tools. When good quality is the minimum that customers will accept, the "emotional quality" of design is the marketing battleground that more companies are choosing for differentiation. Sustainability is driving many design decisions these days, as well, from laptops to countertops and beyond.[7]

Packaging and Labeling

From the customer's perspective, packaging adds value by keeping tangible products safe and in convenient containers until they are used; labeling adds value by communicating product contents, uses, and warnings. Thus, Kellogg breakfast cereals stay fresh and uncrushed in the plastic-lined cardboard packaging, and Motrin pain reliever tablets are kept out of tiny hands by child-resistant containers; both packages bear labels with information about product ingredients and consumption. When planning for labels, check on compliance with regional, national, and local laws and requirements mandating warnings (such as about the health hazards of cigarettes or alcohol), allowable use of certain phrases (such as "low fat"), and even the size or type of words (for warnings or other details).

Packaging can help companies burnish brand image by communicating and delivering benefits that stakeholders value, such as a commitment to sustainability. Coca-Cola's marketing plan, for instance, covers the introduction of sustainable packaging innovations such as bottles made, in part, from plant materials.[8] As another example, sustainable packaging is one way that Walmart is going greener.

PLANNING TIP

Consider channel members' needs and customers' needs when planning packaging and labeling.

> **Walmart.** Walmart's yearly marketing plans include metrics to assure that suppliers continue improving their packaging to incorporate recycled or recyclable materials, minimize waste going into landfills, and minimize the impact on the environment. The company also hosts an annual Packaging Sustainability Expo where hundreds of manufacturers demonstrate their latest eco-friendly packaging for firms that sell products through Walmart and Sam's Club. These and other steps are moving Walmart toward its 2025 goal of eliminating all waste in its 4,100 U.S. stores through redesign, recycling, and reuse.[9]

Packaging and labeling play an important marketing role by highlighting points of differentiation, explaining the product's features and benefits, reinforcing what the brand stands for, and attracting attention among customers and channel partners. In addition, marketers should plan packaging and labeling to "sell" from the shelf, because more than 70 percent of shoppers make their buying decisions while in the store. Finally, test new packaging carefully before making any changes. As mentioned in Chapter 1, sales of Tropicana orange juice plunged 20 percent after the company introduced new packaging and loyal customers couldn't find the familiar half-gallon containers on crowded store shelves.[10]

PRODUCT DEVELOPMENT AND MANAGEMENT

The fourth major element of product strategy is managing movement through the **product life cycle** of introduction, growth, maturity, and decline. Even experts have difficulty predicting the exact length and shape of a product's life cycle, which limits the practical application of this theory. However, you can look at sales trends for clues to a particular product's life-cycle stage: New products with low but growing sales are in the introduction stage, young products with rapidly increasing sales are in the growth stage, existing products with relatively level sales are in maturity, and older products with decreasing sales are in decline.

PLANNING TIP

Aim to have different products in different stages of the life cycle at any one time.

Product life-cycle stages can be influenced by many factors, including competition, consumer lifestyles, and societal attitudes. Household wipes, for instance, were once a red-hot new product, zooming from introduction to growth to maturity in just a few years as the market grew to $1 billion in sales. As competition intensified, companies had to find new ways of differentiating their products and building sales. Now that the product is mature—as are most existing products—major players such as Procter & Gamble and Clorox are fighting for market share and profitability, which complicates the marketing planning process.[11]

As you prepare your marketing plan, build in environmental screening and analysis to understand your product's movement through the life cycle and the marketing challenges you will face at each stage (see Exhibit 6.5). Consider how technology affected the encyclopedia's life cycle.

Idea Generation and Screening	Initial Concept Testing	Business Analysis	Design Prototype	Market Testing	Commercialization
• Based on customer needs and wants, identify new product ideas	• Research customer value of product concepts	• Estimate development, production, and marketing-mix costs	• Design and produce working prototypes	• Test customer reaction through limited market trials or simulated testing	• Plan targeting and timing of launch
• Screen out unprofitable or unsuitable ideas	• Refine concept based on research	• Compare costs with potential share, sales, profitability to identify good candidates	• Test prototype functionality, customer appeal	• Test different marketing-mix combinations for support	• Plan production and marketing-mix support for launch

Introduction	Growth	Maturity	Decline
• Launch the new product	• Enhance product (new features, improved quality, added services, new packaging)	• Add brand or line extensions	• Reposition, reformulate, or cut struggling products
• Support launch with marketing-mix programs to build customer awareness, make product available, and encourage trial	• Support rising sales with expanded channel coverage, pricing for market penetration, and communications to start and reinforce customer relationships	• Defend market share through competitive pricing, channel expansion, communicating differentiation, and promotion to reinforce customer loyalty	• Manage profitability through careful pricing, pruning channel outlets, and minimal or highly targeted communications

EXHIBIT 6.5 Product Strategy through the Life Cycle

Encyclopedia Product Life Cycle. The encyclopedia had been moving from maturity toward decline when technology disrupted the product, its pricing, and its channel arrangements. Encyclopedia Britannica, a pioneer of the encyclopedia, introduced its first multivolume set of books in the late 1700s. For 200 years, encyclopedias remained printed products packed with text and illustrations. Then the evolution of computer technology changed the way people search for authoritative reference material. Encyclopedia Britannica's profitability suffered as it tried different ways to extend the product's life cycle by marketing encyclopedias on CD-ROM and DVD, and through online subscriptions.

The spread of PC ownership caused new competitors to take a fresh look at this mature product. Microsoft created a marketing plan to enter the encyclopedia business in the mid-1980s; by the time it actually launched Encarta, its CD-ROM multimedia encyclopedia, several companies already had competing versions on the market. Sales were sluggish, so Microsoft dropped its price to $99; by the mid-1990s, Encarta was the best-selling CD-ROM encyclopedia. With the rise of the Internet Age, Microsoft added a Web site to provide access to the latest updates and later offered Encarta as an online subscription product. However, it discontinued Encarta in 2009 because by that time, millions of consumers were accustomed to looking up information using free search engines and online encyclopedias.

Encarta's demise came about, in part, because of Wikipedia. Founded in 2001, Wikipedia is a free, online encyclopedia, written by users who collaborate on articles about anything and everything. Wikipedia has 265 different encyclopedia sites in languages as diverse as Cornish, Kongo, and Kashmiri. Although Google wants to become a force in this industry through Knol, its free, user-written online encyclopedia, Wikipedia has a head start with higher brand recognition, more articles, and more visitors. Clearly, the encyclopedia's life cycle is far from over.[12]

The life cycle of the encyclopedia spans two centuries—but it's more compressed for some products, especially in the tech world. The personal digital assistant (PDA), with its calendar, contact, and organizing features, was first introduced in the 1990s and popularized by Palm. As technology advanced, rivals leapfrogged each other with new models every few months. Within a decade, the PDA was headed for decline as smartphones such as the iPhone, wireless devices such as BlackBerry handhelds, and tiny notebook computers took its place. Now Palm has discontinued PDAs in favor of the Pre and other smartphones that feature PDA functions.[13]

New Product Development

When companies like Microsoft and Google plan for a new product, they look closely at potential opportunities for providing value to targeted customers. Marketers also need to build on internal strengths to create competitively superior products and think about how to deal with any weaknesses and external threats. Your marketing plan for new product development must cover these basic steps:

- *Idea generation.* Collect ideas from customers, managers and employees, suppliers, distributors, and other sources. **Crowdsourcing**—inviting customers and others outside the organization to participate by submitting concepts, designs, content, or advice—is an increasingly popular way to generate ideas. Threadless.com uses crowdsourcing to come up with new T-shirt designs.[14] Dell set up IdeaStorm.com to solicit customers' ideas; Best Buy invites customers' ideas through blogs, Twitter, and other social media.[15]

- *Screening of new ideas.* Eliminate inappropriate or impractical ideas early in the process to avoid wasting time and resources later.
- *Initial concept testing.* Test to discover whether customers in the targeted segment understand and like the most promising new product ideas; refine or drop concepts that test poorly.
- *Business analysis.* Assess the business prospects of the remaining ideas and eliminate any that could be too expensive or will not contribute to the marketing plan's objectives.
- *Prototype design.* Design and produce a prototype to determine the practicality and cost. If different technology or skills are needed, making a prototype will bring such issues into focus before full production.
- *Market testing.* Test the new product and various introductory marketing activities to gauge demand and competitive strength. Google thoroughly tests every change to its search services before making a final decision; because everything is online, the company can try different versions and gather feedback to make a decision very quickly.[16]
- *Commercialization.* Introduce the new product in some areas or across the entire market, with the support of channel, pricing, and promotion strategies.
- *Monitoring of customer reaction.* Monitor customer reaction; if a new product does not fare as well as expected, the company faces decisions about changing the marketing mix (including the product), repositioning the product, or pulling it from the market. You can learn many valuable lessons even when customers don't react as positively as you'd hope. For example, General Electric has a marketing process in place to pick the brains of managers whose much-anticipated new products did not perform well.[17]

Here's how Griffin Technology plans new accessory products for customers to use with digital devices such as iPhones and iPods.

Griffin Technology. This Nashville-based company makes a wide range of peripheral products such as power chargers and speakers that go with computers, digital music players, televisions, and other electronics items. Many of its ideas come from customers and employees seeking solutions for a problem such as wirelessly connecting two gadgets. Marketers write a page on each new-product idea and submit it to a category manager, who discusses the concept with designers, researchers, and other internal experts to determine how well it fits with Griffin's customers, capabilities, resources, and goals. "We poke the idea and see if it screams while asking, 'Will people really like this?' or 'How does this fill a need?'" says a Griffin project manager. Through customer research, Griffin evaluates the level of interest and tests possible names and marketing approaches.

If an idea passes both screening and testing, Griffin conducts a business analysis to gauge the market size, competitive prospects, and profit potential. The next step is to build a prototype and refine the design until the product is ready for testing by internal users and selected customers. During this time, marketers plan the rest of the marketing mix to ensure solid, timely support for the product introduction. They also ask key retailers for input and advance orders before setting a launch date. Despite this rigorous development process, occasionally a few products will test well yet have to be dropped before commercialization because of unexpected circumstances such as cost spikes.[18]

In many cases, companies make decisions about new products and life-cycle movement to avoid or minimize **cannibalization**—allowing a new product to eat into sales of one or more existing products. Some cannibalization is inevitable in high-tech markets, where life cycles are relatively short because competitors race to launch the next breakthrough product. Companies often believe that if they don't cannibalize their own products, rivals will seize the opportunity to grab both sales and customer relationships. Rather than completely cannibalize a product, however, the firm may prefer to reposition it for other uses or segments.

PLANNING TIP

Should you cannibalize your own product before a competitor grabs the opportunity?

Product Lines and the Product Mix

The product strategy in your marketing plan should also cover the management of each **product line** (products that are related in some way) and the overall **product mix** (the assortment of all product lines offered). The existing mix is analyzed as part of the current situation; after examining each product and line individually, you can make decisions about the length and width of your lines and mixes. One way to grow is by putting an established brand on a new product added to the existing product line, creating a **line extension.** Another is to plan a **brand (or category) extension,** putting an established brand on a new product in a different category for a new customer segment. Because of the high cost of developing entirely new products, many products being introduced these days are actually extensions.

Shortening or narrowing lines and mixes can help you concentrate your resources on the most promising products and segments for survival, maintenance, or growth. Longer product lines and wider product mixes typically require more resources to develop and sustain, but they help deep-pocketed companies grow and pursue ambitious objectives. This is especially true when a multinational firm such as Sony Electronics formulates marketing plans for products suited to local needs and preferences.[19]

Sony. Stung by losses during the recent recession, Sony Electronics—known for high-end, high-tech devices such as the eBook reader and the PlayStation game console—drew up marketing plans to compete by expanding its product lines and mix. For Japan, Korea, and the United States, where high-speed wireless Internet access is widely available, Sony planned a new line of networked electronic items. For the United States, Sony planned a new line of popularly priced, brightly-colored HD camcorders geared to younger consumers. This line was intended as a competitor to the fast-selling Flip, a palm-sized, easy-to-use and inexpensive camcorder by Digital Technologies. Lessons learned from these product launches will help Sony's marketers lay a solid foundation for future profitability.[20]

PLANNING BRANDING

Branding is the use of words, designs, and symbols to give a product a distinct identity and differentiate it from competitive products. After customers learn to associate a brand with the value created by a particular set of product elements (such as features, benefits, and quality), they simplify the decision-making process by routinely buying that brand rather than stopping to evaluate every alternative on every shopping occasion. Strong brands can help marketers in a number of ways (see Exhibit 6.6).

In terms of branding, a product may carry:

- *Company name and individual brand*, such as Courtyard by Marriott, Marriott Marquis.
- *Individual name* for a product, a category, or targeting a segment. Infiniti and Nissan are separate brands, under Nissan's ownership, geared toward different segments of car and truck buyers.
- *Private-label brand*, used by one retailer or wholesaler, such as Safeway's O Organics food brand. This particular private-label brand is so successful, in fact, that Safeway has begun licensing it to a few retailers in other nations, including Carrefour.[21]
- *Multiple brands*, by *cobranding*, in which two or more organizations put their brands on one product; or by *ingredient branding*, in which an ingredient's brand is featured along with the product's brand, as when Intel computer chips are showcased as part of a Dell laptop. "We want people, when they decide they need a new laptop, to make sure they're going to look at Intel inside," says an Intel executive.[22]

Brands should be recognizable and memorable, capable of being legally protected in the physical world and the digital world, and suitable for international markets if and when the company expands globally.[23] They should also have some meaning for the target market and be appealing (whether expressed in words, images, or sounds).[24] Think of how the stylized peacock and the three-note chime symbolize the NBC network TV brand, for instance. Online brands are not immune to these basic branding guidelines. Amazon.com and Google have become strong, distinctive, and valuable brands through constant, consistent marketing-mix support, whereas online brands without clear differentiation or marketing reinforcement have struggled or been acquired by others. Google

EXHIBIT 6.6 Marketing Advantages of Strong Brands

- Improved perceptions of product performance
- Greater loyalty
- Less vulnerability to competitive marketing actions
- Less vulnerability to marketing crises
- Larger margins
- More inelastic consumer response to price increases
- More elastic consumer response to price decreases
- Greater trade cooperation and support
- Increased marketing communications effectiveness
- Possible licensing opportunities
- Additional brand extension opportunities

regularly appears at or near the top of experts' lists of the world's most valuable brands—and its value continues to rise.[25]

Branding decisions made during the planning process are closely tied to product positioning and other marketing activities for building customer relationships through brand equity, as the next two sections explain.

Branding and Positioning

Every consumer or business product faces some competition in the marketplace, from direct competitors (Huggies disposable diapers compete with Pampers disposables), substitutes (Huggies disposables compete with cloth diapers), or both. The brand not only identifies a particular product; it reminds customers of the value that sets the product apart from all others and makes it both distinctive and competitively superior. The company can influence but not control customer perceptions; however, it can control product features, benefits, design, and other points of differentiation that customers care about. Consistency counts: If a marketing-mix strategy or implementation conflicts with the positioning, customers can become confused about what the brand stands for.

What if a company wants to change the value that its brand stands for? Kia Motors, based in South Korea, is facing that challenge in the U.S. market.

> **Kia Motors.** For years, the main attribute that U.S. car buyers associated with Kia (and its parent, Hyundai) was low price. Now Kia wants younger buyers, in particular, to notice the brand for other reasons, not just price. Introducing stylish new designs like the Soul, a boxy vehicle reminiscent of the Toyota Scion xB, the Honda Element, and the Nissan Cube, is one way it's enhancing its brand image. Kia also has a marketing plan to rename some models as part of the brand image upgrade. For instance, the redesigned Spectra model is now called the Forte. "We want to leave the old baggage behind," says the vice president of marketing. "A lot of people don't know who we are anyway. So why not come out with new names like Forte?"[26]

The Power of Brand Equity

The stronger the brand, the more it encourages customer loyalty and boosts **customer lifetime value,** the total amount a customer spends on a brand or with that company during the entire relationship. The Tabasco brand, owned by the McIlhenny Company, has developed a loyal long-term following among consumers with a taste for pepper sauce (see Exhibit 6.7).

Tabasco also illustrates the power of **brand equity,** the extra value customers perceive that enhances their long-term loyalty to the brand. Customers who like spicy flavors are aware of the Tabasco brand, understand what it stands for, respond positively to it, and want an ongoing relationship with it—all hallmarks of high brand equity (see Exhibit 6.8). The brand has such enormous equity that every year, thousands of visitors flock to Avery Island, Louisiana, to visit the factory. It has even been licensed for peppery-flavored Tabasco Spicy Tequila.[27]

PLANNING TIP

High brand equity can help defend share when a product is mature or faces fierce competition.

Although McIlhenny is the parent company, it is the Tabasco name that brings the value of brand equity to customers and the organization. This is the case with a number of

EXHIBIT 6.7 Marketing Tabasco

consumer product giants such as Procter & Gamble (well known for individual brands such as Pampers and Tide) and Unilever (Dove soap, Lipton tea, and other brands). In contrast, Sony and Honda build the equity of their corporate brands by putting them on diverse product lines and in marketing communications across targeted markets (think Sony PlayStation and Honda Accord).[28] On the other hand, Panasonic earned such equity over the years that its parent, Matsushita, took the brand as its corporate name after 90 years in business.[29]

Address brand equity in your marketing plan because it can insulate your organization against competitive threats and become a driver for long-term growth and prosperity.

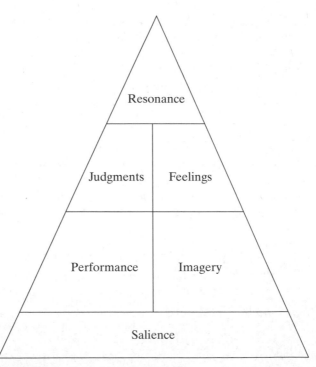

EXHIBIT 6.8 Pyramid of Brand Equity

Look beyond the foundation of brand comprehension and history to plan for customer preference and attachment to your brand.[30] Public corporations may find that their share price performs better when their brands are beloved by customers than when their brands are not well liked, according to recent research.[31]

Often companies put special emphasis on brand equity in marketing plans designed to support growth. For example, consumer packaged goods manufacturer Unilever says that 75 percent of its revenues come from 20 global brands. When it lavished extra marketing attention on six personal-care brands, revenues rose dramatically, despite competition and sluggish economic conditions, which helped Unilever progress toward its long-term growth goals.[32]

Note that brand and line extensions can help a new product achieve customer acceptance, if marketing research shows that the brand has a positive image consistent with the segment's needs, expectations, and perceptions. Yet extending a brand too far from its roots can dilute the image, especially if the new line or product does not completely deliver on the brand's promises of quality, status, need satisfaction, or another point of differentiation. In the end, it is customers who decide what a brand means to them and how they feel about it. You can influence salience, performance, judgments, and resonance, but you don't have direct control over how customers think about, feel about, or act toward your brand.

Summary

In a marketing plan, product strategy covers decisions about features, benefits, and related services; quality and design; packaging and labeling; product development and management; and branding. Products can be tangible goods, services, places, ideas, organizations, or people. Features are the attributes that enable the good or service to perform its intended function and deliver benefits—the need-satisfaction outcomes customers want from a product. Product-related supplementary services deliver valued benefits to satisfy customer needs as part of the product strategy.

Product quality means how well the product satisfies customers, and it is closely linked to design. Packaging and labeling deliver value to customers (providing benefits such as storing products, keeping them safe, and explaining ingredients and usage) and to organizations (by polishing brand image, communicating product features and benefits, and attracting interest). The marketing plan should include planning for the four stages of the product life cycle (introduction, growth, maturity, and decline), for new-product development, and for the management of product lines and the overall product mix. Branding gives a product a distinct identity and differentiates it from competitive products. Moreover, it supports the chosen positioning for a product in a targeted segment and helps build customer relationships for long-term loyalty and brand equity.

Your Marketing Plan, Step by Step

Now that you're ready to plan your marketing mix, use the following questions as starting points for making decisions about product and brand strategy. Document your answers in your marketing plan.

1. Using your knowledge of the market and your targeted segment, identify at least one specific customer need that each of your products (goods or services) is intended to satisfy. What features will each product include, and what benefits will these features deliver? How will these benefits create value for customers by satisfying needs? Be as specific as possible.

2. Take a closer look at the features you've identified. What basic functionality must this product's features deliver to meet customers' needs and their minimum quality expectations? Are any features too expensive to include in a competitively priced product or otherwise inconsistent with your marketing plan objectives? What alternatives might be appropriate in this situation? What is the quality of competing products and should you seek competitive advantage through superior quality?

3. What supplementary services, if any, would enhance the value of your offering? Will you plan to offer supplementary services to any customers, to all customers, or to selected segments? Why and how?

4. Which competitors (if any) compete on the basis of innovative design or packaging? Can or should you design or redesign your product and/or packaging to improve your competitive standing or enhance the aesthetic appeal of your product? What legal requirements must you follow in designing and labeling your product? What packaging or labeling requirements do channel members have for products of this type?

5. Does your new product appeal to some of the same customers as one of your existing products? Can or should you avoid cannibalizing sales of the existing product(s), given your competitive situation? Think about the product's life cycle as you consider this issue.

6. Will you brand with a company name, individual name, private-label brand, or multiple brands? Why? Could you better differentiate your product by modifying your brand or cobranding with another organization? Do your product plans fit with your brand's positioning and image? What can you do to make your brand more memorable, distinctive, recognizable, and appealing? Given your brand, your product plans, and the competitive environment, what can you do to boost brand loyalty and make a difference in customers' lives?

Endnotes

1. Peter Burrows, "Cisco Seizes the Moment," *BusinessWeek,* May 25, 2009, pp. 46–48.

2. Michael J. de la Merced, "Merlin Entertainment Group Plans a Public Offering," *New York Times,* October 24, 2009, www.nytimes.com; "London Eye to be 'Eco-Friendly,'" *BBC News,* May 18, 2009, www.bbc.co.uk; Julie Estrada, "Sea Life's Parent Company, Merlin Entertainment Reports Record Net Earnings," *Zoo and Aquarium Visitor,* May 2009, http://www.zandavisitor.com.

3. "Consumer Creations," *Progressive Grocer,* February 13, 2009, n.p.; Samantha Murphy, "Sweet Sensation," *Chain Store Age,* June 2008, p. 50.

4. "Customer Service, Not Price, Remains Top Cause of Customer Churn," *Accenture Digital Forum,* December 2008, www.digitalforum.accenture.com.

5. Jeffry Bartash, "AT&T's Rivals Still Seek Answer to iPhone," *Wall Street Journal,* November 6, 2009, www.wsj.com; Brad Reed, "Sprint CEO Preaches Patience at JP Morgan Tech Conference," *San Francisco Chronicle,* May 19, 2009, www.sfgate.com.

6. Peter Landers, "Hospital Chic: The ER Gets a Makeover," *Wall Street Journal,* July 8, 2003, pp. D1, D3.

7. Steven Shaw, "Greener Pastures: Product Trend Report," *Kitchen & Bath Design News,* November 2009, www.kitchenbathdesign.com/; Matthew Wheeland, "Greener by Design: Why and How Innovation Matters," *Reuters,* May 19, 2009, www.reuters.com.

8. "Coke Introduces Bottle Made from Plants," *Bevnet.com,* May 21, 2009, www.bevnet.com.

9. Amie Vaccaro, "Greener by Design: A Metrics Driven Approach to Sustainable Business," *Reuters,* May 19, 2009, http://www.reuters.com; Lauren R. Hartman, "Walmart Expo Showcases Sustainability Efforts," *Packaging Digest,* May 4, 2009, www.packagingdigest.com.

10. Ted Mininni, "When It Comes to Innovation, Simplicity Rocks," *MediaPost Marketing Daily,* October 23, 2009, www.mediapost.com/; Natalie Zmuda, "Tropicana Line's Sales Plunge 20% Post-Rebranding," *Advertising Age,* April 2, 2009, www.adage.com.

11. Karen McIntyre, "Household Wipes," *Nonwovens Industry,* February 2009, pp. 22+.

12. Lev Grossman, "Google Wave: Wave New World," *Time,* October 19, 2009, www.time.com; Sindya Bhanoo, "Knol's Expert-Based Formula Fails to Unseat Wikipedia," *Industry Standard,* May 15,

2009, http://www.infoworld.com; "Britannipedia? Wikitannica? A New Sort of Encyclopedic Knowledge," *St. Petersburg Times (Florida)*, February 1, 2009, p. 6P; Randall Stross, "Encyclopedic Knowledge, Then vs. Now," *New York Times*, May 3, 2009, p. BU-3.

13. Tom Krazit, "Can a Palm Pre Multitask Better than an iPhone?" *CNet*, May 7, 2009, www.cnet.com.

14. Andy Oram, "It's All about the Customer," May 18, 2009, www.forbes.com/2009/05/18/oreilly-andy-oram-technology-breakthroughs-andy-oram.html.

15. Nathan Eddy, "Dell Expands Online Resources for Business," *EWeek*, May 12, 2009, www.eweek.com.

16. Miguel Helft, "Data, Not Design, Is King in the Age of Google," *New York Times*, May 10, 2009, p. BU-3.

17. Jena McGregor, "How Failure Breeds Success," *BusinessWeek*, July 10, 2006, pp. 41+.

18. "Before You Buy: How Apple Hardware Is Born," *MacFormat*, May 21, 2009, www.techradar.com; Charlie Sorrel, "Griffin PowerBlock Charger Packs a Spare," *Wired*, May 14, 2009, www.wired.com.

19. Catherine Thomas, "Too Many Products?" *Portfolio*, February 2009, www.portfolio.com.

20. Mariko Sanchanta and Kenneth Maxwell, "Sony Posts Loss, Boosts Outlook," *Wall Street Journal*, October 31, 2009, www.wsj.com; Daisuke Wakabayashi and Yuzo Yamaguchi, "Sony Losses Raise Pressure On Stringer," *Wall Street Journal*, May 15, 2009, p. B1; Daisuke Wakabayashi and Christopher Lawton, "Sony Turns Focus to Low-Cost Video Camera," *Wall Street Journal*, April 16, 2009, www.wsj.com; David Jolly, "Sony Expects to Report $3 Billion Annual Loss," *New York Times*, January 23, 2009, p. B4.

21. Matthew Boyle, "Generics: Making Gains in the Shelf War," *BusinessWeek*, October 30, 2008, p. 62.

22. Alana Semuels, "Intel Ad Blitz Will Focus on Overall Brand, Computer Firm Says," *Los Angeles Times*, May 22, 2009, www.latimes.com.

23. For more about digital brand theft, see Theresa Howard, "'Cybersquatting' Crooks Profit on Marketers' Brand Names," *USA Today*, May 11, 2009, www.usatoday.com.

24. Kevin Lane Keller, *Strategic Brand Management* (Upper Saddle River, NJ: Prentice Hall, 2003), p. 175.

25. Alastair Jamieson, "Google Becomes World's First 100 Billion Dollar Brand," *Telegraph (UK)*, April 30, 2009, www.telegraph.co.uk; "The 100 Top Brands," *BusinessWeek*, September 29, 2008, p. 56.

26. Simone Baribeau and Justine Lau, "Hyundai Leads as US Auto Sector Recovers," *Financial Times*, November 4, 2009, www.ft.com; Moon Ihlwan, "Kia Motors: Still Cheap, Now Chic," *BusinessWeek*, June 1, 2009, p. 58; Chris Woodyard, "Extra-Hot Sales Warm Kia's Soul," *USA Today*, April 27, 2009, p. 6B; Kathy Jackson, "Kia, Courting the Kids, Ponders New Names for All Its Models," *Automotive News*, March 23, 2009, p. 6.

27. "Tabasco Lands on Pizza," *Adweek Online*, January 16, 2009, www.adweek.com; "Hot Time in the Old Tequila Factory," *Packaging Digest*, December 2008, p. 10.

28. Don E. Schultz, "Understanding Total Brand Value," *Marketing Management*, March/April 2004, pp. 10–11.

29. Yukari Iwatani Kane, "For Matsushita, It's All about Panasonic," *Wall Street Journal*, October 1, 2008, www.wsj.com.

30. See Donald R. Lehmann, Kevin Lane Keller, and John U. Farley, "The Structure of Survey-Based Brand Metrics," *Journal of International Marketing*, vol. 16, no. 4, 2008, pp. 29–56.

31. Owen Jenkins, "Gimme Some Lovin,'" *Marketing News*, May 15, 2009, p. 19.

32. Johny K. Johansson and Ilkka A. Ronkainen, "The Brand Challenge," *Marketing Management*, March/April 2004, pp. 54+.

CHAPTER

7

Developing Pricing Strategy

In this chapter:

Preview

Understanding Value and Pricing Today

   Customer Perceptions and Demand

   Value-Based Pricing

Planning Pricing Decisions

   Pricing Objectives

External Pricing Influences

Internal Pricing Influences

   Adapting Prices

Summary

Your Marketing Plan, Step by Step

PREVIEW

Pricing decisions—formulated during Step 5 of the marketing planning process, as shown in Exhibit 7.1—are vital because they directly produce revenue, whereas other marketing functions require investments of money, time, and effort. Another reason to give careful attention to pricing is that you can implement such decisions more quickly and at less cost than implementing changes in the other three marketing-mix components. Depending on developments in the dynamic marketing environment, there will be times when you'll need the ability to change prices on short notice.

   In this chapter, you'll learn about customers' perceptions of value and price, how demand operates, and the role of pricing in the marketing plan. Next, you'll see how to set pricing objectives and which internal and external factors can influence pricing decisions. Finally, you'll take a closer look at why and how your marketing plan should address price adaptation, recognizing that effective pricing is both art and science.

APPLYING YOUR KNOWLEDGE

Once you've completed this chapter, look at the sample plan in this book's appendix, and browse some of the samples in *Marketing Plan Pro* software for ideas about planning for pricing. Then move ahead with your project by answering the questions in "Your Marketing Plan, Step by Step," at the end of this chapter. Refer to this chapter's checklist as you think about your pricing strategy. Document your decisions using *Marketing Plan Pro* software or in your written plan.

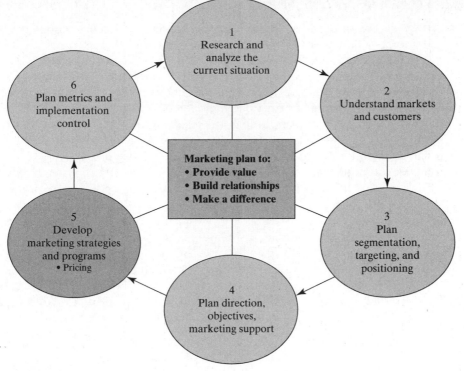

EXHIBIT 7.1   Marketing Planning: Step 5

CHAPTER 7 CHECKLIST   Planning Pricing Strategy

Internal Factors

✔ What do you want your pricing strategy to accomplish for the organization?
✔ How can pricing be used to support positioning, targeting, and product plans?
✔ How do channel and promotion decisions affect pricing?
✔ Will you emphasize price or nonprice competition?
✔ What are each product's costs, and how do they affect the price floor?
✔ How are different prices likely to affect revenues, sales, and breakeven?

External Factors

✔ How do industry customs affect pricing?
✔ How do customers perceive the product's value? Are customers price sensitive?
✔ What are the prices and costs of competing products, and how do they affect price ceilings?
✔ What nonprice alternatives exist for reacting to competitive price changes?

Price Adaptation

✔ What price adaptations are appropriate for achieving pricing objectives?
✔ Is it necessary or advisable to raise prices, and if so, how?
✔ How do resources, capabilities, goals, and direction affect price adaptation?

UNDERSTANDING VALUE AND PRICING TODAY

In the current climate of economic uncertainty, value has assumed special importance in customers' buying decisions and in marketers' plans. As noted in Chapter 1, customers assess the *value* of a product according to the difference between the total perceived benefits they receive and the total perceived price they pay (see Exhibit 7.2). The more weight customers give to benefits in relation to perceived price, the higher the value they perceive in that product. Therefore, as you formulate your marketing plan, prepare to research and analyze value from your customers' perspective; also consider how perceptions of value may be changing and how you will communicate your offering's current value to customers.[1]

In practice, customers don't perceive product value in isolation; instead, they look at value in the context of the benefits and prices of competing or substitute products as well as the context of the marketing environment. Many routinely compare prices online before they make major buying decisions—which affects their value perceptions. Even if customers perceive all products as being priced the same (whether or not their perceptions match reality), no two customers place exactly the same value on the total perceived benefits. To enhance value, your plan should indicate whether you will add to the perceived benefits (e.g., by improving quality or introducing new features) or reduce the perceived price (e.g., by lowering the purchase price or offering more affordable financing).

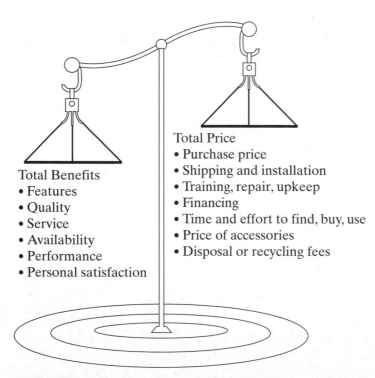

Total Price
• Purchase price
• Shipping and installation
• Training, repair, upkeep
• Financing
• Time and effort to find, buy, use
• Price of accessories
• Disposal or recycling fees

Total Benefits
• Features
• Quality
• Service
• Availability
• Performance
• Personal satisfaction

EXHIBIT 7.2 Perceptions of Total Benefits and Total Price

Lower price, which adds to the perception of higher value, is the appeal of the popular dollar menu.

Dollar menu. McDonald's has marketed a dollar menu for most of the past decade, featuring an ever-changing array of burgers, fries, and other items. Although the restaurants reportedly make a tiny profit of about 6 cents for every $1 cheeseburger sold, the public perception of value—which extends across the entire menu—has helped the company increase sales year after year, even during the worst of the economic crisis.

To compete, other fast-food firms have introduced value menus with prices at or below $1. Taco Bell prices some items as low as 79 cents; Wendy's offers a choice of 99-cent sandwiches; and Burger King sells dollar sandwiches for breakfast, lunch, and dinner. Sonic, which operates 1950s-style drive-in restaurants, launched a dollar menu after seeing sales decline while McDonald's sales were going up. Recently, Walmart initiated a special dollar "menu" of merchandise. Rival Target positions its Dollar Spot merchandise racks in the front of every store.[2]

Your plan should indicate whether you, like McDonald's, will use **fixed pricing,** in which customers pay the price set (fixed) by the marketer—the figure shown on the price tag or the menu—or **dynamic pricing,** varying prices from customer to customer or situation to situation. Most airlines use dynamic pricing, and a few sports teams are experimenting with it. Marketers for the San Francisco Giants baseball team, for instance, adjust ticket prices depending on factors such as the weather, which team is visiting, and which pitchers are starting, all of which affect ticket demand.[3]

Some B2B marketing plans call for **negotiated pricing,** in which buyer and seller negotiate the price. Another way of pricing is through **auction pricing,** in which buyers submit bids to buy goods or services. This may occur through a traditional auction (such as those conducted by Sotheby's), an online auction (such as those on eBay), or other types of auctions. Organizations that rely on negotiated or auction pricing can't predict the precise price they will receive for each product, but they should be able to plan for a minimum acceptable price and profit. In marketing government surplus and seized goods, the U.S. government uses both auction pricing and fixed pricing (see Exhibit 7.3).

Customer Perceptions and Demand

PLANNING TIP

Understand how customers view value and know the value your organization wants to achieve.

When customers act on the basis of their perceptions of price and benefits, their purchases help create demand for a good or service (in combination with supply and other factors). If customers perceive the price to be too high in relation to the benefits, they simply won't buy, which helps to lower demand; if they perceive the price to be too low for the expected benefits or quality, demand also will suffer. On the other hand, if the total perceived benefits of your offering outweigh the total perceived price, customers are more likely to buy from you—or rent, in the case of Zipcar—which helps to increase demand.

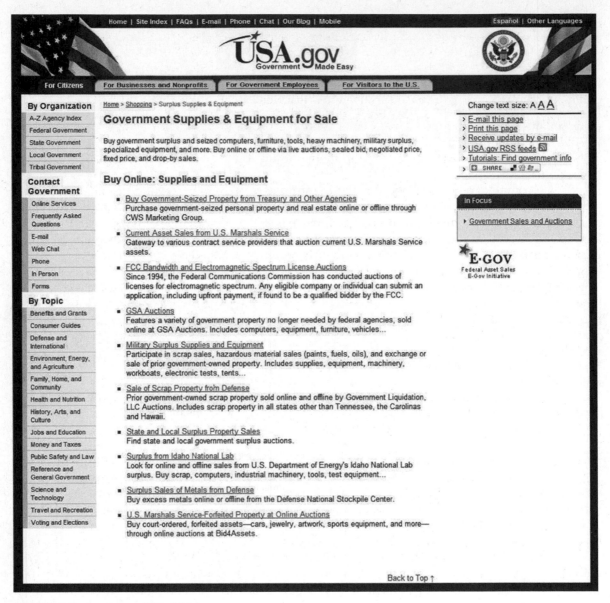

EXHIBIT 7.3 Auction and Fixed Pricing

Zipcar. With the slogan "Wheels When You Want Them," Zipcar represents an economically and environmentally friendly alternative to vehicle ownership. It operates in big cities and near college campuses, pricing car rentals on demand by the hour, day, and week, with different prices for weekdays, weekends, and peak periods. When customers join Zipcar, they receive a Zipcard that wirelessly opens the door to any of the company's 5,500 rental vehicles (including a growing number of Toyota Prius hybrids). These "Zipsters" value the speed and convenience of reserving a car online, picking it up from a reserved parking spot in the area, and returning it to that spot when the rental period is over. Users can even reserve their rental cars using a convenient iPhone app. Zipcar has attracted so many Zipsters that Hertz and Enterprise Rent-A-Car are now entering the "rent on demand" business.[4]

Careful research can help you determine customers' sensitivity to pricing and the level of demand for a product at different price points. This sensitivity is shown by the **price elasticity of demand,** calculated by dividing the percentage change in unit sales demanded by the percentage change in price. When a small price change significantly increases or decreases the number of units demanded, demand is *elastic*; if, for example, you reduced your price by 20 percent, and wound up selling twice the number of units, you'd know that demand for your product is highly elastic. When a price change does not significantly change the number of units demanded, demand is *inelastic*; if you slashed your price by half and your unit sales didn't change, you'd know that demand for your product is highly inelastic. Exhibit 7.4 indicates how different price changes affect demand under elastic and inelastic demand conditions.

Your marketing plan may need to account for testing different price points to see how specific segments react before you make a final decision. In general, customers tend to be less sensitive to a product's price when they[5]

- are buying a relatively small amount;
- are unaware of or can't easily compare substitutes and prices;
- would incur costs or difficulties in switching products;
- perceive that the product's quality, status, or another benefit justifies the price;
- are spending a relatively small amount or are sharing the cost;
- perceive the price as fair;
- are buying products bundled rather than separately.

Customers' price sensitivity and perceptions of value also can be used to deal with imbalances of supply and demand. The idea of managing rush-hour traffic through pricing is catching on in some municipalities.

EXHIBIT 7.4   How Pricing Affects Demand

Change in Price	*Under Inelastic Demand*	*Under Elastic Demand*
Small increase	Demand drops slightly	Demand drops significantly
Small reduction	Demand rises slightly	Demand rises significantly

Pricing to Relieve Traffic Congestion. To minimize highway congestion, Florida charges tolls on new I-95 express lanes in and out of Miami during rush hour. Drivers who perceive value in the benefit of getting to their destinations more quickly will pay the express-lane charge; those who believe the price outweighs the benefit will not. Twenty percent of drivers entering or leaving Miami are choosing to pay for access to the express lanes, which are free to hybrid gas-electric vehicles, buses, motorcycles, and carpool vehicles.

As another example, London charges drivers the equivalent of more than $12 to enter certain parts of the city during peak periods (electric and hybrid vehicles pay nothing). Pricing helps balance supply and demand during busy periods, which in turn prevents traffic tie-ups, moves vehicles along, and minimizes air pollution. Since initiating the congestion charge in 2003, London has not only reduced downtown traffic by 20 percent, it has generated significant revenue for public transportation projects.[6]

Value-Based Pricing

Researching and analyzing how customers perceive the value of a product should be the first step in formulating an appropriate pricing strategy to build demand and meet internal objectives. Nagle and Hogan[7] note that this is not the typical approach to pricing. The most common way is to start with the product and its cost, set a price that covers the cost plus a particular percentage for profit, and then communicate the value to customers. The membership retailer Costco does this, "based on the idea that a business can operate on a fair markup and still pay all of its bills," says one executive. Pricing "is determined by carefully examining true costs, and profits are maintained by stringently controlling costs."[8] Although cost-based pricing works well for Costco, it fails to take into account how customers perceive the value of the offering.

In contrast, the starting point for **value-based pricing** is research about customers' perceptions of value and the price they are willing to pay. Then the company finds ways of making the product at a reasonable cost (**target costing**) to return a reasonable profit or achieve other marketing plan objectives based on the value price.[9] Exhibit 7.5 contrasts traditional cost-based with value-based pricing.

Consider how IKEA, the global home furnishings retailer, plans for value-based pricing.

PLANNING TIP

Research customers' perceptions so you can use target costing to best advantage.

Cost-Based Pricing

PRODUCT ⟶ COST ⟶ PRICE ⟶ VALUE ⟶ CUSTOMERS

Value-Based Pricing

CUSTOMERS ⟶ VALUE ⟶ PRICE ⟶ COST ⟶ PRODUCT

EXHIBIT 7.5 Cost-Based versus Value-Based Pricing

IKEA. More than 50 years after Ingvar Kamprad opened his first store in Sweden, IKEA continues to "offer a wide range of well designed, functional home furnishing products at prices so low that as many people as possible will be able to afford them." It can value-price its products because it uses target-costing to control expenses at every point in the supply chain. Before any new item goes into production, IKEA's designers analyze every detail of its materials and components, discuss the requirements and timing with its 1,300 suppliers, and redesign or change specifications if necessary to meet cost targets. Over the years, IKEA has also driven down costs and enhanced perceived value by going green. Company officials visit every supplier several times a year to check on progress in shaving costs, improving quality, and operating in environmentally sound ways.[10]

From a strategic perspective, price decisions must be value based, profit driven, and proactive. In other words, simply reacting to the market is not an effective approach; you must proactively develop appropriate pricing strategies based on how customers perceive value and how your firm can profitably achieve its objectives through pricing.[11]

PLANNING PRICING DECISIONS

When planning pricing, first determine what this strategy is intended to achieve, given the marketing, financial, and societal objectives set in your marketing plan. Also investigate the various external influences (customers; competitors; channel members; and legal, regulatory, and ethical concerns) and internal influences (costs and breakeven; targeting and positioning strategy; product strategy; and other marketing decisions) that can affect pricing decisions.

Pricing Objectives

Because a product's price is the organization's source of revenue, you should establish specific objectives for all pricing decisions. These objectives must be consistent with each other and with the overall mission, direction, goals, and marketing plan objectives. Not long ago, as the economic crisis continued, Morgan Stanley, Charles Schwab, and several other brokerage firms temporarily waived or reduced fees to retain large clients and avoid loss of market share.[12] Remember that you may have to trade off one pricing objective for another. Rarely can a company boost profitability while simultaneously raising its market share to a much higher level, for example.

Verizon Wireless, one of the largest U.S. cell phone carriers, uses pricing for customer retention as well as for financial objectives.

Verizon Wireless. Like most cell phone carriers, Verizon Wireless traditionally minimized customer churn by charging a hefty early-termination fee if a contract was canceled. It recently doubled the early-termination fee for smartphone contracts because the company subsidizes the pricing of those more expensive models. On the other hand, Verizon Wireless also reduces all termination fees little by little over the course of a contract, encouraging customers to stay with the company. It also uses "triple play" pricing to sell multiple services (voice, Internet access, and TV access) to customers, increasing the likelihood that they will remain loyal because they have so many ties to the company. Today, Verizon Wireless has one of the best retention records of any wireless service provider—and often tops the industry in satisfaction, as measured by the American Customer Satisfaction Index.[13]

In some industries, one additional percentage point of market share can translate into millions of dollars in higher sales, which is why certain companies put share ahead of profit when setting pricing objectives. Over the long term, however, companies cannot survive without profits. Exhibit 7.6 shows a number of pricing objectives that firms may set in their marketing plans.

External Pricing Influences

Many factors outside the organization—and outside its control—come into play when making decisions about pricing. In addition to customers, pricing can be influenced by competitors, channel members, and legal, regulatory, and ethical considerations. Because not every external influence is equally important for each product, targeted segment, or market, carefully analyze each within the context of other marketing plan decisions and the organization's situation.

CUSTOMERS   Perceptions of value, behavior, and attitudes all affect a customer's reaction to pricing. In consumer markets, research shows that customers are willing to buy a good or service if the price falls within a range they view as acceptable for that type of product.[14] This suggests that consumer marketers have some pricing latitude if they stay within the accepted range or change the product to change its perceived value. Even digital items such as a depiction of a gift, for instance, are perceived as having value on Facebook or other sites, and therefore can be priced. The price may be only a dollar or two, but revenues can add up as more people buy.[15]

PLANNING TIP

Analyze these influences for each geographic region if you plan to price market by market.

Remember that price is a big factor in customers' decisions to regularly buy from a particular marketer, as the auto repair chain Monro Muffler Brake & Service knows. Seeing customer loyalty as vital for long-term profitability, Monro Muffler uses pricing to encourage

EXHIBIT 7.6   Sample Pricing Objectives

Type of Objective	*Sample Pricing Objectives*
Financial	• For profitability: Set prices to achieve gross profit margin of 27 percent on this year's sales. • For return on investment: Set prices to achieve full-year ROI of 13 percent.
Marketing	• For higher market share: Set prices to achieve a market share increase of 5 percent within 6 months.
Societal	• For charitable fund-raising: Set prices to net $5 per item for donation to chosen cause.

repeat purchasing, rather than pricing for short-term gain. The CEO explains: "We're lower priced on oil changes, but we're not lower priced on everything. Once you build up trust with the customer, price becomes less important in the equation." Monro Muffler's results show that new customers satisfied with the cheap oil changes are returning for different repairs, lifting both sales and profits. Because of customer trust and loyalty, the company has been able to expand, increase prices on many services, and improve profit margins to a level above that of most competitors—even during poor economic times.[16]

Economic reverses may slow but don't eliminate *conspicuous consumption*, the purchasing of goods or services to convey the buyer's importance, wealth, or status, as luxury marketers have found.

Luxury Pricing. Sotirio Bulgari can price a limited-edition wristwatch with hand-sewn alligator strap above $200,000 because customers view it as a desirable status symbol. Knowing that few are being manufactured, buyers expect the watch to be a collector's item in the coming years. Maserati commands prices over $100,000 because its cars are perceived as distinctive, high-style, and high-performance. Rolls-Royce cars are also perceived as status symbols, for which customers will pay $400,000 and up. The company recently introduced a smaller $300,000 model to appeal to current customers who want a smaller car as well as to attract new customers eager for Rolls-Royce prestige—but at a lower price.[17]

In business markets, customers frequently search for the lowest price to minimize their organizational costs, and some switch suppliers constantly to pay less for parts, materials, components, or services. Globalization has only increased customers' choices and opportunities to obtain better prices. Rather than emphasizing low prices, many B2B marketers build relationships by communicating benefits such as how the product saves customers money in the long run or how it enhances quality.

PLANNING TIP

Research how customers perceive the total benefits and total costs of competing products.

COMPETITORS   Customer behavior is one external clue to an acceptable price range (the ceiling, in particular). The competitive situation provides another external clue. By analyzing the prices, special deals, and probable costs of competing products, you get a better sense of the alternatives that are available to customers and insight into your competitors' pricing objectives and strategies. Home Depot, for instance, electronically compares the prices of key products to the prices charged by competitors. Its marketing managers look at these comparisons, plus internal records, sales trends, and other information, when setting prices by product, store, and market.[18]

Pricing is a highly visible competitive tool in many industries, often exerting downward pressure on profits and limiting pricing options. Yet no two companies have exactly the same objectives, resources, costs, and situations, which means competitors cannot simply copy each other's pricing. To illustrate, because of strong and direct competition in the United States, Coca-Cola and Pepsi-Cola soft drinks remain close in price—nor have their prices risen much in two decades.[19] Marketers need not always match or beat competitors' prices, but they do have to ensure that their product's price fits into the value equation as perceived by customers and makes economic sense for the company.

CHANNEL MEMBERS   Companies that reach customers through wholesalers or retailers must take into account these intermediaries' pricing expectations and marketing objectives. Changes in a channel member's pricing can have a significant influence on its suppliers. During the height of the economic crisis, Saks Fifth Avenue slashed prices on luxury merchandise to avoid being left with a lot of inventory. Delighted customers stocked up—and angry suppliers protested that the discounts dented their high-end brand images and their ability to sell at full price through other upscale stores. The next time Saks held a huge sale, Gucci and many other luxe brands opted out. "The idea is to maintain pricing coherence in the regions in which our products are sold, regardless of channel of distribution," a Gucci official said.[20]

A sample progression of how a consumer product might be priced by the producer, wholesaler, and retailer is in Exhibit 7.7. In this sample, the producer charges the wholesaler $20 for the product and the wholesaler sells it to the retailer for $24, twenty percent above the producer's price. The retailer sells the product to the consumer for $36, which is 50 percent above the price paid by the retailer and 80 percent above the price paid by the wholesaler.

Of course, the actual number of participants in the outbound side of the value chain will vary according to product, industry, market, and segment, affecting the prices paid by intermediaries and the ultimate customer. Note that when a participant performs more functions or enhances the product in a unique way, it may be able to set a higher price (and make more profit) because its immediate customers perceive more value in the offering. Also consider the effect of the Internet on your product's channel pricing. In many categories, wholesale and retail prices are coming down, thanks to more efficient transaction capabilities, convenient price comparisons, and more intense competition.

LEGAL, REGULATORY, AND ETHICAL CONCERNS   Whether planning for domestic or international marketing, all companies need to comply with a variety of pricing laws and regulations. In the United States and many other areas, competing firms are not allowed to collude in setting prices and are not allowed to take other anticompetitive pricing

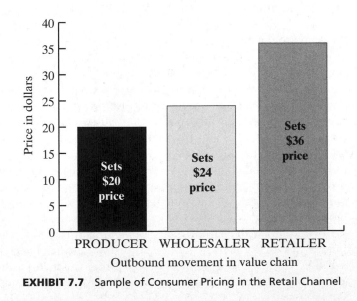

EXHIBIT 7.7   Sample of Consumer Pricing in the Retail Channel

actions. The United States also outlaws predatory pricing—the aggressive use of low pricing to damage a competitor or reduce competition.

In addition, a company usually cannot charge different prices for essentially the same product at the same time in the same market unless the lower price is available through discounts or allowances that are open to all. However, different prices may be allowed if the company has different costs, is responding to competition, or is clearing outdated merchandise.[21] Your marketing plan should also account for any legal limits on the highest price that can be charged for certain products; Canada, for instance, sets a ceiling on prices of prescription drugs.

Since a 2007 Supreme Court ruling, U.S. companies have been permitted to enforce a minimum retail price among channel members. If a store discounts a brand below the supplier's minimum price level, the supplier can cut off shipments to that store. The ruling suggested that price-setting agreements between suppliers and retailers be examined case by case to prevent a negative impact on competition. Now eBay and other retailers are pressuring the federal government to outlaw such *resale price maintenance*, saying it leads to higher prices for consumers.[22]

Apart from applicable laws and regulations, consider the ethic dilemmas in pricing. Is it ethical to raise prices during an emergency, when products may be scarce or especially valuable? Should a company set a high price for an indispensable product, knowing that certain customers will be unable to pay? What are a company's ethical responsibilities regarding full disclosure of prices for upkeep, updates, or replacement parts? How far in advance should customers be notified of planned price increases? As difficult as the ethical aspects of pricing may be, carefully think through the consequences on customer relationships and brand image when you prepare your plan.

Internal Pricing Influences

Within the organization, costs and breakeven are critical influences on pricing. Targeting and positioning strategy, product strategy, and other marketing decisions must also be factored into pricing plans.

COSTS AND BREAKEVEN   Costs typically establish the theoretical floor of the pricing range, the lowest price at which the organization will avoid losing money. Even the largest company cannot afford to price products below cost for an extended period, although (where legal) it may do so to combat a competitive threat or achieve another objective over a limited period. Cost containment is, in fact, a high priority for many companies today, not just to achieve quarterly profit targets but to prepare for future market conditions.

For planning purposes, you'll need to know your costs and how to calculate the **break-even point**—the sales level at which revenue covers costs. Costs and breakeven are more easily calculated for existing products in existing market segments, because you can use historical results as a basis for future projections. For new products and segments, you'll usually rely on research-based forecasts and expert estimates of costs and sales volume (see Chapter 10). When detailed or timely information is unavailable, make an educated guess about costs as you plan.

The total cost of a product consists of *fixed costs*—overhead expenses such as rent and payroll, which do not vary with volume—plus *variable costs*—expenses such as raw materials, which do vary with volume. As one example, corporate rent is a fixed cost and steel is a variable cost for auto

PLANNING TIP

If you don't know your costs, estimate for now and start tracking costs for next year's plan.

manufacturers. After Nippon Steel negotiated a 30 percent price cut for iron ore from its suppliers, Toyota immediately asked for (and received) a reduction in the price paid for steel, a major cost component in its cars and trucks.[23]

Once you know a product's total costs, calculate the average cost of producing a single item (total costs divided by production) at various output levels, corresponding to different assumptions about demand. This reveals cost changes at a number of output levels and indicates how low the company might price the product at each level to at least cover its costs. Next, calculate the break-even point to see how a price will affect revenues and profits at different sales levels.[24] The break-even formula is as follows:

$$\text{Break-even volume} = \frac{\text{fixed cost}}{\text{price} - \text{variable cost}}$$

Exhibit 7.8 illustrates a sample break-even analysis for a company that manufactures specialized software for dentists. In this example, the price (unit revenue) is $995, the variable cost is $45 per unit, and the fixed cost totals $40,550. Thus, the calculation is as follows:

$$\text{Break-even volume} = \frac{40,550}{995 - 45} = \frac{40,550}{950} = 42.6\,\text{units (rounded up to 43)}$$

TARGETING AND POSITIONING STRATEGY   A product's price must be appropriate for the organization's targeting and positioning strategy. To illustrate, because Dollar General targets the segment of price-sensitive shoppers, charging high prices would be inconsistent (and would alienate customers). Conversely, if the luxury goods manufacturer Louis Vuitton put low-price tags on its handbags and accessories, the target segment of affluent consumers would question the products' positioning as symbols of status, style, and quality. In fact, Vuitton refuses to mark down its handbags for clearance, on the basis that low pricing would conflict with the positioning.[25]

PLANNING TIP

Price multiple products in the context of achieving your plan's overall objectives.

PRODUCT STRATEGY   Marketers should not only examine every pricing decision in the context of costs, targeting, and positioning, they should set prices in line with their product strategy. In particular, pricing can be used to manage the product's movement through the life cycle:

- *Introduction.* Some companies use **skimming pricing,** pricing a new product high to establish a top-quality image or highlight unique value and more quickly recover development costs in line with profitability objectives. Apple does this with its Macintosh computers. Other marketers prefer **penetration pricing,** pricing products relatively low to penetrate the market more quickly. Tata Motors used penetration pricing to launch its tiny Nano car; the unusually low price attracted 203,000 buyers in the first three weeks.[26] These two approaches are compared in Exhibit 7.9.
- *Growth.* Pricing is important for competitive strategy during the growth stage, when rival products challenge the new product or service. During growth, companies also use pricing to stimulate demand while moving toward the break-even point.
- *Maturity.* With sales growth slowing, companies can use pricing to defend market share, retain customers, pursue profitability, or expand into additional channels. For instance, Procter & Gamble is doing this in mature categories by introducing lower-priced "basic" versions of its branded products, such as Bounty Basic paper towels.[27]

Fixed Costs		
Creation of printed material graphics and text	$	3,200
Creation of CD-ROM graphics	$	750
Initial set up fee for CD	$	1,600
Initial set up fee for printed materials	$	1,250
Production of 2,000 demo units	$	33,750
Estimated Fixed Costs	$	40,550
Per-unit variable costs (to fulfill orders sold)	$	45
Per-unit revenue	$	995
Breakeven (in Units)		43

Break-Even Analysis:		
Assumptions:		
Average Per-Unit Revenue	$	995
Average Per-Unit Variable Cost	$	45
Estimated Fixed Costs	$	40,550
Units Breakeven		43
Sales Breakeven	$	42,471

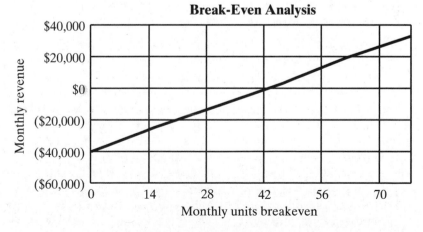

Break-Even Analysis

Units breakeven point = where line intersects with $0

EXHIBIT 7.8 Break-even Analysis

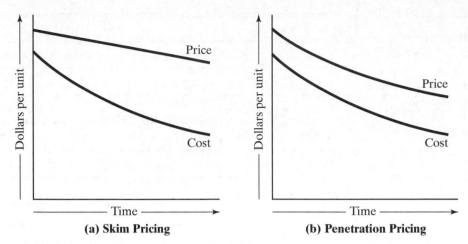

FIGURE 7.9 Skim Pricing and Penetration Pricing

- *Decline.* Pricing can help clear older or outdated products to make way for new ones, stimulate sales to prevent or at least slow a product's decline, or maximize profits. Yet prices do not necessarily drop during decline: Scarcity may make a product more valuable to certain customers and therefore justify a higher price.

Remember 100-calorie snack packs? The price was right when consumers had the money to pay for the value of prepackaged portions.

---

100 Calorie Packs. Catering to consumers who wanted to control portion size, food marketers began introducing 100-calorie snack packs in 2004. The convenient snack packs were priced higher than the equivalent amount of food in a larger package, and returned 20 percent more profit than the larger package. The category quickly grew into a highly profitable $200 million-a-year opportunity, with dozens of new 100-calorie food packages being introduced every year. By 2009, however, category volume was declining as consumers beset by economic woes sought to save money by packing their own snack bags rather than paying more for the grab-and-go 100-calorie packages.[28]

Moreover, pricing is vital for managing the strategy of products in a single line and in the overall mix. After researching customers' perceptions, marketers may set different prices to signal the value of the features and benefits of different products and to differentiate among multiple lines and brands in the product portfolio. When a new model of the Flip pocket camcorder is introduced, the price of older models is reduced—not just to sell the old models off but also to reflect the improved technology of the new model. The biggest temptation, which Flip marketers are resisting, is adding a lot of new features that will drive the price up and blur the differentiation between Flip and its competitors.[29]

Sometimes a marketing plan calls for pricing one product to encourage purchases of other products in the line or mix. Two marketers of laser printers and replacement cartridges, Hewlett-Packard and Xerox, are approaching this pricing opportunity in opposite ways.

> **Hewlett-Packard vs. Xerox.** Hewlett-Packard's marketing plan projects ongoing profits from sales of ink and toner cartridges after customers have bought its ink-jet printers and laser printers. The replacement cartridges carry very hefty profit margins and make a significant contribution to HP's bottom line. Even when consumers who buy for home printers slow down their purchasing, HP's business and industrial customers buy replacement ink cartridges in volume to keep up with printing needs.
>
> Xerox, which makes heavy-duty printers for businesses, has seized on the high cost of replacement cartridges as a problem to be solved by its ColorQube laser printers, which use solid ink. Buyers save money because they don't have to spend as much on replacement ink. Isn't Xerox worried about cutting into sales of its traditional color laser printers? "We are more concerned that there is significantly more opportunity to attack our competition," its president says. "The best way to grow our business sometimes is to cannibalize our own, or to cannibalize a technology."[30]

OTHER MARKETING DECISIONS   The marketing plan's direction will strongly influence the organization's pricing strategy. For survival, the organization's prices should cover costs at the very least; for bankruptcy, organizations can use pricing to liquidate stock and raise money quickly. For aggressive growth, the company may decide to set prices that return slim or no-profit margins in the short run.

Pricing is also influenced by decisions about suppliers and logistics. In terms of promotion strategy, higher-priced products aimed at higher-income customer segments are often promoted in different media and with different messages than lower-priced products aimed at lower-income segments. Finally, pricing is a big challenge for companies that market through personal selling, especially when customers expect to negotiate prices with salespeople. This is why many companies train sales personnel in profitability requirements and set a floor for price negotiation to prevent sales that generate little or no profit.

Adapting Prices

If internal factors suggest the price floor and external factors suggest the price ceiling, price adaptation helps companies modify and fine-tune prices within an acceptable range—or even beyond. Marketers may use price adaptation to make changes in support of their objectives:

PLANNING TIP

Consider which adaptations are traditional—and nontraditional—in your industry or channel.

- *Discounts.* Many companies offer quantity discounts for buying in volume and seasonal discounts for buying out of season. Business customers also may earn a cash discount for prompt payment; intermediaries may earn a functional discount when they perform specific channel functions for a producer.
- *Allowances.* Wholesalers and retailers may receive discounts, extra payments, or extra product allocations for participating in special promotions. Some companies offer trade-in allowances for businesses or consumers who bring in older products and buy newer ones.
- *Bundling or unbundling.* You may enhance customer perceptions of value by bundling one product with one or more goods or services at a single price.

Unbundling can be used if the bundle price is perceived as too high and individual products will sell well on their own.

- **Product enhancement.** Enhancing the product to raise its perceived value can help the company maintain the current price or perhaps increase the price.
- **Segment pricing.** Pricing may be adapted for certain customer segments, such as a children's menu (segmenting by family composition), a senior discount (segmenting by age), or a delivery charge (segmenting by need for service). To illustrate, the New York drug retailer Duane Reade prices disposable diapers for newborns to yield a higher profit margin than pull-up disposables for toddlers. Why? Its research shows that the new-parent segment is less price sensitive than the toddler-parent segment.[31]

Changes in consumer behavior may also prompt price adaptation, as the team-buying phenomenon is doing in China.

Team Buying. Chinese shoppers are increasingly shopping together so they can bargain as a group for better prices, a practice known as *tuangou* (team buying). The trend started when online chatters found that they were planning purchases of similar products and decided to strengthen their buying power by visiting stores together. Now numerous Web sites have sprung up to help consumers co-ordinate their buying trips. "Sometimes we call the shop," says one participant, "but often we just surprise them. Shopkeepers argue, but in the end they want the business." When 500 consumers converged on an electronics superstore, the retailer turned away other shoppers, agreed to cut its prices by 10–30 percent on TVs, DVD players, and other items, and even gave the team buyers a goody bag when they left.[32]

Specific pricing tactics can help marketers achieve specific marketing or financial objectives. Loss-leader pricing, for instance, with popular or new items priced near cost, is a common way to build store or Web-site traffic. Objectives for customer acquisition might be supported by short-term pricing cuts or tactics that temporarily enhance value, such as low interest rates during select periods. The chosen adaptation depends on the company's resources and capabilities, its goals and strategic direction, and its marketing plan objectives.

Be sure your plan accounts for the short-term and long-term effects of price competition. If every company matches or beats the price of its rivals and a price war ensues, customers will soon perceive few if any differences and be less brand-loyal. Research shows that in more than two dozen product categories, customers give more weight to price than to brand because they perceive few differences among brands. In contrast, they give more weight to brand than to price when buying automobiles and alcoholic beverages, which have more perceived differences.[33] See Exhibit 7.10 for some alternative reactions to competitive price cuts. Stressing product, promotion, or channel differentiation, along with value-based pricing, will confer the strongest advantage, given that prices are easily matched but non-price-related points of difference are not.

EXHIBIT 7.10 Alternative Reactions to Competitive Price Cuts

Strategic Options	Reasoning	Consequences
1. Maintain price and perceived quality. Engage in selective customer pruning.	Firm has higher customer loyalty. It is willing to lose poorer customers to competitors.	Smaller market share Lowered profitability
2. Raise price and perceived quality.	Raise price to cover rising costs. Improve quality to justify higher prices.	Smaller market share Maintained profitability
3. Maintain price and raise perceived quality.	It is cheaper to maintain price and raise perceived quality.	Smaller market share Short-term decline in profitability Long-term increase in profitability
4. Cut price partly and raise perceived quality.	Must give customers some price reduction but stress higher value of offer.	Maintained market share Short-term decline in profitability Long-term maintained profitability
5. Cut price fully and maintain perceived quality.	Discipline and discourage price competition.	Maintained market share Short-term decline in profitability
6. Cut price fully and reduce perceived quality.	Discipline and discourage price competition and maintain profit margin.	Maintained market share Maintained margin Reduced long-term profitability
7. Maintain price and reduce perceived quality.	Cut marketing expense to combat rising costs.	Smaller market share Maintained margin Reduced long-term profitability
8. Introduce an economy model.	Give the market what it wants.	Some cannibalization but higher total volume

Summary

From a customer's perspective, value is the difference between the total perceived benefits and the total perceived price of a product. Marketers care about customers' price perceptions because they influence the number of units demanded. Price elasticity, which indicates customers' price sensitivity, is calculated by dividing the percentage change in unit sales demanded by the percentage change in price. Marketers should use value-based pricing rather than cost-based pricing to formulate a strategy that will drive demand and satisfy company objectives.

As you plan pricing strategy, determine what you want to achieve in the context of the marketing plan's marketing, financial, and societal objectives. Next, factor in key external influences (customers; competitors; channel members; and legal, regulatory, and ethical concerns) and key internal influences (costs and breakeven; targeting and positioning strategy; product strategy; and other marketing decisions) when making pricing decisions. Finally, consider when and how to adapt prices.

Your Marketing Plan, Step by Step

Answer the following questions as you work on the pricing part of your marketing plan.

1. Look back at the marketing-plan objectives you've set. How will pricing move you closer to these objectives? What, specifically, do you want to accomplish through pricing? List at least two objectives for your pricing strategy, checking to be sure that they don't conflict with your other objectives or with your targeting and positioning decisions.

2. List the elements that contribute to your offering's total benefits and total price, as shown in Exhibit 7.2. Be sure to include elements that aren't obvious, such as the benefit of status. Now do the same for the top three competing offers. How do their offers and prices compare with yours? For planning purposes, how can you research customers' perceptions of your offer's value versus the value of competing offers?

3. What do you know about the price elasticity of demand for offerings such as yours? What public information can you find about the reaction when the prices of competing offers (or goods/services in this category) have increased or decreased? What are the current and projected trends of supply in your industry? What do you know or suspect about the price sensitivity of customers in your targeted segment(s)? What are the implications for your pricing decisions and your marketing mix?

4. What expectations or customs of channel members must you factor into your thinking about pricing your offer? For instance, do wholesalers or retailers typically expect a certain profit margin from the sale of products such as yours? Should pricing be adapted to accommodate seasonal demand or promotions in your channel? What legal, regulatory, and ethical concerns apply to your pricing strategy?

5. Do you know or can you estimate your fixed costs, variable costs, and total costs? Are these costs likely to change during the period covered by your plan? If so, how and why? Using the formula for calculating break-even volume, can you estimate the sales level you must achieve to cover your costs? How does this level relate to the objectives in your marketing plan?

6. If you're introducing a new good or service, will you use skimming or penetration pricing, and why? If your product is in a later stage of its life cycle, how will you use pricing? When, how, and how often should you adapt your price to achieve your pricing objectives? Be sure to calculate the effect of price adaptation on projected sales and profits. Also consider whether price or nonprice competition makes sense for your marketing situation. Review Exhibit 7.10 as you write about what you might do if a competitor slashes its price and you are forced to respond.

Endnotes

1. John Hogan, "Is Your Pricing Strategy a Tactical Anchor or a Strategic Lever for Growth?" speech delivered at the American Marketing Association Strategic Marketing Conference in Chicago, May 11, 2006.

2. Mike Hughlett, "McDonald's Lays Plans to Take Dollar Menu to Breakfast Nationwide," *Chicago Tribune,* November 6, 2009, www.chicagotribune.com/business; Lauren Shepherd, "Restaurants Cut Lunch Prices to Bring in Diners," *Associated Press,* May 27, 2009, www.associatedpress.com; Douglas A. McIntyre, "Inspired by McDonald's, Wal-Mart Creates Its Own Dollar Menu," *Time,* May 15, 2009, www.time.com; Heather Chambers, "Sonic Driving Its New Dollar Menu Into Area," *San Diego Business Journal,* March 23, 2009, p. 12; Emily Bryson York, "McD's Secret Sauce: It Embodies Value," *Advertising Age,* February 2, 2009, p. 3.

3. Ken Belson, "Baseball Tickets Too Much? Check Back Tomorrow," *New York Times,* May 18, 2009, www.nytimes.com.

4. Peter Ha, "Zipcar App," *Time,* November 2, 2009, www.time.com; Elizabeth Olson, "Car Sharing Reinvents the Company Wheels," *New York Times,* May 6, 2009, www.nytimes.com; Rupal Parekh, "Zipcar Finds a Niche in Turbulent Economy," *Advertising Age,* January 26, 2009, p. 15; Mark Levine, "Share My Ride," *New York Times Magazine,* March 8, 2009, pp. 34+.

5. Thomas T. Nagle and John E. Hogan, *The Strategy and Tactics of Pricing,* 4th ed. (Upper Saddle River, NJ: Prentice Hall, 2006), p. 130.

6. Michael Turnbell, "With New Express Toll Lanes, Interstate 95 Traffic Is Moving Faster," *South Florida Sun Sentinel,* May 18, 2009, www.sunsentinel.com; Brendan Sainsbury, "Charge Ahead," *Alternatives*

Journal, January–February 2006, pp. 34+; Robert W. Poole, Jr., "What the Traffic Will Bear," *Forbes,* May 10, 2004, p. 44.

7. Nagle and Hogan, *The Strategy and Tactics of Pricing,* chapter 1.

8. "From the Editor's Desk," *The Costco Connection,* March 2009, p. 5.

9. For more about target costing, see: Mohan Gopalakrishnan, Janet Samuels, and Dan Swenson, "Target Costing at a Consumer Products Company," *Strategic Finance,* December 2007, pp. 37+.

10. Steve Banker, "In-Store Logistics at IKEA," *Logistics Viewpoints,* November 5, 2009, http://logis-ticsviewpoints.com/2009/11/05/in-store-logistics-at-ikea/; Mark Albright, "Woven into IKEA Fabric," *St. Petersburg Times (Florida),* April 29, 2009, p. 1B: "IKEA Grows Despite Slowdown," *Business Daily Update,* April 7, 2009, n.p.; Zoe Wood, "The Friday Interview: War on the Home Front as IKEA Chief Tempts Flatpack-phobic," *The Guardian (London),* January 23, 2009, p. 33; Larissa Brass, "IKEA Sources 'Green' Furniture from Dandridge, Tenn.," *Knoxville News-Sentinel,* January 19, 2009, n.p.

11. Nagle and Hogan, *Strategy and Tactics of Pricing,* pp. 8–9.

12. Aaron Lucchetti, "Brokerages Drop Fees to Retain Top Clients," *Wall Street Journal,* May 30, 2009, www.wsj.com.

13. "Verizon to Double Its Cancellation Fees," *Washington Post,* November 5, 2009, www.wash-ingtonpost.com; Calvin Azuri, "Verizon Wireless Customers Are the Most Satisfied, Survey Says," *TMCnet,* May 20, 2009, www.tmcnet.com; "Verizon Wireless Offers Additional 'Worry-Free' Guarantees," *The America's Intelligence Wire,* November 20, 2006, n.p.; Kevin Fitchard, "Untethering the Bundle," *Telephony,* August 14, 2006; Yuki Noguchi, "Verizon Wireless to Lower Exit Fee," *Washington Post,* June 29, 2006, p. D1.

14. Wayne D. Hoyer and Deborah J. MacInnis, *Consumer Behavior,* 3rd ed. (Boston, MA: Houghton Mifflin, 2004), p. 262.

15. Rob Walker, "Immaterialism," *New York Times Magazine,* May 3, 2009, p. 28.

16. "Monro Muffler 4Q Pft Up 57%; Boosts Div 17%, Announces Buy," *Wall Street Journal,* May 28, 2009, www.wsj.com; James Covert, "Monro Muffler Puts Focus on Trust," *Wall Street Journal,* June 11, 2003, p. B5G.

17. "The New High-end Consumer: 'Please Put My Bottega Veneta Wallet in a Plain Bag,'" *Knowledge at Wharton,* May 27, 2009, http://knowledge.wharton.upenn.edu/article.cfm?articleid=2248; Patricia Marx, "Face Value," *The New Yorker,* May 25, 2009, pp. 32–36.

18. Matt Nannery, "Digital Depot," *Chain Store Age,* January 2004, pp. 18A+.

19. Geoffrey Colvin, "Pricing Power Ain't What It Used to Be," *Fortune,* September 15, 2003, p. 52.

20. Christina Binkley, "Death to Discounts? The Designers Rebel," *Wall Street Journal,* April 16, 2009, www.wsj.com.

21. See Nagle and Hogan, *The Strategy and Tactics of Pricing,* chapter 14.

22. Joseph Pereira, "Price-Fixing Makes Comeback After Supreme Court Ruling," *Wall Street Journal,* August 18, 2008, p. A1; "EBay, Others Want End to Retail Price-fixing," *Industry Standard,* May 19, 2009, http://www.thestandard.com/news/2009/05/19/ebay-others-want-end-retail-price-fixing.

23. Vivian Wai-yin Kwok, "Passing on the Savings in Steel," *Forbes,* May 27, 2009, www.forbes.com.

24. See Chapter 9 and Appendix 9A in Nagle and Hogan, *Strategy and Tactics of Pricing,* for more detail on break-even formulas and calculations.

25. Carol Matlack, "The Vuitton Machine," *Business Week,* March 22, 2004, pp. 98+.

26. "India Flips for Bargain-priced Tata Nano," *NW Autos,* May 15, 2009, www.nwsource.com.

27. "P&G Tries to Absorb More Low-End Sales," *Brandweek,* September 26, 2005, p. 4.

28. Elaine Wong, "100-Calorie Packs Pack It In," *Brandweek,* May 26, 2009, www.brandweek.com; Jeremy W. Peters, "Fewer Bites, Fewer Calories, Lot More Profit," *New York Times,* July 7, 2007, P. C1, C4.

29. Michael Dinan, "Interview: Pure Digital's Anti-iPhone Approach to Flip Camcorders," *TMCNet,* April 30, 2009, www.tmcnet.com.

30. Cliff Edwards, "HP Gets Tough on Ink Counterfeiters," *BusinessWeek,* May 28, 2009, www.businessweek.com; Franklin Paul, "Xerox Keeps Up R&D, Risks Cannibalization," *Reuters,* May 19, 2009, www.reuters.com.

31. Victoria Murphy Barret, "What the Traffic Will Bear," *Forbes Global,* July 3, 2006.

32. Christopher S. Tang, "United We May Stand," *MIT Sloan Management Review,* May 12, 2008, http://sloanreview.mit.edu/business-insight/articles/2008/2/5024/united-we-may-stand/; "Shop Affronts," *The Economist,* July 1, 2006, p. 59.

33. "The Commoditization of Brands and Its Implications for Businesses," *Copernicus* and *Market Facts,* December 2000, pp. 1–6.

8 Developing Channel and Logistics Strategy

In this chapter:

PREVIEW

Although video on demand is nothing new, *print on demand* is another "on demand" movement gaining strength as authors, publishers, book stores, and libraries look for new ways to make books available to readers where and when they want them. The Northshire Bookstore and the New Orleans Public Library are two of a growing number of institutions that use the Espresso Book Machine to print a full-size book on demand, in less than five minutes. In fact, the number of print-on-demand books published in a year now exceeds the number of books published by traditional publishers.[1]

The idea of delivering a good or service "on demand" is changing channel and logistics strategy, meaning how, when, and where marketers distribute goods and services—all part of Step 5 of the marketing planning process (see Exhibit 8.1). This chapter discusses the channel and logistics decisions you must address when preparing a marketing plan. First you'll explore the connections and flows in the value chain and consider how various participants add value to the offering. The next section explains the major influences on channel strategy and the decisions you must make about channel functions, levels, and members. The closing section looks at logistics strategy, including how to approach key decisions about transportation, storage, inventory management, and other functions vital to marketing.

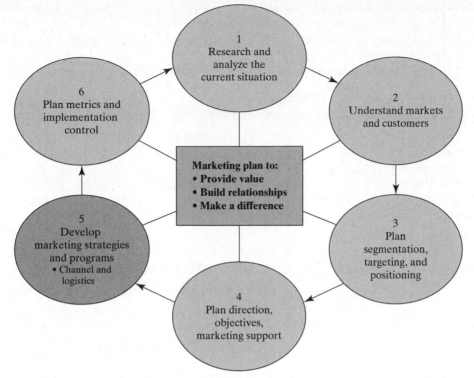

EXHIBIT 8.1   Marketing Planning: Step 5

APPLYING YOUR KNOWLEDGE

After reading this chapter, review the channel and logistics entries in this book's sample plan and in a few of the sample plans bundled with your *Marketing Plan Pro* software. Next, answer the questions in "Your Marketing Plan, Step by Step," at the end of this chapter, as you think about channel and logistics. This chapter's checklist summarizes channel and logistics issues to consider during the planning process. Continue documenting your ideas with *Marketing Plan Pro* software or in your written plan.

CHAPTER 8 CHECKLIST   Channel and Logistical Issues

Channel Issues

✔ How do product, data, and money flow through your value chain, and how can participants add more value for your customers?

✔ How do goals and objectives, resources, direction, need for control, and marketing-mix decisions affect channel choices?

✔ Which channels and members perform the best, and at what cost to the organization?

✔ How do product characteristics and life cycle, positioning, targeting, market issues, and competitive factors affect channel choices and costs?

✔ How do customers expect or prefer to gain access to the product, and what is the impact on channel decisions?

✔ How many levels/members are needed/desirable to get offering to targeted segments?

Logistical Issues

✔ What logistical functions must be performed and by which channel members?

✔ Who will transport and store supplies, parts, and finished products—how, where, and when?

✔ Who will manage inventory, orders, billing, shipping, payment—and how?

✔ How do production- and sales-related objectives affect logistical plans?

✔ How are logistics affected by customer needs/preferences, channel/company capabilities, product plans, and marketing plan objectives?

PLANNING FOR THE VALUE CHAIN OF TODAY AND TOMORROW

PLANNING TIP

Think ahead: altering channel arrangements can be difficult and time consuming.

Books, videos, and other goods and services are marketed as part of a **value chain,** also known as a *supply chain,* a series of interrelated, value-added functions plus the structure of organizations performing them to get the right product to the right markets and customers at the right time, place, and price. The marketer (shown as "producer" in Exhibit 8.2) manages supplier relationships and logistics on the inbound side to obtain the inputs (such as parts, shipment dates, and cost figures) needed for creating goods and services. On the outbound or demand side, the marketer manages logistics and **channels** (also called *distribution channels*), the functions that allow you to meet demand by making a product available to customers in each market.

During the planning process, you need to analyze how value is added at each connection in this chain, from inputs on the inbound side to finished products moving outbound to the point at which customers pay and take possession. To illustrate, Godiva buys chocolate, heavy cream, butter, sugar, nuts, and other ingredients from suppliers around the world (this adds value inbound to producer, as in Exhibit 8.2). The company produces its luxury chocolates in different facilities—including some in Belgium, where the company was founded—and then uses temperature-controlled shipments to deliver

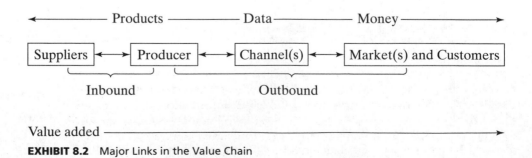

EXHIBIT 8.2 Major Links in the Value Chain

the chocolates to its own stores and to other fine retailers that carry Godiva products. On the outbound side of value chain, Godiva ensures that its chocolates go through appropriate channels to reach each target market.

As you plan, remember that the value chain you have today may not be the same as the one you'll need tomorrow. Changes in the internal and external environment can bring changes to both channel arrangements and channel members. Chrysler dealers found this out the hard way when the company went bankrupt and severed ties with nearly 800 dealers, giving just a few weeks' notice.[2]

Increasingly, marketers are looking ahead to tomorrow's efficiencies by hiring experts to connect with suppliers, manufacture products, and get shipments directly into outbound channels. Li & Fung, based in Hong Kong, adds to the value chain by doing this for many marketers, although its participation is invisible to customers on the demand side.

Li & Fung. What do J. C. Penney, Target, Timberland, Kohl's, Macy's, Walmart, and Liz Claiborne have in common? All contract with Li & Fung to make and deliver products under their various brand names. Liz Claiborne designs and markets Juicy Couture, Kate Spade, and other fashion brands but leaves all the manufacturing and shipment details to Li & Fung, which finds the right fabrics, supervises the sewing, packages the garments, and fulfills orders from retailers. In 2004, Li & Fung rang up revenue of $12 billion; today, its annual revenue from 80 facilities in 40 countries is nearly $20 billion. In fact, so many companies want to hand over their supply, production, and delivery functions that Li & Fung is seeking to acquire suppliers and outsourcers to accommodate higher volume.[3]

Whether you're developing a marketing plan for a retailer, manufacturer, or another kind of marketer, be aware that you have the long-term option of changing the players in your value chain and/or changing the way each adds value, the way Chrysler was forced to do. As you explore the possibilities, consider whether an outside player—such as Li & Fung—might, in the future, manage certain functions more efficiently or effectively than your organization. Conversely, you might want to bring some functions in-house to gain more control or for other purposes.

Flows in the Value Chain

Channel and logistics strategy involves managing three value-chain flows. The flow of products refers to physical items such as raw materials and product packaging (on the inbound side) and finished products (on the outbound side) plus other items that move from outbound to inbound (such as products returned for repair). The flow of data refers to information such as the number of items ordered (moving inbound or outbound), customer requirements and feedback (passed along from channel members or directly from customer to producer), and other information that adds value through effectiveness and efficiency. The flow of money refers to payments for supplies (on the inbound side), reseller or customer payments for finished goods (on the outbound side), and other money movements between participants.

PLANNING TIP

Diagram the value chain to see where value is added and find areas for improvement.

Map the flows in your value chain so your marketing plan will cover the movement of all three flows in both directions. Sometimes you'll have to consider movement between noncontiguous links in the value chain, such as the flow of a rebate check from a producer directly to a customer who has purchased a product from a retailer. Note that the inbound side of the value chain is always B2B. For example, Dancing Deer, which makes cakes, cookies, and brownies, is a business customer to the suppliers that sell it chocolate, butter, and other ingredients. After producing its baked goods, Dancing Deer makes them available to targeted customers through its Web site and through selected specialty stores, all part of the outbound channel. New product information and other details flow between producer and suppliers as well as between producer and its outbound channel partners. Money also flows from producer to suppliers and from markets/customers to channel partners to producer.

Adding Value through the Chain

As you plan, take into account how each participant adds value to satisfy the needs of the next link (the immediate customer) as well as the needs of the customer at the end of the value chain. Thus, the retailers that market Godiva's products will put its chocolates on display and have sufficient quantities in stock when customers want to buy. The price paid by each successive participant reflects the value added by the previous link; customers at the end of the chain ultimately pay for the combined value added by all participants, an element of pricing strategy that was discussed in Chapter 7.

Think creatively about the functions that must be performed at every stage of the chain, which participant will perform each function, and how that participant will be paid. The marketing plan for FreshDirect's vending-machine meals reflects a creative approach to an old distribution method.

FreshDirect. This Web-based grocery delivery service in New York City has branched out into top-quality prepared entrees, ready in four minutes, distributed through vending machines placed in major Manhattan office buildings. The company chose high-tech vending machines that can be monitored remotely to take inventory, confirm operational status, and transfer electronic payment data. The equipment vendor had to allow for sending electronic receipts on request, because employees sometimes need these to be reimbursed for meals eaten while working overtime at the office. It also had to arrange for the machines to accept credit or debit payment only, so FreshDirect could avoid the headaches of restocking bills and coins and taking cash to the bank. FreshDirect's marketing plan recognized that these enhancements would add convenience for customers and for the company alike.[4]

FreshDirect put the heating and dispensing function as far downstream in the value chain as possible—allowing customer demand to trigger these functions, which are handled by the vending machine when activated by an order. The flow of money and data from the vending machine to FreshDirect is vital; without them, the company wouldn't know what to restock, what to stop selling, and how much revenue is generated. Again, these flows are managed through network links with the vending machine. Although your marketing plan may not have the same flows as FreshDirect, you can see how careful and creative value-chain planning makes a difference to the organization and its customers.

Services and the Value Chain

If you're planning for a restaurant, a financial service, or another intangible product, you also need to map all the flows within your value chain. The inbound flows relate to ordering, paying for, and receiving shipments of supplies that support service delivery (such as foods or office supplies). The outbound flows help customers arrange to receive the service (such as making airline reservations). Because services are usually produced and used simultaneously, marketers must plan flows to match supply and demand. Citibank, for instance, must stock each ATM with sufficient $20 bills and receipt paper for the anticipated daily usage.

Value for services, like tangible products, is added inbound through the chain as the producer incorporates a variety of inputs. Outbound, channel members add value by promoting the service, communicating with the customers, making appointments or selling tickets, managing payments and paperwork, and handling other functions to give customers access to the service at an appropriate price, place, and time. Consider the channel for convenient medical services, a channel that has been changing to accommodate patients' busy lives.

Medical Clinics. MinuteClinic, which offers walk-in medical care for minor illnesses, operates dozens of small clinics located inside the drug stores of its parent company, CVS. Take Care Health Clinic, owned by Walgreens, maintains walk-in clinics in many of its parent drug stores. And Walmart is partnering with local hospitals to open walk-in clinics in dozens of its U.S. stores, which are also equipped with retail pharmacies.

Why this change in channel strategy? The clinics benefit from access to the retailers' customer base, store location, and pharmaceutical services. They're especially busy in fall and winter, when people request flu shots or need treatments for coughs, infections, and similar ailments. Customers value the convenience of quick medical attention and access to prescription drugs, at an accessible location and at a reasonable price. And the stores benefit from customers buying pharmaceuticals, medical supplies, or other merchandise before or after a visit for medical care.[5]

PLANNING CHANNEL STRATEGY

How can channel strategy help your organization achieve its marketing plan objectives? Although many aspects of this strategy are invisible to customers, it plays a major part in the marketing mix of every business. You must decide which channel functions will be covered, who will handle each function, how many channel levels to use, and how many and what type of channel members to choose. (In addition, you'll face decisions about logistics, as discussed later in the chapter.)

PLANNING TIP

Ideally, ask each channel partner to show how it will market your product.

Channel Functions

As you know, the channel as a whole must perform a variety of value-added outbound functions such as matching the volume, amount, or offer to customer needs; providing intermediaries and customers with product and market information; contacting and negotiating with customers to maintain relationships and complete sales; and transporting and storing products prior to purchase.

During planning, identify the channel functions needed for each product, determine which functions intermediaries should handle, and estimate the compensation each channel member should receive for the value it adds. Some producers prefer to assume many or all of the functions themselves because they want more control over customer contacts, pricing, or other elements; others, such as Liz Claiborne, delegate selected functions to reduce costs and focus resources on other tasks. Even within the same industry, a channel strategy that works for one company may not be suitable for its competitors. Liz Claiborne has Li & Fung handle delivery from factories to stores, whereas some other firms manage these channel arrangements on their own.

Channel Levels

PLANNING TIP

Use research to stay in touch with customers' needs when using two- or three-level channels.

How many channel levels are needed or desirable? The higher the number of channel levels, the more intermediaries are involved in making the product available (see Exhibit 8.3). Each channel level adds value in some way by having the product in a convenient place for purchase, for instance, or providing information and demonstrations. In exchange, each level expects to profit from the sale to the next level or to the final customer, costs that must be factored into the ultimate selling price.

A *zero-level channel* refers to a direct channel linking seller and buyer. Amazon uses this approach for its Kindle e-book reader, marketing directly to consumers and bypassing

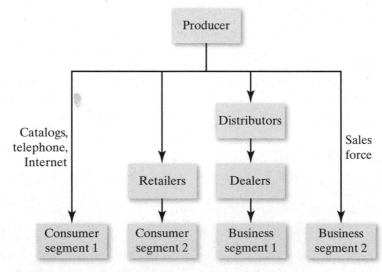

EXHIBIT 8.3 Channel Levels

wholesalers and other retailers. An entrepreneurial venture such as Kogi Korean BBQ may begin with a zero-level channel to get close to its customers and build its brand.

Kogi Korean BBQ. Mark Manguera, a fan of Korean food and tacos, cooked up the idea of selling Korean barbecue on taco shells from a roving catering truck. He got the truck, enlisted a chef as partner, and began planning his route through Los Angeles. Instead of stopping randomly and waiting for customers to happen by, however, Manguera and his partners use Twitter and blogs to let 50,000 followers know when and where the truck will stop. After reading Kogi's posts, as many as 300 people line up in anticipation of the truck's arrival on any given day. Kogi's success led to the purchase of additional trucks and to the opening of a new channel in which its BBQ tacos are featured on the menu of the Alibi Room restaurant in Los Angeles.[6]

Sometimes complex or novel products need considerable support from channel members, which may mean using a one-level, two-level, or even three-level channel for certain markets or segments. In a *one-level channel,* the seller works with a single type of intermediary to build strong channel relations and facilitate product, data, and financial flows through the value chain. Some products, such as automotive parts, are customarily distributed through two- or three-level channels. Apple uses multiple channel levels, marketing through selected retailers and catalog merchants as well as through its own stores. If the product covered by your market plan is new, you'll need to find ways of breaking into established channels to reach your targeted segments, which is not always easy with an unproven product or brand.

Movies are currently expanding the number of channel levels and members used to reach the viewing and buying public. This trend may be applicable to a variety of goods and services.

PLANNING TIP

Add or eliminate levels depending on the product, buying patterns, and other factors.

Channels for movies. At one time, major movies debuted in first-run theaters and then were shown in a much larger, wide-release network of theaters. Independent movies achieved modest distribution through "art" cinemas in selected cities. These days, independent and popular movies are increasingly available on demand— sometimes simultaneously with theater release—through cable or satellite providers. A growing number are downloadable or viewable through the iTunes online store and the Hulu.com entertainment portal. The world's most-watched video site, YouTube, is adding 15 hours of movie content *every minute,* in its bid to make itself more attractive to advertisers.

Consumers who prefer to rent have many channel options. Redbox, for instance, is a red boxlike vending machine that rents DVDs for $1 per night. Catering to impulse rentals and customers seeking convenience, each of the 21,000 Redbox kiosks installed in supermarkets and other retail locations nationwide holds

700 DVDs. Netflix, an online-only subscription service that offers DVDs by mail and offers instant viewing, has already captured 7 percent of the U.S. rental market and is expected to hold up to 10 percent by 2013. Blockbuster has a significant store empire and an online presence for movie rental. However, competition from Netflix, Redbox, on-demand services, and other distribution alternatives has hurt Blockbuster's growth and profits in recent years. Now the company is closing hundreds of stores and placing its own DVD rental kiosks in high-traffic locations. In the future, will studios make movies available directly to consumers?[7]

Reverse Channels

In some industries or countries, a company's marketing plan also must allow for reverse channels to return products for exchange, repair, or recycling. Reverse channels can even be used to build relationships with customers and the community. To illustrate, Nokia accepts mobile handsets for recycling at centers across India; it takes the phones apart to recycle 80 percent of the parts and components. For each phone it recycles, Nokia plants a tree in the community.[8] Marketers must investigate applicable laws or regulations, such as the European Union's strict rules mandating recycling of certain products and materials, when planning channels in various markets.

Reverse channels present profit and relationship opportunities for enterprising companies such as ReCellular.

ReCellular. Based in Michigan, ReCellular has built its business on recycling old cell phones. Of the 5.5 million units it receives for recycling every day, approximately half are stripped to reclaim the batteries, plastic parts, and other components for use in manufacturing other products; the others are refurbished for resale in 40 nations around the world. The company encourages customers to recycle their old handsets through channel partners such as Best Buy and Verizon Wireless.

ReCellular also strengthens relationships with the community by paying nonprofit groups for used cell phones they collect. Last year alone, its donations to nonprofits topped $4 million. As an example, ReCellular recycles used phones collected by the nonprofit Cell Phones for Soldiers. For each cell phone recycled, the nonprofit receives enough cash to buy an hour of prepaid phone time for a soldier serving abroad.[9]

Channel Members

How many and what type of channel members will be needed at each channel level? Customers' needs and habits are important clues to appropriate channel choices and to identifying creative new channel opportunities for competitive advantage. Financial considerations are another key factor. Channel members have certain profit expectations, and customers have their own perceptions of a product's value; both affect the marketer's pricing strategy and profit potential. In addition, the choice of channel members depends on the product's life cycle, the positioning, and the targeted segment (see Exhibit 8.4).

EXHIBIT 8.4 Intensive, Selective, and Exclusive Distribution

	Value to Marketer	*Value to Customer*	*Planning Considerations*
Intensive distribution (in many outlets for maximum market coverage)	Increase unit sales, market impulse items, cover more of each market, reduce channel costs per unit sold.	Convenient, wide access to frequently used or impulse products; price may be lower due to competition.	• Will service be adequate? • Will product be displayed and sold properly? • Will conflict arise between outlets?
Selective distribution (in a number of selected outlets)	Cover specific areas in each market, reduce dependence on only a few outlets, supervise some channel activities, control some channel costs.	See product and receive sales help in more outlets within each market, obtain some services as needed.	• What is the optimal balance of costs, control, and benefits? • Will outlets be convenient for customers? • Do sales reps understand the product and customers' needs?
Exclusive distribution (in a few outlets for exclusivity within each market)	Choose specific outlets to introduce an innovative item, support positioning, build closer channel relationships, better supervise service, etc.	Receive personalized attention; access to delivery, alterations, customization, and other services.	• Will channel costs be too high? • Will product be available to all targeted segments? • Will price be too high, given channel profit requirements? • Will outlets be committed marketing partners?

At introduction, an innovative new product may be offered in a very limited number of outlets (*exclusive distribution*) to reinforce its novelty and enable store staff to learn all about features and benefits. In maturity, the company may try to keep sales going by getting the product into as many outlets as possible (*intensive distribution*). In decline, companies may sell through fewer channel members (*selective distribution*) to keep shipping costs down.

Relations with channel members should be reexamined periodically to be sure the organization is achieving its objectives and to determine whether channel members and customers are being satisfied. IBM, for example, sets sales and fulfillment targets for its own sales force and for channel members, monitors weekly progress, and has a structured process to get channel members the leads, products, education, and support they need to achieve objectives. Its marketers calculate return on investment to assess the financial payback of the channel strategy and to consider changes. They also hire researchers to survey thousands of channel members twice a year in each market. The purpose is to solicit feedback about IBM's support and training, reseller margins, and responsiveness as a business partner—in short, to find out whether channel members are satisfied with value-chain flows and if not, what can be done to increase satisfaction and loyalty.[10]

PLANNING TIP

Use channel resources creatively to add value for competitive advantage.

Influences on Channel Strategy

All the channel decisions discussed earlier are influenced by a number of internal and external factors, summarized in Exhibit 8.5. The major internal factors for marketers to consider during this part of the planning process include the following:

- **Direction, goals, and objectives.** The channel strategy must be consistent with the organization's chosen direction, its higher-level goals, and its marketing plan objectives. Companies with green marketing objectives need to plan appropriate channels for getting products to green-oriented customers as well as reverse channels for reclaiming recyclable products or parts.
- **Resources and capabilities.** If the company has the resources and competencies to handle certain channel functions, it may do so while keeping costs in line by hiring others for different functions. Companhia Brasileira de Distribuição, the largest retailer in Brazil, has the resources to manage quality and inventory by storing seafood products in one specialized distribution center and flowers and plants in another. The retailer has also acquired an electronics retail chain for added competencies and diversified merchandising.[11]
- **Marketing mix.** Channel decisions must work with the organization's product, pricing, and promotion strategies. Unusual or unexpected combinations (like Cottage Hill Nursery marketing live wisteria trees through QVC) can be successful, but require careful planning and top-notch implementation. Cottage Hill first sold its trees and flowers through QVC in 2001; it now sells more through QVC than through any other channel, packaging its plants carefully for the trip to customers who have called or clicked to buy.[12]
- **Control.** Does the company want or need tight control over channel functions for quality or image reasons? Can the company afford this kind of control, or must it give up some control in exchange for other benefits, such as lower costs or wider coverage in certain areas?

The major external factors influencing decisions about channel strategy are as follows:

- **Customers.** Channel choices should be consistent with what customers want, prefer, expect, or will accept. John Deere sells riding lawnmowers through Home

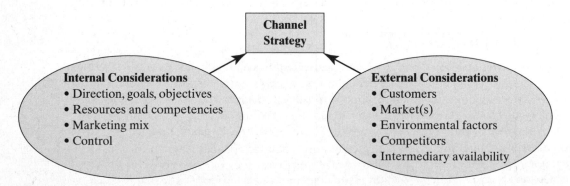

EXHIBIT 8.5 Influences on Channel Strategy

Depot and other retail chains because "that's where our customers are going," says a sales executive. Yet Stihl advertises that its chain saws and other power tools are available through 8,000 independent dealers but not home-improvement giants like Home Depot. "Sometimes telling someone where you're not available is more effective than telling where you are," notes the marketing manager. For convenience, Stihl invites customers to find the nearest dealer or request assistance by texting the company.[13]

- *Market(s).* Companies are finding new ways to reach far-flung markets. For example, Western Union is expanding its money transfer services into new domestic and global markets by partnering with banks, check-cashing firms, and other channel members. As a result, customers of Garanti Bank in Turkey can now transfer money (in euros or in dollars) to any of Western Union's 334,000 offices worldwide.[14]

- *Environmental factors.* Channel choices should reflect the marketer's analysis of technological, legal-regulatory, social-cultural, and other factors in the environment. This is especially important with offerings that cannot be sold to certain segments, may become obsolete quickly, are fashion oriented, or are heavily regulated. To illustrate, alcoholic beverages are subject to rules regarding where and when they may be marketed, which clearly affects channel decisions.

- *Competitors.* How can the company use channel strategy to gain a competitive edge? Fashion brands walk a tightrope between availability and exclusivity and must choose their channel partners with care. The Buckle stores are popular with teenagers, but that's not the only attraction for producers. The retailer also offers free alterations, an important amenity for customers who buy form-fitting fashions such as MEK Denim jeans.[15] Sometimes going outside the usual channels can be more effective than using the same channel members as most competitors, if customer behavior and costs allow. Build-A-Bear Workshop has a B2B sales division to market customized stuffed animals as specialty items for corporations, dressed in T-shirts bearing the company's logo.

- *Availability of intermediaries.* What intermediaries are available in each market, what are their strengths and weaknesses, and what is their reach? Marketers with frequently purchased consumer products often seek distribution through large retail chains, for instance, but each chain has its own locations, strategy, and so on. Just a decade ago, organic food companies had relatively limited choices; now specialized grocery chains such as Whole Foods Market are expanding and even mainstream Walmart stocks a wide array of organic foods, increasing distribution opportunities.

PLANNING FOR LOGISTICS

The mechanics of managing the flows through the value chain from point of origin to point of production and then outbound to point of sale or consumption are addressed by **logistics.** You want a logistics strategy that is responsive to customer needs yet meets your internal financial targets. This is a delicate balancing act: Companies do not want to overspend to get supplies and products, information, and payments where and when they should be. On the other hand, they risk losing customers if they take too long to fill orders, have too few units or the wrong assortment on hand to fill orders, have a confusing or complex ordering process, cannot easily track orders and shipments, or make it difficult for customers to return products.[16]

PLANNING TIP

Estimate the total cost of logistics for each service level before making a final decision.

Still, responding to customers' needs entails some costs (for delivery, inventory, order confirmation, etc.). Thus, when planning for logistics, you should weigh the total cost of logistics against the level of customer responsiveness that is appropriate to meet your organization's marketing plan objectives.

Walmart, the world's largest retailer (a producer of private-label merchandise and a major player in the outbound section of many manufacturers' value chains), keeps logistics costs low so it can keep prices low for competitive advantage.

Walmart. "Logistics is the lifeblood of Walmart," observes a Walmart regional vice president. It's so important to Walmart that CEO Michael Duke and two previous CEOs each took a turn running the retailer's logistics earlier in their careers. Even as the retailer unpacks 4.7 billion cartons of merchandise to stock the shelves and serve 180 million shoppers worldwide every week, it cuts prices and boosts margins. Buying from manufacturers rather than from wholesalers when possible saves time and money.

By forecasting demand months in advance, sharing forecasts with suppliers, and calculating and customizing inventory levels for each store, the retailer ensures enough time to plan timely, cost-effective transportation and delivery. Because Walmart never wants to run out of fast-selling products like toothpaste, it warehouses and transports high-turnover goods separately from slower-selling merchandise. It also has plans in place to deal with spikes in demand for bottled water, nonperishable foods, and other merchandise when a hurricane or other extreme weather is on the way. If a store sustains storm damage, Walmart sends disaster vans to provide telecommunications capabilities, track inventory, manage debit and credit card transactions, and handle other vital functions until normal operations can be restored.[17]

Logistical Functions

Walmart minimizes the total cost of logistics and operates self-service stores, a balance that supports its market share and profit objectives. Like Walmart, you must consider four main logistical functions when preparing your marketing plan (see Exhibit 8.6):

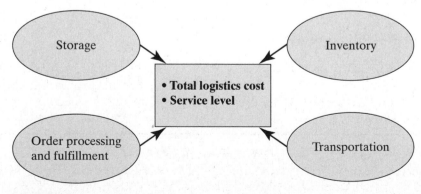

EXHIBIT 8.6 Logistics Decisions

- **Storage.** Where will supplies, parts, and finished products be stored, for how long, and under what conditions? Sometimes suppliers agree to warehouse goods; sometimes the marketer warehouses goods until needed to fill customer orders. More storage facilities means higher costs, but faster response times. Walmart locates its huge distribution centers no more than one day's drive from each cluster of stores so it can replenish shelf stock quickly. In addition, each outlet has refrigerated storage and other special storage arrangements for perishable, tiny, outsized, or fragile products.
- **Inventory.** How many parts, components, and supplies must be available inbound for production? How many finished goods are needed on the outbound side to meet customer demand and organizational objectives? How do projected inventory levels affect storage and transportation decisions? Lower inventory means lower costs but may cause delays in filling customers' orders if products are out of stock. Weyerhaeuser, which makes wood and paper products, researches customers' future needs and revises sales forecasts every month so it can plan inventory levels for the coming 6–24 months. During a recent slowdown in housing construction, Weyerhaeuser had about a week's worth of softwood lumber on hand; if not for its precise forecasting, the company would have had up to a three weeks' supply on hand.[18]
- **Order processing and fulfillment.** Who will be responsible for taking orders, confirming product availability, packing products for shipment, tracking orders in transit, preparing invoices or receipts, and handling errors or returns? How will these tasks be accomplished and relevant information be tracked, and in what time frame? Such tasks are as vital to companies with intangible offerings as they are to companies offering tangible products. Apple's App Store makes things simple for developers who use it to sell their applications (games, organizing tools, etc.) made for iPhones and iPods. The App Store handles order processing, fulfillment, and payments; it receives 30 percent of the retail price for its work and sends the remaining 70 percent to the firm or entrepreneur who developed each app—people like David Coyle, who designed the Deckster virtual card game.[19]
- **Transportation.** How will supplies, parts, and finished products be transported inbound and outbound? Who will pay? Where and when will goods or materials be picked up and delivered? For door-to-door pickup and delivery, marketers often use truck transport. When schedules are flexible and products are heavy or bulky, they may choose less-costly rail or water transport; when deadlines are short and products are perishable or precious, marketers may use fast (but expensive) air transport.

Influences on Logistics Decisions

One factor that can influence your planning for logistics is the organization's approach to social responsibility, as Give Something Back's experience indicates.

PLANNING TIP

Benchmark against best practices in several industries to improve your logistics.

Give Something Back. After seeing how Newman's Own raised money for charity by marketing food products, Mike Hannigan and Sean Marx started Give Something Back (GSB) to market office supplies and donate the profits to charity. Now GSB is the largest independently owned office-supply firm in California, with multiple distribution centers and a retail Web site that competes head-to-head with Staples and Office Depot. Although GSB offers many of the same items as its competitors—and free next-day delivery, like they do—it stocks more than 6,000 environmentally friendly products, as well.

Being socially responsible has affected GSB's logistics strategy. Recently the firm decided to start a free e-waste pickup service for customers. "We send a fleet of trucks out every morning full of stuff, and they come back empty," explains Hannigan. "So we'll fill them with e-waste and bring it back to our warehouse. It's leveraging [assets]—our trucks and people—without additional cost, to allow customers to do something that they wanted to do anyway."[20]

Cost constraints are another factor to consider. Online businesses often provide a choice of delivery options with associated prices, allowing customers to decide how much they're willing to spend for faster delivery. In some cases, businesses simply build delivery costs into the price of their products. Finally, be prepared to justify your logistics budget to decision makers.

Even on a smaller scale, logistics decisions can make a real difference in any marketing plan. Note that the marketing plan need not contain every detail of the logistics strategy, but it should contain a general outline, explain the balance of total costs versus responsiveness, and indicate how logistics functions will support your other marketing decisions.

Summary

Products reach markets at the right time, place, and price through the value chain, a series of interrelated, value-added functions and the structure of organizations performing them. Each organization adds value to satisfy the needs of the next link (the immediate customer) as well as customers at the end of the chain. The marketer manages suppliers and logistics on the inbound side to obtain inputs, then manages channels and logistics to meet demand on the outbound side. Plan for the movement of products, information, and money in both directions along the value chain. Service marketers also need to understand all the flows in the chain, determine how value is added and by which participant, and manage flows to balance supply and demand.

Channel strategy covers decisions about which channel functions must be performed and by which participant; how many channel levels to use; how many and what type of channel members to choose. Influences on channel strategy include direction, goal, and objectives; resources and core competencies; other marketing-mix decisions; control issues; customers' needs and preferences; market factors; environmental factors; competitors; and intermediary availability. Logistics involves managing the mechanics of products, data, and information flows throughout the value chain, based on objectives that balance total costs with customer responsiveness levels. The four main logistics functions are storage, inventory, order processing and fulfillment, and transportation.

Your Marketing Plan, Step by Step

To get started on planning for channel and logistics, answer the following questions. Take a moment to review the channel and logistics entries in the SonicSuperphone sample plan in this book's appendix. Also browse the sample plans bundled with the Marketing Plan Pro *software for ideas. Document what you decide in your written plan or using* Marketing Plan Pro.

1. If you're planning for an existing good or service, study and map the product, information, and money flows through the value chain. If you're planning for a new offering, map the value-chain flows you would like to have. Identify any special needs or situations that would affect any of the flows at one or more links in the chain. If possible, approximate the value-chain flows of two major competitors to spot possible areas where your organization can improve or even gain an edge.

2. Consider the demand side of the value chain. Based on your knowledge of your target markets and customers, how, when, and where do consumers or businesses expect or prefer to gain access to your offering? What demand peaks and valleys should your value chain accommodate? How does the demand side affect the supply side of your value chain, including suppliers, production, and preparation for handoff to channel partners?

3. Looking at your entire value chain, what functions must be performed inbound and outbound? Which will your organization handle and which will you have outsiders handle—and why?

4. How many channel levels will you plan for? Is your type of offering usually marketed directly to customers or through intermediaries? If you want to use one or more channel levels, identify the types of intermediaries in each and note how each will make your offering available to the ultimate buyer, a consumer or a business customer. Will you need reverse channel(s)? What will the flow be in that channel?

5. Will you choose intensive, selective, or exclusive distribution? Why is your choice appropriate for your offering, your organization, your market, and your customers? What criteria will you use to evaluate channel members (potential or existing)?

6. Before you finalize your channel decisions, reexamine your ideas with the following factors in mind: your organization's direction, goals, objectives, resources, capabilities, and need for control; the marketing mix you're recommending in your marketing plan; your customers' preferences and requirements; the markets you're targeting; environmental and competitive factors; and availability of intermediaries.

7. Now plan for logistics. How will you balance the need to be responsive to customers with the need to meet internal financial targets? List each of the four main logistical functions; next to each, write a few sentences about the main issues to be considered and how you will address each. Reread your notes with an eye toward cost. Also look at how your logistics will help you achieve the financial, marketing, and societal objectives already recorded in your marketing plan. Do you see any conflicts?

Endnotes

1. Larry Marsh, "Espresso Book Machine Offers Hot Book with Your Coffee," *Kansas City Star,* October 17, 2009, http://voices.kansascity.com; Jim Milliot, "Number of On-demand Titles Topped Traditional Books in 2008," *Publishers Weekly,* May 19, 2009, www.publishersweekly.com; Rrishi Raote, "Hot off the Press," *Business Standard,* May 30, 2009, www.business-standard.com.

2. Ken Bensinger, "Chrysler Allowed to Terminate Dealerships Today," *Los Angeles Times,* June 9, 2009, http://www.latimes.com.

3. Jeffrey Ng, "Li & Fung Apparel Deal Boosts U.S. Expansion," *Wall Street Journal,* October 19, 2009, www.wsj.com; Bruce Einhorn, "How Not to Sweat the Retail Details," *BusinessWeek,* May 21, 2009, pp. 52–54; Frank Longid and Wing-Gar Cheng, "Li & Fung Seeks 'Major' Deal to Meet 3-Year Targets," *Bloomberg,* May 13, 2009, www.bloomberg.com.

4. Aili McConnon, "The Issue: FreshDirect Focuses on Customer Service," *BusinessWeek,* July 1, 2009, www.businessweek.com; Emily Jed, "FreshDirect Positions Vending as a Fine Dining Destination,"

Vending Times, March 2009, www.vendingtimes. com; Douglas Quenqua, "Eating Healthy, Even at Your Desk," *New York Times,* December 17, 2008, www.nytimes.com.

5. Jon Chavez, "Retailers' Clinics Aim to Boost Health of Clients, Bottom Lines," *Toledo Blade,* October 18, 2009, http://toledoblade.com; Bruce Japsen, "Walgreens, CVS Roll Out New Medical Services," *Sun-Sentinel (Florida),* June 9, 2009, www.sun-sentinel.com; "Wal-Mart Pharmacy Programs Prompt Dialogue," *Drug Topics,* May 28, 2009, www.modernmedicine.com.

6. Nancy Luna, "More Gourmet Food Trucks Coming to O.C.," *Orange County Register,* November 9, 2009, www.ocregister.com; Katy McLaughlin, "Food Truck Nation," *Wall Street Journal,* June 5, 2009, www.wsj.com; Jessica Gelt, "Kogi Korean BBQ, A Taco Truck Brought to You by Twitter," *Los Angeles Times,* February 11, 2009, www. latimes.com.

7. Dorothy Pomerantz, "Why Redbox Terrifies Hollywood," *Forbes.com,* October 26, 2009, www.forbes.com; "Movie Kiosks Are Booming, but Hollywood Studios Aren't Pleased with Low Price," *Chicago Tribune,* October 21, 2009, www. chicagotribune.com; Kristen Schweizer, "YouTube Wins Global Movie Premiere as Dog Tricks Don't Sell Ads," *Bloomberg.com,* June 4, 2009, www. bloomberg.com; "Distributing Independent Films: Saved by the Box," *The Economist,* May 23, 2009, p. 68; Phil Villarreal, "Redbox: $1-a-day Kiosks Turning Up All Over," *Arizona Daily Star,* June 4, 2009, www.azstarnet.com; Eric Savitz, "Netflix: Will Streaming Economics Change for the Worse?" *Barron's Tech Trader Daily,* May 13, 2009, http:// blogs.barrons.com/techtraderdaily/2009/05/ 13/netflix-will-streaming-economics-change-for-the-worse; Ben Fritz, "Blockbuster Sales Drop 20% in First Quarter," *Los Angeles Times,* May 15, 2009, http://www.latimes.com/business/la-fi-ct-blockbuster15-2009may15,0,5306249.story.

8. "Mobiles for a Greener Earth," *ExpressBuzz.com,* June 9, 2009, http://www.expressbuzz.com/edition/ story.aspx?Title=Mobiles+for+a+greener+earth&a rtid=n0NFdlLMs0w=&SectionID=lifojHIWDUU=& MainSectionID=wIcBMLGbUJI=&SectionName= rSY∣6QYp3kQ=&SEO=.

9. Wendy Leonard, "Drop Off Old Cell Phones for Recycling to Help U.S. Troops," *Deseret News (Salt Lake City),* May 24, 2009, www.desnews. com; Anjali Fluker, "Shifting Technology Helps ReCellular Grow from Humble Roots," *Crain's Detroit Business,* November 20, 2006, p. 12; James S. Granelli, "Laws to Give New Life to Used Cellphones," *Los Angeles Times,* July 1, 2006, p. C1; www.recellular.com.

10. David Strom, "Wired for Power," *VARbusiness,* March 15, 2004, pp. 54+.

11. "Brazil's CBD Forecasts '09 Gross Sales Of BRL23 Billion, +10% On Year," *Dow Jones Newswires,* June 9, 2009, money.cnn.com; Kerry A. Dolan, "Outmuscling Wal-Mart," *Forbes,* May 10, 2004, pp. 80–81.

12. Katherine Sayer, "Blooming Business: QVC Sales Have Irvington Nursery Booming," *Press-Register (Alabama),* May 17, 2009, www.al.com/news/ press-register/metro.ssf?/base/news/124259677 489240.xml&coll=3.

13. Timothy Aeppel, "Too Good for Lowe's and Home Depot?" *Wall Street Journal,* July 24, 2006, p. B1; http://mobile.stihlusa.com.

14. "Garanti, Western Union in Cooperation," *Hurriyet Daily News,* May 26, 2009, www.hurriyet.com.

15. Nicholas Casey, "Teen Idols: Aeropostale, Buckle Post Big Gains as Rivals Swoon," *Wall Street Journal,* May 22, 2009, www.wsj.com.

16. Sunil Chopra and Peter Meindl, *Supply Chain Management,* 2nd ed. (Upper Saddle River, NJ: Prentice Hall, 2004), p. 73.

17. Lisa Baertlein, "Wal-Mart on the Move," *Reuters,* June 5, 2009, www.reuters.com; Mark Albright, "Big Retailers Plan for Hurricane Season with Military Precision," *St. Petersburg Times,* June 7, 2009, www.tampabay.com; "Wal-Mart to Customize Stores to Boost Neighborhood Appeal," *Los Angeles Times,* September 8, 2006, p. C3; William Hoffman, "Mixing It Up," *The Journal of Commerce,* May 29, 2006, pp. 64A.

18. Jim Carlton, "Weyerhaeuser's Supply-Side Strategy," *Wall Street Journal,* June 27, 2006, p. B4.

19. "Apex Techie Says His App Is Real Deal," *TMCNews,* June 10, 2009, www.tmcnet.com/ usubmit/2009/06/10/4220007.htm.

20. Cameron Scott, "Doing Good by Doing Well," *San Francisco Chronicle,* June 5, 2009, www. sfgate.com; Eve Kushner, "Mike Hannigan: Give Something Back," *The Monthly,* December 2006, http://themonthly.com/feature12-06-mike.html.

Developing Marketing Communications and Influence Strategy

In this chapter:

PREVIEW

To connect with customers, you have to communicate with them, whether by advertising, sales promotion, public relations (PR), direct marketing, and/or personal selling. The purpose is to forge relationships and, over time, influence customers' thoughts and feelings about and behavior toward your brand, offering, or organization. In the past, marketing communications usually consisted of one-way messages from the organization to its customers and prospects; today, the purpose is to encourage ongoing dialogue through messages and media that engage audiences and invite interaction.

Preparing your strategy for communications and influence is part of Step 5 in the marketing planning process (see Exhibit 9.1). This chapter discusses planning for communications and influence, including the latest social media, word-of-mouth techniques, and buzz marketing. You'll also learn about choosing the target audience, setting objectives and budget, examining relevant issues, selecting specific communications tools, and preparing for research before and after a promotion or campaign. Finally, you'll take a closer look at planning for the five main tools marketers use to communicate with audiences and the need for coordinating all messages and all media.

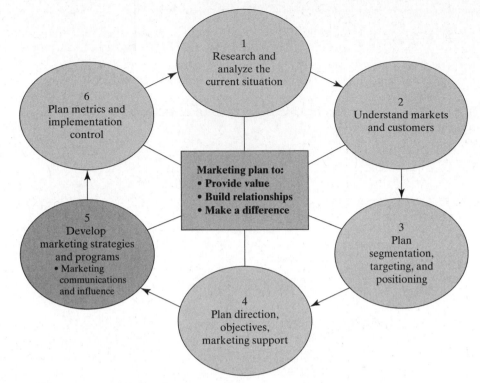

EXHIBIT 9.1 Marketing Planning: Step 5

APPLYING YOUR KNOWLEDGE

Read this chapter, then look at the marketing communications ideas in this book's sample plan and in some of the sample plans bundled with your *Marketing Plan Pro* software. Answer the questions in "Your Marketing Plan, Step by Step," at the end of this chapter as you think about influencing your customers. This chapter's checklist summarizes key communications issues to consider. Continue documenting your ideas with *Marketing Plan Pro* software or in your written plan.

CHAPTER 9 CHECKLIST   Planning Marketing Communications

Audience Analysis

✔ What is the profile of a typical audience member?
✔ How do the audience's behavior, characteristics, and media usage affect media and message choices?

Objectives and Budget

✔ What are your marketing communications intended to achieve?
✔ How do the objectives support the marketing plan's objectives?
✔ Is the budget sufficient to achieve the objectives with the chosen tools and media?

Issues

✔ What legal, regulatory, and ethical issues affect the audience, geographic region, media, or messages?
✔ What social, cultural, competitive, and technological issues must be considered?

Research

✔ What does research reveal about the market, audience, and communication preferences?
✔ How can you pretest communications and research postimplementation awareness and response?

PLANNING TO COMMUNICATE WITH AND INFLUENCE AUDIENCES

You're part of the audience for many marketing messages, so you already know that the purpose of such communications is to influence your consumer decisions. **Customer-influence strategies** are strategies for engaging customers through marketing communications and influencing how they think, feel, and act toward a brand or offering.[1]

The rise of **social media**, online media designed to facilitate user interaction, has added a powerful new dimension to today's communications and influence strategies. Social media such as YouTube, Facebook, Twitter, and blogs promote engagement because their content is largely or entirely created by the users, who post written messages, videos, podcasts, photos, and so on, and respond to posts and comments by other users. Many marketers have a presence on social media, and they encourage interaction to get dialogues going with customers. However, because usage is free and users post what they wish, marketers lack the kind of control over social media that they have over the content of a TV ad they pay to produce and air, for instance.

Social Media, Word of Mouth, Buzz, and Influence

Interaction among users of social media can spark positive or negative **word-of-mouth (WOM) communication,** people telling other people about a company, a brand, an offering, or something else they have noticed. Information spread by WOM (or *word-of-mouse* online) has more credibility because it comes from a personal source rather than being controlled by a company or an agency. As a result, the outcome of WOM is unpredictable and often cannot even be accurately measured.

A video or an ad or another message goes *viral* when it gains a large audience through people sending it (or a link to it) to others online. This, in turn, can influence how consumers or business customers think about and feel and act toward the subject of the viral message—the company, offer, issue, or person mentioned or depicted in it. Opening a viral message and forwarding it are two actions that indicate a level of interest and can influence attitudes and behavior, such as encouraging agreement with the view expressed in the message or prompting the purchase of the featured brand.

Businesses and nonprofits use social media to reach audiences and influence what members say and feel about, and act toward, a brand or an offering or an idea. Here's how the Centers for Disease Control, a U.S. government agency, uses social media to get the word out about health matters.

Centers for Disease Control. The U.S. Centers for Disease Control and Prevention (CDC) has found social media such as blogs, Facebook, and Flickr to be effective for instant public outreach in many situations. When the government announced a recall of foods containing contaminated peanut butter, the CDC used its Web site as a central distribution point for media releases, podcasts, photos, and other updates targeting consumers and reporters. It also created *widgets* (bits of software that audience members install to bring specific content to their computers or social media site such as a blog or Facebook pages) with reminders to avoid eating the recalled peanut products.

As the H1N1 swine flu swept the world, the CDC expanded its use of social media. Its Twitter page for emergency notices, launched a few months before the outbreak, attracted more than 1 million followers as the agency posted links to state-by-state statistics, podcasts with experts, and other information. The agency also participated in Second Life virtual events to raise awareness of flu risks. "American's prime source of health information is still the news media, so that's still a great effort and will always be important," explains a CDC official. "But we also think that we can extend our reach and the impact of our information by combining traditional media with social media and viral media."[2]

With **buzz marketing,** the company seeks to generate more intense WOM, knowing that the buzz may fade as quickly as it starts; sometimes marketers provide communicators with incentives such as samples or coupons (or, occasionally, payments).[3] Buzz marketing, whether face-to-face, electronic, or through publicity, has been used to stimulate WOM for all kinds of products, from vehicles and videos to detergent and DVDs—even chicken.

KFC. KFC hoped for buzz when it asked Oprah Winfrey to post coupons for free samples of its new grilled chicken on her Web site—and that's what it got. The offer prompted a run on the product, with long lines and traffic jams snarling streets around some KFC outlets. This, in turn, caused newspapers, radio, and TV stations to pick up the story, which built even more buzz. Although some disappointed consumers had to settle for a rain check to try the chicken later, KFC ultimately achieved its objective of launching the new product with more than 4 million free samples. "The critical thing was to get people to eat the chicken, whatever it took," KFC's president said. The promotion was so successful, in fact, that KFC repeated it six months later.[4]

As you work on your marketing communications and influence strategy, start by defining your target audience. Then establish objectives and a budget, analyze pertinent issues, and select appropriate tools. Your final step before implementation will be to plan research to test communications and evaluate the effectiveness of your campaign(s).

Choose the Target Audience

The target audience might consist of customers and prospects or, when image building is part of the marketing plan, it may consist of employees, community leaders, local officials, and a number of other key stakeholders. Some communication strategies used to achieve

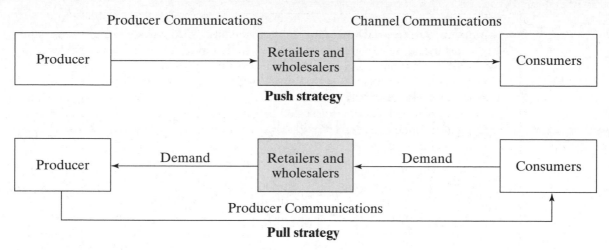

EXHIBIT 9.2 Push and Pull Strategies

market share and sales objectives can be characterized in terms of "push" or "pull" (see Exhibit 9.2).

PLANNING TIP

Review the customer analysis for clues to communicating with your audience.

In a **push strategy,** you target intermediaries, encouraging them to carry and promote (push) the product to business customers or consumers. In a **pull strategy,** you encourage consumers or business customers to ask intermediaries for the product, building demand to pull the product through the channel. Although companies often combine push and pull strategies, they tend to budget more for pull activities.[5] The decision to use push or pull must fit with channel decisions and be appropriate for the product, its pricing, and its positioning. Fox's Biscuits, like many marketers, uses both push and pull strategies.

Fox's Biscuits. Owned by Northern Foods, a top UK food manufacturer, Fox's Biscuits uses TV advertising, radio, PR, and social media in pull strategies to build demand for cookies such as Fox's Crunch Creams and Fox's Chocolatey. One integrated campaign encouraged consumers to e-mail each other customized video and audio messages featuring the star of Fox's TV commercials, Vinnie the Panda. This campaign also increased brand involvement by inviting consumers to post questions for Vinnie on special Facebook and Twitter pages. On the push side, the company has targeted convenience stores, in particular, to increase the amount of shelf space devoted to Fox's biscuits and expand the number of stores that carry the products. "This is becoming increasingly important for us," observes the brand category manager.[6]

When you plan for reaching your audience, look beyond generalities and develop a profile of a typical audience member in as much detail as possible, including gender; age; lifestyle; media, product, and payment preferences; attitudes; timing of buying decisions; and so on. Digging for such details reveals nuances to help shape what the messages should say, and how, when, and where to say it. As an example, knowing that many consumers and business customers are heavy users of cell phones, a growing number of firms are using **mobile marketing** to send information, directions, coupons, and other messages to customers through text and e-mail received on cell phones as well as through Web sites optimized for handset screens.[7]

Set Objectives and Budget

You can use marketing communications to move your target audience through a series of responses corresponding to beliefs, behavior, and feelings about your product, brand, or company. As Exhibit 9.3 shows, marketers of low-involvement products such as inexpensive items first want to influence the audience's beliefs, then the audience's actions, and, finally, its feelings. If a consumer sees value in a certain beverage (beliefs), she may buy a bottle and try it (behavior) and then decide whether she likes the taste (feelings). Marketers of high-involvement products such as cars also start by influencing the audience's beliefs; then they strive to influence feelings and behavior. In contrast, marketers who emphasize the consumption experience initially try to influence the audience's feelings, followed by the audience's actions and then its beliefs.

Clearly, these are simplified response models; in reality, target audiences are exposed to multiple messages in multiple media—often simultaneously, as when someone listens to the radio while surfing the Web.[8] Thus, you should research and understand the response model for a given product or category when setting objectives tied to your marketing plan's objectives.

If you want to acquire new customers, then your audience must be aware of your offer (influencing beliefs). One communication objective might be to "achieve 25 percent awareness of Product A among the target audience within 4 months," with the exact percentage and timing dependent on the marketing objective, the promotion investment, and knowledge of the customer's buying process. Related objectives might be to "have 900 prospects request an information package about our services before June 30" and "generate 300 qualified leads for the sales staff by March 15."

Marketing research provides critical background for setting objectives. If research shows that the segment is aware of the product but has no strong preference for it (feelings), the objective might be to "achieve 18 percent preference for Product E among the target audience within 3 months." If research indicates that customers like the product enough to try it (behavior), the aim might be to "achieve 9 percent trial of Product C among the target audience within 6 months" or "have 200 customers request samples of

Low involvement model:

Communications ⟶ Influence beliefs ⟶ Influence behavior ⟶ Influence feelings

High involvement model:

Communications ⟶ Influence beliefs ⟶ Influence feelings ⟶ Influence behavior

Experiential model:

Communications ⟶ Influence feelings ⟶ Influence behavior ⟶ Influence beliefs

EXHIBIT 9.3   Models for Audience Response

Product B during September." Using communications to enhance image, the objective might be to "make 55 percent of the target audience aware of the corporation's philanthropic donations by December 31" or to "double the percentage of the target audience having positive attitudes toward the corporation within 12 months."

A number of factors should be considered when devising a marketing communications budget, including the overall marketing budget, the objectives to be achieved, environmental trends, choice of advertising or other tool(s), the number of markets to be covered, the competitive circumstances, the potential return on investment, and so on. Because organizational resources are finite, be realistic about the situation, have definite short- and long-term objectives in mind, and budget creatively.

Some small businesses with modest budgets are including social media in their marketing plans instead of or in addition to traditional communications.

Small Businesses and Social Media. Social media can stretch a small business's budget without breaking the connection with customers. When the economy was faltering, Julie Metallo, who runs the Rita B Salon in Denver, decided to cut her communications spending. She kept running some print ads but also put her company on Facebook and MySpace. Soon she had a loyal following of several hundred customers checking her Web site and social media posts for news about special promotions and upcoming events. As another example, after 52Teas.com began using Twitter and Facebook to announce its handcrafted tea blend of the week, the company doubled its sales of the featured blend. Now more than 6,000 people follow 52Teas on Twitter and Facebook, and sales are going strong.[9]

See Chapter 10 for more about budgeting.

Examine Issues

Your communications strategy can be affected by a variety of legal, regulatory, technological, ethical, cultural, and competitive issues. For example, it is illegal for companies in the United States, United Kingdom, and some other nations to make false claims for a product or describe a food as "low fat" if it does not meet certain criteria.[10] Communications for products such as prescription drugs must comply with strict rules; sometimes messages must include health or product-use warnings, and the company must be prepared to safeguard customer privacy in particular ways.

PLANNING TIP

Plan ethical communications to earn your audience's trust.

Companies that communicate ethically and, where possible, follow voluntary industry ethics codes are more likely to build trust with target audiences and polish their image. This is an especially challenging issue for those who use social media, because legal and regulatory guidelines are still evolving. For example, is it ethical for a marketer to pay bloggers to post messages about particular brands or offerings? The Federal Trade Commission has just clarified guidelines calling for disclosure of such payments.[11] Forrester Research suggests that in the case of such "sponsored conversations," bloggers should disclose that they are being paid and be free to write what they think about the offering, positive or negative.[12] The Word of Mouth Marketing Association and the Blog Council, two industry groups, have already adopted voluntary guidelines emphasizing transparency for advertisers using social media.[13]

Although specific social issues affecting communication will vary from product to product, all marketers should understand the public's perception of promotions. In one U.S. survey, 60 percent of the respondents said their view of advertising was "much more negative than just a few years ago," and 54 percent said they "avoid buying products that overwhelm them with advertising and marketing."[14]

Consider competitive issues, as well. How can you use communications to play up a meaningful point of difference setting your offering apart from those of rivals? How can you counter campaigns from competitors with much larger budgets and better-established brands or products? Are new technologies available to pinpoint target audiences more accurately regardless of competitive campaigns? How can you attract attention despite a cluttered marketing environment?

PLANNING TIP

Consider new ways to convey your message and stimulate response.

Choose Communication Tools

There are five basic categories of marketing communication tools (see Exhibit 9.4). Here is a brief overview; highlights of planning for each will be examined later in the chapter.

- *Advertising.* Advertising is cost-effective for communicating with a large audience, with the marketer in complete control of message and media. Marketers often use advertising to introduce and differentiate a product, build a brand, polish the organization's image, communicate competitive superiority, or convey an idea.
- *Sales promotion.* This marketer-controlled tool can be used to target consumers, businesses, or channel members and sales representatives. It is particularly useful for accelerating short-term sales results; combating competitive pressure; provoking product trial; building awareness and reinforcing other communication activities; encouraging continued buying and usage; and increasing the offer's perceived value.

EXHIBIT 9.4   Major Communications Tools

Tool	Use	Examples
Advertising	Efficiently get messages to large audience	Television and radio commercials; Internet, magazine, and newspaper ads; paid search engine links; product and company brochures; billboards; transit ads; ads delivered by cell phone and e-mail
Sales promotion	Stimulate immediate purchase, reward repeat purchases, motivate sales personnel	Samples; coupons; premiums; contests, games, sweepstakes; displays; demonstrations; trade shows and incentives
Public relations	Build positive image, strengthen ties with stakeholders	Event sponsorship; news releases, briefings, and podcasts; speeches and blogs; public appearances
Direct marketing	Reach targeted audiences, encourage direct response	Mail, e-mail, telemarketing campaigns; printed and online catalogs; direct response television and radio
Personal selling	Reach customers one-to-one to make sales, strengthen relationships	Sales appointments; sales meetings and presentations; online chat sales help

- *Public relations.* Public relations has more credibility than other promotion tools because the audience receives the message through media channels perceived to be more objective than sources controlled by the organization. However, marketers can neither control what the media will report nor guarantee that the company or product will get any media coverage. Marketers use PR when they want to present the product and company in a positive light; build goodwill and trust; and inform customers, channel members, and other stakeholders about the product and its benefits.
- *Direct marketing.* A highly focused, organization-controlled tool, direct marketing facilitates two-way interaction with a specific audience, allows for pinpoint targeting, and accommodates offers tailored to individual needs and behavior. Marketers can easily measure the outcome and compare it with objectives to determine effectiveness and efficiency. Direct marketing helps organizations start, strengthen, or renew customer relationships; increase sales of particular products; test the appeal of new or repositioned products; or test alternate marketing tactics such as different prices.
- *Personal selling.* Personal selling is an excellent organization-controlled tool for reaching business customers and consumers on a personal basis to open a dialogue, learn more about needs, present complex or customized information, or obtain feedback. Companies selling expensive goods or services or customizing products for individual customers frequently rely on personal selling. However, it is labor intensive and expensive, which is why many products are not marketed in this way. On the other hand, a number of consumer products are being successfully marketed through personal selling at home parties.

Plan Research

If you have the time and money, your marketing plan should allow for pretesting and postimplementation research to evaluate communications. The point of pretesting is to find out whether the target audience understands the message and retains information about the brand or product. It also shows whether your audience responds as expected: Do beliefs, attitudes, or behavior change as a result of communications? Such results help in fine-tuning the format, content, delivery, timing, duration, and context of communications before the bulk of the campaign is implemented.

PLANNING TIP

When pretesting, allow time for testing changes before launching the campaign.

Postimplementation research will show whether the communications strategy accomplished its objectives and which activities were particularly effective in supporting your marketing plan. As you select your communications tools, think about how you will measure and evaluate performance. Unilever, for instance, planned a test to deliver coupons for Dove soap to consumers' cell phones. During the test, it checked that the on-screen coupons could be read by supermarket scanners and that results would be available for in-depth analysis.[15]

USING COMMUNICATION TOOLS TO ENGAGE AUDIENCES

Marketing plans usually cover the use of various tools in one or more campaigns to engage audiences and achieve communications objectives; the details and explanations are generally shown in an appendix or other documents rather than in the body of the plan. Before selecting specific tools and planning programs, use your audience analysis to understand customers' interests, habits, and preferences. If possible, prepare a SWOT analysis of what your competitors are doing to communicate with and exert influence on customers. As you plan, apply the principle of integration and consider the overall effect when you use any combination of advertising, sales promotion, PR, direct marketing, and personal selling.

Advertising

For the purposes of developing a marketing plan, advertising's two basic decisions concern the message (what content will be communicated?) and the media (what vehicle or vehicles will deliver the message, and when, where, how, and how often?). These decisions must be in keeping with the target audience's characteristics, needs, behavior, and receptivity; the budget allocated for advertising; relevant issues affecting communications strategy; and the objectives set (e.g., awareness or purchase of the product). Audiences are attracted to creative messages, but messages that are too extreme or outlandish will not be effective. Research therefore suggests: "Creativity needs to stay ahead of the curve—but clearly not too far."[16]

Your messages and media have to work together: If, for example, your plan calls for product demonstration, a visual medium like the Internet or television will be the best choice—but only if the budget allows and the chosen vehicle reaches the target audience. The ad's wording, format and design, graphics, sound, and other medium-specific elements will communicate the appeal of the message. A message with an **emotional appeal** relies on feelings (fear, love, anger, happiness, or another emotion) to motivate audience response.

Some messages rely on a **rational appeal,** using facts and logic to stimulate response by showing how the product solves a problem or satisfies a need. Many B2B ads, in particular, are based on rational appeals linked to the specific benefits that business buyers seek. This is how Citrix Online uses rational appeals in B2B advertising.

Citrix Online. This high-tech company, based in Santa Barbara, California, uses rational appeals in TV and radio commercials to play up the benefits of its online meeting and remote-computer-access services. It advertises that its GoToMeeting site "is the easiest, most secure, and cost-effective solution for conducting online meetings." Its GoToMyPC site "provides fast, easy, and secure remote access to your PC from any Web browser," important benefits for road warriors who need to access certain files when they're out of the office. Citrix Online is also engaging its audience by inviting submissions of 30- or 60-second videos to be used as commercials on TV and online, with cash prizes for the winning videos. By showing how it can solve specific problems of business customers, this division of Citrix has grown to $100 million in annual sales.[17]

Each medium has characteristics that convey the message in a different way; the Internet offers sight, sound, motion, and interactivity, whereas print ads can offer color, longer life, and the ability to communicate more details. To achieve marketing communication objectives, even the most creative message must be presented in a specific medium or vehicle (such as a certain magazine or Web site) that will reach the target audience (see Exhibit 9.5).

In particular, in-store television is becoming a medium of choice for consumer packaged goods because the message reaches shoppers when and where they buy. Unilever,

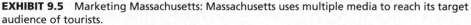

EXHIBIT 9.5   Marketing Massachusetts: Massachusetts uses multiple media to reach its target audience of tourists.

PLANNING TIP

Be sure a message's
creative execution will
work in each medium
under consideration.

for example, is among the many companies that advertise on Walmart's in-store TV network, which has 27,000 screens in 3,000 Walmart stores. Target, Kroger, and other big retailers also sell advertising time on in-store TV networks.[18]

Two key decisions in planning media choices are how many people to reach during a certain period (known as **reach**) and how often to repeat the message during that period (known as **frequency**). Reaching more people is costly, as is repeating the message multiple times. Thus, the marketer must determine how to allocate the budget by balancing reach with frequency, based on knowledge of the target audience. Some marketers are advertising at the movies to reach target audiences during specific periods. Kia Motors did this when it launched its Soul subcompact car. Why air commercials at the movies? "The mindset of people watching movies is much different than the mindset of people watching TV," says Kia's director of advertising.[19]

The choice of where to advertise—in geographic terms—depends on where the product is available or will be introduced during the course of the marketing plan (see Exhibit 9.6). In terms of timing, a message or campaign might run continuously (reminding the audience of benefits or availability), during periods of seasonal or peak demand (when the audience is interested in buying), or steadily but with sporadic intensity (along with sales promotions or other marketing activities).

Finally, look at whether you should use **keyword search advertising,** also known as **paid search,** a form of online advertising in which the company pays to have its site listed in the search results for specific words or brands. Sony recently changed to year-round use of paid search instead of paying for keyword ads during product launch periods. "People search all year round, so from now on we're looking at being 'always on,'" a marketing executive explains.[20]

Sales Promotion

It takes time to build a brand, cultivate customer loyalty, or reinforce commitment among channel members, but sales promotion can help by reducing perceived price or enhancing perceived value for a limited time. Among the sales promotion techniques that marketers can plan to use when targeting customers and prospects are sampling, couponing, rebates and refunds, premiums, sweepstakes and contests, bonus packs, and loyalty programs. Among the techniques that marketers can use when targeting channel members and

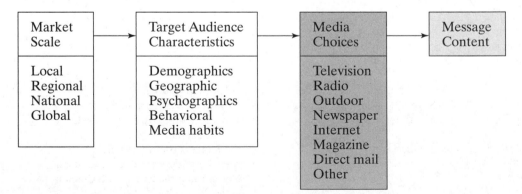

EXHIBIT 9.6 The Media Mix

salespeople are allowances and incentives, sales contests, training and support, and point-of-purchase materials. Exhibit 9.7 describes the purpose of each and highlights issues to be considered during planning.

PLANNING TIP

Consider sales promotion for internal and external marketing.

Objectives for sales promotion activities targeting customers and prospects may include building awareness, encouraging product trial or usage, encouraging speedy response, reinforcing loyalty, supporting advertising or other communications, and defending against competitors. Objectives for sales promotion activities targeting channel members and sales representatives may include enhancing product knowledge,

EXHIBIT 9.7 Sales Promotion Techniques

Technique and Purpose	Issues
Sampling—Allow prospects to examine and experience product without risk.	• Does the budget allow for sampling? • How, when, and where will samples be distributed?
Couponing—Reduce the perceived price of a product.	• Will coupons be redeemed by loyal customers rather than prospects? • Will coupons be redeemed properly?
Rebates and Refunds—Reduce the perceived price and lower the perceived risk.	• Is the organization prepared for the mechanics? • How will returning money to customers affect financial objectives?
Premiums—Offer something extra for free or for a small price to enhance product's value.	• How will the premium affect the plan's financial objectives? • Will the premium be unattractive or too attractive?
Sweepstakes, contests, and games—Attract attention and build excitement about a product or brand.	• What legal and regulatory rules apply? • Does the budget allow for prizes, operational mechanics, and communications support?
Bonus packs—Bundle two or more products together for a special price, lowering the perceived price.	• Does the budget allow for special packaging? • Will customers perceive sufficient added value?
Allowances and incentives—Give retailer or wholesaler financial reasons to support the product.	• Will intermediaries offer their customers special prices as a result? • Will intermediaries overorder now and order less later?
Sales contests—Reward salespeople for selling a certain product.	• Will the product receive adequate attention after a contest is over? • Will the budget cover the cost of prizes and administration?
Training and support—Educate salespeople about product and support the sales effort.	• How often is training needed? • How much support does a product or channel member need?
Point-of-purchase materials—Use signs, other methods of in-store promotion.	• Will retailers use the materials? • Does the budget allow for providing different intermediaries with different materials?

building commitment, reinforcing focus and loyalty, encouraging speedy response, supporting channel and other communications, and defending against competitors. Here's how McDonald's Japan uses consumer sales promotion.

McDonald's Japan. One reason McDonald's uses sales promotion is to motivate customers in Japan—especially families—to return to its restaurants again and again. It recently teamed up with Nintendo to provide free content to customers who go online with their DS handheld game consoles in certain areas of each restaurant. Each time they come, customers can download their choice of free Nintendo collectable game characters and click to receive McDonald's discount coupons, as well.

Not long ago, it introduced a new breakfast hot dog with special point-of-purchase materials during the annual World Baseball Classic sports event. As one of the event's sponsors, McDonald's linked its advertising and new-product promotion to the Japanese team's winning performance, and set a one-day record for chainwide sales in Japan.[21]

Many marketers include sales promotion in their marketing plans as a way of accelerating response over a set period, with clearly measurable results (such as counting the number of coupons redeemed and the number of units sold). However, overuse can lead customers or channel members to be more price sensitive when buying certain types of products, posing a potential threat to brand equity and profitability.[22]

PLANNING TIP

Identify the target audience for each PR objective you set.

Public Relations

The purpose of PR is to open the lines of communication and develop positive relationships with one or more of the organization's stakeholder groups. Target audiences (the *public* in public relations) usually include some combination of customers and prospects, employees and job applicants, channel members, suppliers, government officials, local community groups, special interest groups, and the financial community.

Some of the objectives that you may set for PR are as follows:

- *Understanding stakeholders' perceptions and attitudes.* Public relations can help take the public's pulse and identify concerns about products and operations, social responsibility, and other issues. Whether feedback comes in through letters, e-mails, phone calls, or interaction with company personnel, you can learn what your audiences care about and see your organization through the public's eyes—then plan to respond.
- *Manage image.* Shaping and maintaining the company's or brand's positive image generates goodwill and sets the stage for strong relations with target audiences. One way to do this is by having management and employees participate in community events, charitable causes, and other local activities. Public relations is also used to minimize image damage if the company makes a mistake or is involved in a crisis such as suspected product contamination.
- *Communicating views and information.* Sometimes PR is used to correct public misperceptions or clarify a company's stand or action on a particular issue.
- *Building brand and product awareness.* Through news conferences, special events, and other techniques, PR can spotlight a brand or a product line.

Many companies plan to build product awareness through a combination of PR and other communications. Citrix, for example, uses advertising for its GoToMeeting and other offerings, but it also relies on PR to maintain a high profile for its brands and products. The company's online media center includes a digital media kit with fact sheets and photos of managers and offerings, downloadable news releases, links to online news mentions of the company and its products, and quotes from industry analysts covering the company.[23]

Direct Marketing

In direct marketing, the organization reaches out to customers and prospects through mail, broadcast and print media, the Internet, and other media. This communications tool is cost-effective for targeting and the use of customized messages, offers, and timing—even one recipient at a time if enough information is available about each individual's needs and characteristics. Because the audience responds directly to the organization, you can easily measure results and see whether objectives have been met—and change the message or medium fairly quickly if necessary. The marketing plan should summarize the objectives, the expected response, how results will be measured, any use of research, relevant issues, and the connection with other communications objectives. To be effective, the direct marketing message must be relevant to the target audience and not be perceived as junk mail or spam.

PLANNING TIP

Research the audience's needs and receptivity as you plan content, media, message, and timing.

Many direct marketing programs aim for an immediate sale; other objectives may be building awareness, influencing perceptions and attitudes, continuing customer relationships, obtaining leads for sales staff, and encouraging prospects to take the next step toward buying. Not-for-profit organizations typically set objectives such as generating contributions and signing up volunteers.

> **Teletón.** Teletón, a charity in Mexico that operates 11 rehabilitation centers for children with disabilities, uses direct marketing to reach donors during its annual radio and TV telethon and uses commercials on Spanish-language TV networks in the United States. More than three-quarters of Teletón's donations are received by phone, although it also solicits donations online and through keyword text messages that charge the contribution to the donor's cell-phone account. In addition, Teletón engages donors through its presence on Facebook, Twitter, and YouTube.[24]

Personal Selling

Personal selling is appropriate if the target audience requires customized goods or services, needs assistance assessing needs, makes large purchases, or requires individual attention for other reasons. This is an important tool for pharmaceutical firms, equipment manufacturers, and many other B2B marketers, as well as for some marketers that target consumers. The one-to-one nature of personal selling (in person or by phone) supports strong customer relationships; therefore, the emphasis may not be on making an instant sale but on building connections for the future. "Focus on developing a win-win relationship for both the company and the customer," advises Larry Panattoni, a sales representative for Servatron in Spokane, Washington, and "orders will follow."[25]

PLANNING TIP

Support personal selling with communications to build awareness, interest, and demand.

Decisions you will face in planning for personal selling include the following: whether to hire salespeople or work with an outside sales agency; how to recruit, train, manage, motivate, and compensate sales staff; how many salespeople are needed; and how to organize the sales force (for example, by product, market, or type of customer).

A number of decisions about structuring the sales process draw input directly from the marketing plan:

- *Identifying and qualifying prospects.* Based on earlier segmentation and targeting decisions, management identifies the audience for personal selling activities and determines how prospects will be qualified for sales contact.
- *Planning the presales approach.* Details from earlier market and customer analyses inform the approach that a salesperson plans in contacting prospects.
- *Making sales contact.* Based on the prospect's needs and the firm's positioning, the salesperson opens a dialogue with a prospect, determines specific needs, and explains how the offering will provide value.
- *Addressing objections.* Using knowledge of the product, the prospect's needs, and the competition, the salesperson responds to specific concerns and questions raised by the prospect.
- *Closing the sale.* The salesperson completes the sale, arranges payment, and schedules delivery with an understanding of pricing and logistics strategies.
- *Following up after the sale.* To continue building the relationship, the salesperson must understand the customer service strategy, the customer's needs, and applicable communications support, such as frequent-buyer programs.

If you have sales personnel, your marketing plan should provide for ongoing, two-way communications to strengthen relationships and track results. Here's what Avon Products is doing.

Avon Products. Because Avon markets cosmetics and personal care products to consumers through independent sales representatives, its marketing plan puts considerable emphasis on using technology to communicate with and support these people. At stake is $10 billion in revenue from sales made by 6 million reps in 100 nations. In countries such as Turkey, where few people have Internet access from their homes, Avon reps go to Internet cafés to correspond with the company via e-mail and to place orders online. Avon's sales leaders, who manage groups of reps, can use smartphones and PCs to tap into a special system for monitoring sales productivity and following up on payments due to the company.[26]

Integrated Marketing Communication

For maximum effect, plan to coordinate the content and delivery of all marketing communications for your offering, brand, and organization to ensure consistency and support your positioning and direction. This approach is known as **integrated marketing communication**.

Integration not only avoids confusion about the brand and the benefits, it reinforces the connection with the sports or lifestyle activities and sparks instant recognition when people in the target audience are exposed to the firm's logo or product name. The total effect of your communications makes an impact by differentiating your products and communicating their value in a crowded competitive arena. It also contributes to the level of influence you may be able to exert on your audiences, whether that influence is to make a favorable brand impression or to encourage buying of certain products.

Several factors make carefully planned and coordinated communications even more crucial to marketing success.[27] These include the following: maturing markets, a decline in the effectiveness of mass-media advertising, consumers' perceptions of brand parity, an increase in consumers' choices and information sources, global competition, and changes in channel power. In any case, whether you use a combination of advertising, sales promotion, PR, direct marketing, and personal selling, or only one of these tools, integration of all messages in all media will help you leverage and focus your efforts to better effect.

Summary

Planning marketing communications and influence strategy involves the use of advertising, sales promotion, PR, direct marketing, and/or personal selling to engage target audiences and influence how they think and feel about and how they act toward a brand or offering. A growing number of marketers use social media, word of mouth, and buzz, when appropriate, to connect with audiences and influence them. A push strategy addresses the channel as the target audience; a pull strategy pulls products through the channel by addressing customers as the target audience; a strategy that combines push and pull targets both customers and the channel.

Start by choosing and analyzing the target audience, setting your objectives and budget, and examining key issues such as legal, regulatory, technological, and competitive circumstances. Depending on the plan's overall objectives, communications may be used to move the target audience through responses corresponding to beliefs, behavior, and feelings about the product or brand. After deciding on the communications tools for your campaign, allow for pretesting and postimplementation research to evaluate and fine-tune the strategy and specific programs. Integrated marketing communication means coordinating the content and delivery of all messages and media to ensure consistency and support the positioning and direction.

Your Marketing Plan, Step by Step

Answering the following questions will help you think through the decisions you face in planning communications and influence strategy. Review the communications ideas in the SonicSuperphone sample plan (see Appendix) and browse some of the sample plans bundled with the Marketing Plan Pro *software for more ideas. Then document what you decide in your written plan or using* Marketing Plan Pro.

1. Who, specifically, is your target audience? What do you know about these people that can help you communicate with them? Look at the primary and secondary research, segmentation data, and other information you've gathered so far for your marketing plan as you write a paragraph or two about your target audience. How can you learn more about your target audience's media usage,

   lifestyle, preferences, and other details that relate to communications and influence?

2. What do you want to accomplish by communicating with your target audience(s)? Will you use a push strategy, a pull strategy, or a combination? You'll need separate objectives when you target customers in a pull strategy and when you target intermediaries in a push strategy. Look at Exhibit 9.3 as you

establish objectives for influencing your audience's response to your communications. List at least two specific objectives for communicating with and influencing each audience. How do these objectives support the marketing, financial, and societal objectives in your overall plan? If possible, look at the outcome of previous communications strategies to see whether objectives were achieved and if not, why not. Also estimate the communications budget needed to meet your objectives in the coming year, knowing you can fine-tune the budget later in the planning process.

3. What legal, regulatory, ethical, cultural, competitive, and technological issues are likely to affect your ability to reach your audience or to use certain messages or media? Write a few sentences summarizing the communications opportunities and threats presented by the issues you've identified, based on research and your firm's previous experience, if any. How are competitors communicating with your target audience, and what are the strengths and weaknesses of their communications and influence strategies? Write a

brief SWOT analysis of your main competitor's communications and influence strategy, and draw conclusions about the implications for your strategy.

4. With your objectives and budget in mind, which communications tools are most appropriate for engaging your target audience, based on your audience analysis? Write a few sentences about each of the five main tools, indicating why you will or won't include it in your communications strategy, and explaining your rationale for your choices. Now dig deeper to consider how you will use your chosen tools. Outline the highlights of your marketing communications strategy, and indicate how you will integrate your messages and media.

5. Will you pretest your communications? What postimplementation research will you plan to evaluate the outcome of your strategy? How will you know whether your communications have been received, understood, and acted upon by your target audience? How will you know whether you have influenced the audience's thinking, feelings, and behavior? Be sure to explain your answers in your plan.

Endnotes

1. See Michael Levens, *Marketing Defined, Explained, Applied* (Upper Saddle River, NJ: Pearson Prentice Hall, 2010), p. 167.
2. Josh Goldstein, "Social Media Explored as Tool for Health Experts," *Philadelphia Inquirer,* November 8, 2009, www.philly.com/inquirer; Anya Martin, "Health Data Proves Contagious on Social Media," *Wall Street Journal,* May 27, 2009, www.wsj.com; Gautham Nagesh, "As Social Media Becomes a Hit with Agencies, GSA Plans More Offerings," *Nextgov,* May 22, 2009, www.netgove.com. For more about widgets, see Larry Weber, *Sticks & Stones* (Hoboken, NJ: Wiley, 2009), p. 63.
3. Larry Yu, "How Companies Turn Buzz into Sales: The Good Word from Devoted Customers May Not Always Be the Most Effective Promotional Tool," *MIT Sloan Management Review,* Winter 2005, pp. 5+.
4. Christa Hoyland, "KFC Holds Free-Piece Grilled Giveaway, El Pollo Loco Counters with Contest," *QSRWeb,* October 26, 2009, www.qsrweb.com.
5. Roger J. Best, *Market-Based Management,* 4th ed. (Upper Saddle River, NJ: Pearson Prentice Hall, 2005), p. 312.
6. "Council Workers Given Advice on How to Eat Biscuits," *The Telegraph (UK),* October 20, 2009, www.telegraph.co.uk; Robert McLuhan, "Field Marketing Report—FMCG Brands and Convenience Stores," *Marketing,* June 9, 2009, www.marketing.co.uk; Danielle Long, "Fox's Biscuits Uses Online to Push Vinnie the Panda," *New Media Age,* May 26, 2009, www.nma.co.uk; "Vinnie Goes Viral," *Talking Retail,* May 29, 2009, www.talkingretail.com.
7. Kristina Knight, "MMA: Mobile to Jump 25% in 2009," *Biz Report,* June 8, 2009, www.bizreport.com.
8. "Media Multi-Taskers," *Marketing Management,* May–June 2004, p. 6; Don E. Schultz, "Include SIMM in Modern Media Ad Plans," *Marketing News,* May 15, 2004, p. 6.
9. Jennifer Alsever, "Tweeting for Profit," *Fortune,* June 15, 2009, www.fortune.com; Greg Avery, "Social-Media Marketing Pushes Aside Usual Methods," *Denver Business Journal,* March 13, 2009, http://denver.bizjournals.com.
10. Lexie Williamson, "Healthcare: Consumer Health," *PR Week (UK),* September 19, 2003, p. 14.

11. Amy Schatz, "Advertisers Call for a Do-Over on FTC Blogger Rules," *Wall Street Journal,* October 15, 2009, www.wsj.com; Douglas MacMillan, "Blogola: The FTC Takes on Paid Posts," *BusinessWeek Online,* May 20, 2009, www.businessweek.com.

12. Josh Bernoff, "Why Sponsored Conversation—AKA Paid Blog Posts—Can Make Sense," *Groundswell Forrester blogs,* March 2, 2009, http://blogs.forrester.com/groundswell/2009/03/by-josh-bernoff.html.

13. See the WOMMA Ethics Code at http://womma.org/ethics/code/ and the Blog Council's Disclosure Best Practices Toolkit at http://blogcouncil.org/disclosure/.

14. Stuart Elliott, "A Survey of Consumer Attitudes Reveals the Depth of the Challenge that the Agencies Face," *New York Times,* April 14, 2004, p. C8.

15. Andrew Lavalle, "Unilever to Test Mobile Coupons," *Wall Street Journal,* May 29, 2009, www.wsj.com.

16. Douglas C. West, Arthur J. Kover, and Albert Caruana, "Practitioner and Customer Views of Advertising Creativity: Same Concept, Different Meaning?" *Journal of Advertising,* Winter 2008, pp. 35+.

17. Jack M. Germain, "Citirix Online Brings SMBs into the Virtual Meeting Room," *E-Commerce Times,* June 15, 2009, www.ecommercetimes.com; Kate Maddox, "No Small Comfort; As Small Businesses Try to Make Sense of the Reeling Economy, B-to-B Marketers Reach Out with Offers of Understanding and Assistance," *BtoB,* November 10, 2008, p. 28.

18. Teresa F. Lindeman, "Remaking Wal-Mart," *Pittsburgh Post-Gazette*, October 28, 2009, www.post-gazette.com; "Wal-Mart Digitizes TV Network," *Brandweek,* September 8, 2008, p. 4; Mya Frazier, "Rush Is on to Rule In-Store TV Ads," *Advertising Age,* June 26, 2006, p. S-13.

19. Jon Fine, "Where Are Advertisers? At the Movies," *BusinessWeek,* May 25, 2009, pp. 65–66.

20. "Sony Expands Search Budget for an 'Always On' Strategy," *New Media Age,* April 23, 2009, p. 6.

21. Hiroko Nakata, "McDonald's Starts DS-User Service," *The Japan Times,* June 16, 2009, www.japantimes.co.jp; "Official Team Japan and World Baseball Classic DVDs on Sale in Japan," *Major League Baseball Releases,* June 10, 2009, http://mlb.mlb.com/news/.

22. Belinda Gannaway, "Hidden Danger of Sales Promotions," *Marketing,* February 20, 2003, pp. 31+; Philip Kotler, *A Framework for Marketing Management,* 2nd ed. (Upper Saddle River, NJ: Prentice Hall, 2003), pp. 318–319.

23. Rich Karpinski, "Marketing Budgets in Flux," *BtoB,* May 4, 2009, p. 12; www.citrixonline.com.

24. "Hispanic Donors; Playing Up Family Ties in Appeals," *Nonprofit Times,* May 2009, www.nptimes.com; "Teleton MexAmerica Raises Largest One Day Amount to Date," *Science Letter,* March 24, 2009, n.p.; www.teleton.org.mx.

25. Chris Penttila, "The Art of the Sale," *Entrepreneur,* August 2003, pp. 58+.

26. Steve Hamm, "Cloud Computing's Big Bang for Business," *BusinessWeek,* June 15, 2009, pp. 42–43; "Ding Dong! Empowerment Calling," *The Economist,* May 28, 2009, www.economist.com; J. Alex Tarquinio, "Selling Beauty on a Global Scale," *New York Times,* November 1, 2008, p. B2.

27. See Kenneth E. Clow and Donald Baack, *Integrated Advertising, Promotion, and Marketing Communications,* 3rd ed. (Upper Saddle River, NJ: Pearson Prentice Hall, 2007), p. 15.

10 Planning Metrics and Implementation Control

In this chapter:

PREVIEW

When you started your marketing plan, your first step was to understand the current situation of your brand, offering, and organization. Knowing that change is both constant and inevitable, you must have measures and procedures in place for addressing unexpected challenges and assessing progress toward objectives after you put your plan into action. Therefore, the final step in marketing planning is to prepare for tracking results and controlling plan implementation (see Exhibit 10.1).

In this chapter, you'll learn about the four tools for checking performance during the period covered by your marketing plan: metrics to gauge movement toward achieving objectives, forecasts of future sales and costs, budgets allocating financial resources, and schedules identifying the timing of marketing tasks. Also, you'll learn how to plan for marketing control to identify, analyze, and correct variations from the expected results.

APPLYING YOUR KNOWLEDGE

After you read this chapter, review the metrics and control entries in this book's sample plan and in some of the sample plans bundled with the *Marketing Plan Pro* software. Also answer the questions in "Your Marketing Plan, Step by Step," at the end of this chapter as you plan for measuring marketing performance. Think about the questions in this chapter's checklist when planning a marketing audit. Finally, document your ideas, including any contingency plans you develop, using *Marketing Plan Pro* software or in a written plan.

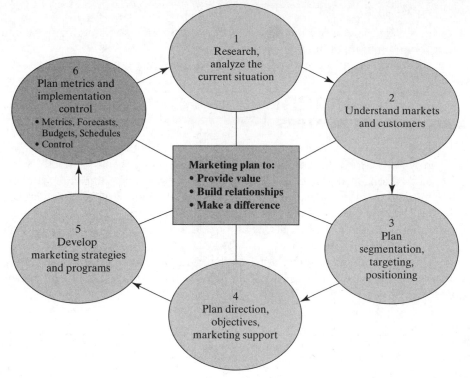

EXHIBIT 10.1 Marketing Planning: Step 6

CHAPTER 10 CHECKLIST   Planning a Marketing Audit

Marketing Strategy

✔ Does the mission focus on market and customer needs?
✔ Are marketing-mix strategies appropriate in light of the situation analysis?
✔ Do all marketing objectives support the strategies, goals, and mission?
✔ Do employees understand the marketing plan and have the skills, resources, and time to implement it?

Marketing Operations and Results

✔ Is the organization ready to track and report results and trends to marketing decision makers?
✔ Does the organization have suitable systems for managing marketing-mix activities?
✔ Does the organization have good relationships with customers, channel members, salespeople, suppliers, and partners?
✔ Can the organization benchmark against industry or world-class standards?
✔ How are performance problems analyzed, and how is control applied?

Stakeholder Relations

✔ How are stakeholders' comments, feedback, and priorities obtained, analyzed, and incorporated into marketing decisions?

✔ How do customers and other stakeholders perceive the brand/product/company, and how have their perceptions and attitudes changed over time?

MEASURING WHAT MATTERS

How can you measure the desired outcomes of your marketing strategies and programs? How can you measure progress week by week or month by month toward long-term outcomes? The time to establish checkpoints and standards for measuring interim performance is during the planning process. Once implementation is underway, you can monitor these measures and analyze results over time to diagnose any variations and make any changes needed to get back on track toward future success.

Major corporations with multiple marketing plans in place have an especially tricky time measuring progress. Here's a look at Procter & Gamble's challenge in moving toward its overall goal.

Procter & Gamble. The CEO of Procter & Gamble defines the company's overall goal as "winning with consumers." To "win" is to make a difference with consumers, whose purchases, in turn, determine whether P&G wins sales and profits (which make a difference with its shareholders). With more than $83 billion in annual worldwide sales of brand giants such as Tide, Bounty, and Pampers, P&G has a lot at stake. To see whether its marketing plans are helping it win big with consumers, P&G monitors hundreds of measures day by day, week by week, and boils the results down to four basic questions:

- Is the number of households that buy a given P&G brand or product increasing?
- What percentage of consumers who buy a P&G product once buy the same product again?
- Do consumers consider a specific P&G brand a good value?
- How do P&G brands compare with their best competitors in the hearts and minds of consumers?[1]

Every day, P&G has new opportunities to move closer to its goal through marketing that encourages more consumers to buy its brands, become loyal buyers, understand the value in P&G brands, and beat the competition. This is why P&G's marketers are constantly measuring results, comparing results with objectives, and seeking to improve performance by tweaking their plans when necessary.

Marketing plans typically include four main tools for measuring progress toward the desired results: (1) metrics, (2) forecasts, (3) budgets, and (4) schedules (see Exhibit 10.2).

EXHIBIT 10.2 Tools for Measuring Marketing Progress

Tool	Application
Metrics	Used to establish measures for specific performance-related outcomes and activities and then track results against measures
Forecasts	Used to predict future sales and costs as checkpoints for measuring progress
Budgets	Used to allocate funding across programs in specified periods and then track expenditures during implementation
Schedules	Used to plan and coordinate the timing of tasks and programs

PLANNING METRICS

Metrics are numerical measures of specific performance-related activities and outcomes used to see whether the organization is moving closer to its objectives and goals. Metrics focus managers and employees on activities that make a difference, set up performance expectations that can be objectively measured, and lay a foundation for internal accountability and pride in accomplishments. Consider what happened when Malaysia Airlines instituted profitability as its primary metric.

> **Malaysia Airlines.** When Malaysia Airlines was struggling to recover from heavy losses, its managers had no time for testing small changes—they needed "big results fast." They chose the metric of profitability to gauge how well each route was doing. After extensive analysis, they identified ways to improve the profitability of many routes, but they dropped others that were found to be hopelessly unprofitable because of lack of sufficient capacity or for other reasons. Now every day at 5 P.M., top managers receive a summary of that day's profitability by region and, within each region, by route and individual flight. This helps the company assess the financial results of marketing programs such as the Global Low Fares campaign, designed to introduce the airline to new customers worldwide and fill more seats on each flight.[2]

Exhibit 10.3 shows the main categories of metrics often used to assess marketing performance. Look back at what P&G's CEO said about wanting to win with consumers, and you can see that it's using metrics to assess its share of hearts, minds, and markets. Note that the marketing plan need not include all metrics for all activities—but it should show the most important metrics and explain the connection between those measurements and the organization's objectives.

PLANNING TIP

Review recent and previous year's metrics measurements in your situational analysis.

Marketers who use social media generally establish awareness-related metrics such as the number of video views or the number of blog visitors during a particular period. Because marketing is accountable for results, they also need metrics for measuring effectiveness in achieving financial objectives. When the Common Wealth Credit Union in Lloydminster, Canada, started a social media outreach campaign on Facebook, YouTube, and a blog, the bank didn't just count the number of fans, friends, or views. Its metrics included number of new accounts and amount of new deposits. By those measures, the bank's outreach was successful: It brought in 2,300 new accounts and millions of dollars in new deposits.[3]

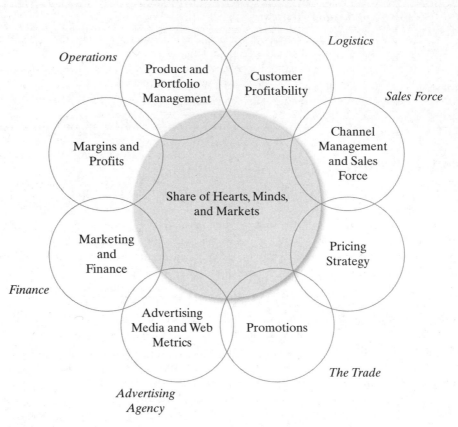

Customers and Market Research

Operations

Logistics

Sales Force

Product and Portfolio Management

Customer Profitability

Channel Management and Sales Force

Margins and Profits

Share of Hearts, Minds, and Markets

Marketing and Finance

Pricing Strategy

Finance

Advertising Media and Web Metrics

Promotions

The Trade

Advertising Agency

EXHIBIT 10.3   Main Categories of Marketing Metrics

Many organizations monitor key results using a **marketing dashboard,** a computerized, graphical or digital presentation that helps management track important metrics over time and spot deviations from the marketing plan.[4] Like a car dashboard, the marketing dashboard helps marketers see the situation at a glance, based on a limited number of data inputs, so they can make decisions quickly to improve effectiveness or efficiency.[5] Discover Financial Services uses a marketing dashboard to track sales and other key metrics, and then uses the data to analyze the impact of communications and plan for future campaigns.[6] Kodak uses a marketing dashboard to monitor metrics such as return on marketing investment, changes in market share, and changes in sales revenue.[7]

Identifying Metrics

How can you identify suitable metrics? One approach is to work backward from the mission, goals, and objectives to find specific outcomes and activities that signal progress (think both short-term and long-term progress). For example, companies pursuing growth need metrics to measure changes in customer relationships and sales. Such metrics might include measurements of customer acquisition, customer retention, customer defection, customer satisfaction, customer lifetime

EXHIBIT 10.4 Sample Metrics for Marketing Plan Objectives

Type of Objective	Sample Metrics
Marketing	• To acquire new customers: Measure number or percentage of new customers acquired by month, quarter, and year. • To retain current customers: Measure number or percentage of customers who continue purchasing during a set period. • To increase market share: Measure dollar or unit sales divided by total industry sales during a set period.
Financial	• To improve profitability: Measure gross or net margin for a set period by product, line, channel, marketing program, or customer. • To reach breakeven: Measure the number of weeks or months until a product's revenue equals and begins to exceed costs.
Societal	• To make products more environmentally friendly: Measure the proportion of each product's parts that are recyclable or have been recycled during a set period. • To build awareness of a social issue: Research awareness among the target audience after the program or a set period.

value, and sales trends by customer or segment.[8] Exhibit 10.4 shows some sample metrics for a number of marketing plan objectives.

Metrics that reveal increases in the customer base and customer satisfaction can serve as early indicators of future sales performance. Conversely, lower scores on these metrics are warning signs of problems that must be addressed. Some companies are using the *Net Promoter Score,* popularized by Bain & Company's Fred Reichheld, to gauge customer loyalty. This metric identifies the percentage of customers that are "promoters" (highly likely to recommend the firm to friends and colleagues) and the percentage that are "detractors" (unlikely to recommend the firm). Users find value in investigating why detractors won't recommend the company. Planet Tan, a Dallas-based chain of tanning salons, contacted customers who were detractors and learned that they were confused by its pricing. In response, Planet Tan changed its pricing and now offers monthly memberships.[9]

Good performance as measured by customer satisfaction, market share, competitive ranking, social responsibility targets, and other nonfinancial metrics sometimes means accepting the trade-off of lower short-term financial performance.[10] In terms of financial outcomes, common metrics are return on investment (ROI) and gross or net profit margins for each marketing activity, products and lines, channels, promotions, and price adjustments, among other measures. Note, however, that while marketers believe such measures are vital, the way certain outcomes are measured can vary from company to company; moreover, finance executives may be accustomed to using different metrics than marketing executives use.[11]

PLANNING TIP

Plan for metrics needed by top-level executives and marketing managers.

Not-for-profit organizations frequently use metrics to quantify the immediate and long-term results of marketing initiatives. Common metrics are donations received (to show effectiveness and efficiency of fund-raising by program and source), number of people being helped (to demonstrate use of service by segment or location), and public image (to gauge awareness among and attitude of stakeholders). The Centers for Disease Control and Prevention uses the metric of number of forwards to assess how any people are sending and receiving its e-cards with public health messages (see Exhibit 10.5).

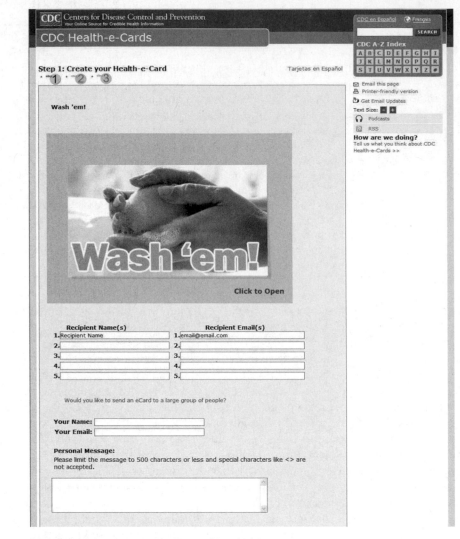

EXHIBIT 10.5 The CDC Markets Public Health

The nonprofit Big Brothers Big Sisters uses a number of metrics to measure progress toward its marketing plan objectives.

Big Brothers Big Sisters of America. This organization has been matching children with adult mentors in local communities for more than 100 years. Three key metrics it uses to measure the results of advertising campaigns, outreach programs, and cause-related marketing partnerships are the following: the number of children being mentored, the amount of money raised to support activities, and the number of media mentions to build awareness and participation.

During the past decade, the group's marketing has increased the number of children mentored nationwide from 138,500 to 255,305. Local affiliates use similar metrics: Big Brothers Big Sisters of Northern Nevada, for instance, matched 125 children with adult mentors in 2001; by 2009, it had matched 850 children with adult mentors. Big Brothers Big Sisters also monitors the number of media mentions in a given year, such as being the focus of a clue in the *Jeopardy* game show. In addition, corporate contributors such as Arby's and Jack in the Box use metrics to track their progress in raising donations for the nonprofit.[12]

A second way to identify metrics is by looking for key components or activities related to customer buying behavior, using research gathered during the situation analysis. This means finding measurements that signal customer movement toward a purchase. Although many firms measure brand preference as an indicator of future buying behavior, this metric is not right for all organizations. Once customers start buying, the company can use metrics to measure sales by transaction or by segment, customer or segment purchase frequency, sales by channel or intermediary, and so forth. Exhibit 10.6 presents sample metrics keyed to some basic stages in the buying process (compare with the audience response models in Exhibit 9.3).

Businesses that rely on personal selling usually set up metrics to measure the sales pipeline, such as number of prospect inquiries, number of qualified leads generated, number of meetings with qualified leads, number of bids accepted, percentage of prospects converted to customers, and number of orders received. Hewlett-Packard's Technology Solutions Group tracks number of leads generated by each marketing activity, from online seminars and industry trade shows to event sponsorships and public relations.[13] Channel productivity may be judged using metrics such as number or percentage of customers or sales generated per channel or intermediary, cost and profits per sale by channel or intermediary, speed of order fulfillment, and percentage of stock-outs. Of course, the exact metrics depend on each organization's situation and priorities.

PLANNING TIP

Determine whether last year's metrics make sense for this year's plan.

EXHIBIT 10.6 Metrics Based on Customer Behavior

Behavior	*Sample Metrics*
Customer becomes aware of an offering.	Measure customer awareness of offering and competing offers, by segment.
Customer learns more about an offering.	Measure number of information packets or catalogs requested, number of hits on Web site or YouTube video, number of people who visit store or showroom.
Customer has a positive attitude toward the offering.	Measure customer attitudes toward the offer and competing offers, by segment; feedback from hotlines, blogs, letters, e-mails, channel, etc.
Customer tries the offering.	Measure number of people who receive free samples or redeem coupons for trials.
Customer buys the offering.	Measure sales by transaction, segment, channel, payment method; conversion from trials and information requests.
Customer is satisfied.	Measure customer satisfaction by offering and by segment; satisfaction feedback from hotlines, blogs, letters, tweets, e-mails, channel, etc.
Customer becomes loyal.	Measure customer retention and churn; size and frequency of repeat purchases; utilization of frequent buyer program.

Using Metrics

Although metrics start with periodic measurements of marketing plan activities and outcomes, they are most valuable when viewed in the context of the following:

- *Expected outcomes.* How do the outcomes measured by metrics compare with the expected outcomes in the marketing plan? If the metric is dollar sales by segment, the marketer will compare actual segment sales over a given period with expected segment sales for that period to evaluate progress.
- *Historical results.* How do the outcomes measured by metrics compare with the actual outcomes in previous periods? Because marketers review previous results as part of their internal environmental analysis, they have the data to weigh current outcomes against previous outcomes, which can reveal unusual trends and suggest possible problems that could affect performance. Verizon Wireless, Sprint, AT&T, and all of the 200 firms that participate in the American Consumer Satisfaction Index examine short- and long-term trends as reflected in the company and industry rankings in the yearly survey.[14]
- *Competitive or industry outcomes.* How do the outcomes measured by metrics compare with competitors' outcomes or average outcomes for the industry? When comparable competitive or industry information is available, marketers can check these against their own organization's outcomes to gauge relative performance and reveal strengths and weaknesses. Because competitors operate under different circumstances and have very different goals, costs, and outcomes, competitive comparisons are useful only in relative terms. The online retailer Zappos.com doesn't track how long its reps spend on customer calls, although that's a key metric for marketers concerned with call-center efficiency. Instead, Zappos—now owned by Amazon.com—aims to strengthen customer relationships by encouraging reps to be friendly and chatty.[15]
- *Environmental influences.* How do the outcomes measured by metrics appear in relation to environmental trends, such as an economic boom or a parts shortage? Marketers need to interpret metrics in the context of everything else affecting the organization. If metrics indicate that sales objectives are barely being achieved when an economic boom has dramatically boosted demand, the organization should reevaluate its metrics or create new ones to find out why sales aren't higher still.

Many companies check performance metrics on a monthly basis, although some check weekly, some daily, or more often, when they have access to fresh data and know they can gain or lose a sale at the click of a mouse. Remember that metrics are merely tools to track the progress of programs after implementation, nothing more. Management must make decisions and take action when metrics show that the expected results are not being achieved.

One of the most common metrics for measuring marketing success in financial terms is return on investment in marketing (ROMI):

$$\frac{\text{Net profit attributable to a marketing activity (\$)}}{\text{Marketing investment (\$)}}$$

ROMI can be applied to individual marketing activities as well as to the overall marketing investment made by an organization. If a sales promotion returns a net profit of $20,000 and it costs $6,000, the ROMI calculation would be:

$$\frac{\$20,000}{6,000} = 333\%$$

Remember that activities geared toward marketing and societal objectives may not demonstrate immediate paybacks. In fact, not every marketing-plan outcome or activity can be measured, nor is every possible metric actually meaningful. For example, if a company lacks the budget to conduct valid attitudinal research, it cannot use customer attitudes as a metric. Another potential problem is that marketers will simply aim to meet each metrics target without watching the overall effect on strategic outcomes.[16]

PLANNING FORECASTS, BUDGETS, AND SCHEDULES

In addition to specifying metrics for measuring interim performance, your marketing plan should include forecasts, budgets, and schedules.

Forecasting Sales and Costs

Forecasts are future projections of what sales and costs are likely to be in the months and years covered by the plan. To do a good job of forecasting, companies must weigh external factors such as demand, threats, and opportunities as well as internal factors such as goals, capabilities, and constraints. Many marketers prepare forecasts for the best-case, the worst-case, and the most likely scenario. Not-for-profit organizations may prepare forecasts of future contributions, overall need for services, and projected service use, along with future estimates of associated costs. Forecasts can never be more than good estimates, and in fact you must allow for some forecast error because these are only projections. Still, forecasts should be as accurate as possible, because the organization relies on them when developing strategies and planning the resources needed to implement the marketing plan.

PLANNING TIP

The specific forecasts you prepare depend on your firm and its priorities.

Here's how the movie rental company Netflix uses forecasting.

Netflix. With wider availability of broadband Internet in the United States, millions more consumers every year have the ability to order movies and programs streamed from Netflix's servers. That's a good thing for Netflix, which forecasts a widening gap in the cost of fulfilling a customer's order by mail versus online streaming. Currently, Netflix pays 80 cents for mailing a DVD to and from a customer but only 5 cents for streaming a two-hour movie. As the price of postage rises, Netflix's costs rise.

Moreover, consumers are increasingly drawn to on-demand delivery. Redbox, the movie-rental kiosk chain, is growing rapidly because renters enjoy choosing a movie and watching it right away, and Blockbuster is moving into kiosks even as it closes stores. "By the end of the year, kiosks will likely be our No. 1 competitor," Netflix's Hastings confirms. "There are already more kiosks in America than video stores." Other competitors include online entertainment sites such as Hulu.com and cable subscription services such as Comcast. Small wonder that by 2015, according to Netflix's forecasts, only a sliver of its sales revenue will come from renting movie DVDs by mail. Netflix's future depends on marketing plans that encourage customers to subscribe to entertainment delivered online to home PCs, TVs, DVD players, and game consoles.[17]

Plan to review your forecasts often because internal or external shifts can influence sales, costs, and marketing performance at any time. Forecasting must account for the effect that marketing activities will have on the direction and velocity of sales. For example, you may forecast higher sales for a new product if you plan to use penetration pricing to encourage rapid adoption. On the other hand, if you use skimming pricing to skim profits from the market, your forecast for introductory sales volume may be lower than with penetration pricing. Why does this matter? Relying on a forecast that underestimates sales could leave you with insufficient inventory or staffing to satisfy demand; on the other hand, relying on an overestimate could lead to overproduction and other costly problems.

Here's how the online retailer Amazon.com uses forecasting in its marketing plans.

Amazon.com. Amazon forecasts sales and costs for different days of the week, as well as for every week, month, and quarter, so it can be ready with appropriate staffing and inventory levels. Amazon's forecasts also allow for the effect of holidays, seasonality, economic conditions, competitive actions, and other elements that influence demand. And when it introduces new products of its own, such as its Kindle electronic book reader, it forecasts sales and plans production accordingly. However, when Amazon introduced its first Kindle and again when it launched a model with a larger screen, its forecasts were too low. Demand was so strong and immediate that the Kindle sold out very quickly, frustrating would-be buyers who had to settle for adding their names to a long waiting list. Rival Barnes & Noble had a similar experience during the launch of its electronic book reader, with orders outstripping supply for a time.[18]

TYPES OF FORECASTS   The most commonly used types of forecasts are as follows:

- *Forecasts of market and segment sales.* The company starts by projecting a market's overall industrywide sales for up to five years, using the definition created during the market analysis. This helps size the entire market so managers can set specific share objectives (as discussed in Chapter 5) and estimate the share competitors will have in future years. If possible, the company also should forecast year-by-year sales in each targeted segment.
- *Forecasts of company product sales.* Based on market and segment forecasts, market and customer analysis, direction decisions, and marketing strategies, the company now projects the number and dollar amount of product (or product line) sales for each market or segment. These are usually presented month by month for

a year or for the period covered by the marketing plan and sometimes longer. Toyota, for example, projects sales model by model; one recent forecast calls for selling 1 million Prius hybrid cars a year within five years. It also creates separate year-by-year forecasts for each new vehicle to track those sales more closely.[19]

- *Forecasts of cost of sales.* Here, management forecasts the costs associated with company product sales forecasts, based on data gathered for the analysis of the current situation and on data about cost trends. These forecasts may be adjusted after marketing budgets have been prepared.

- *Forecasts of sales and costs by channel.* When companies sell through more than one channel level or intermediary, they may want to project monthly unit and dollar sales by product by channel and, if feasible, costs per channel. These forecasts focus attention on channel cost efficiency and provide a yardstick for measuring and analyzing actual channel results and expenses. Coach forecasts sales by product, product category, and store for its company-owned stores and the department stores that stock its upscale leather goods.[20]

Next, the marketer calculates the month-to-month and year-to-year change for the figures in each forecast to examine trends (such as how much growth in sales is being projected for the coming 12 months) and rate of change (such as how quickly costs are rising). Forecast projections and trend calculations can be used to check on target markets, review objectives, reallocate resources, and measure actual against expected results. Given the rapid rate of change in many markets, many companies update forecasts monthly or more often to reflect current conditions; many also collaborate with key suppliers and channel members for more precise forecasting.

SOURCES AND TOOLS FOR FORECASTING DATA   Often companies obtain data for forecasting purposes from their value-chain partners. Marketers can also tap primary research sources such as studies of buying patterns and buying intentions that suggest demand levels by market, segment, category, or product. However, marketers must use judgment, remembering that customers may not buy in the future as they have in the past, nor will they necessarily make future purchases even though they told researchers they would do so.[21] Trade associations, government statistics, and industry analysts' reports can be valuable secondary sources of data.

Some marketers predict future sales by applying causal analysis methods such as regression analysis, econometric models, and neural networks or using time series methods such as smoothing and decomposition. They may also apply judgmental forecasting tools such as sales force estimates, executive opinion, the Delphi method, and online prediction markets, as shown in Exhibit 10.7. Because these tools may be subject to human error or bias, marketers generally use a combination of judgment and statistical analysis updated with estimates from knowledgeable sources for increased accuracy.

As difficult as forecasting can be for existing products, planners face even more challenges in forecasting for new products. Some companies use the Bass model for forecasting initial purchases of new products; this is appropriate when (1) the company has been able to collect sales data for even a brief period, or (2) the product is similar to an existing product or technology with a known sales history.[22]

When a product is so innovative that it establishes a new product category—such as the electronic book reader—marketers have no historical or industry data to factor into

EXHIBIT 10.7 Judgmental Tools for Forecasting

Forecasting Tool	Use
Sales force estimates	Composite projection based on estimates made by sales personnel; convenient but accuracy depends on instincts, experience, and objectivity of salespeople.
Executive opinion	Composite projection based on estimates made by managers; convenient but accuracy depends on instincts, experience, and objectivity of managers.
Delphi method	Composite projection based on successive rounds of input from outside experts, who ultimately come to consensus on estimates; time consuming but sometimes helpful when forecasting new-product or new-market sales.
Online prediction market	Composite projection based on combined judgment of employees or stakeholders who indicate their confidence in certain marketing predictions through online "trading" in a mock stock market; efficient but may involve bias toward longer-term predictions.

their forecasts. (As you saw earlier, Amazon's forecasts for the Kindle were too low, and the product sold out much more quickly than anticipated.) Instead, some predict sales using the results of simulated test marketing research, while others look at sales patterns of products with similar market behavior for clues to the new product's future sales. Once forecasts are in place, marketers create budgets to allocate resources and prepare to track expenses.

Budgeting to Plan and Track Expenses

Budgets are time-defined allocations of financial outlays for specific functions, programs, customer segments, or geographic regions. Budgeting enables marketing managers to allocate expenses by program or activity over specific periods and compare these with actual expenditures. Some organizations insist that budget preparation follow internal financial calendars; some specify profit hurdles or particular assumptions about expenses and allocation; some mandate particular formats or supporting documentation; and some require budgets based on best-case, worst-case, and most likely scenarios. A growing number of businesses are no longer fixing budgets annually but instead are adjusting budgets monthly based on market realities or tying budgets to longer-term performance.[23]

PLANNING TIP

Combine bottom-up and top-down budget input when allocating marketing funds.

BUDGETING METHODS FOR MARKETING SPENDING How much money should be budgeted for marketing programs? Smaller companies often deal with this question using **affordability budgeting,** simply budgeting what they believe they can afford, given other urgent expenses. Affordability budgeting may work for start-ups in the early days, when many entrepreneurs have little to spend. However, this is generally not a good way to budget, because it doesn't allow for the kind of significant, ongoing investments often needed to launch major new products or enter intensely competitive markets. In effect, budgeting based on affordability ignores the profit payback that comes from spending on marketing to build sales.

Ideally, the size of the marketing budget should be based on careful analysis of the link between spending and sales (and for not-for-profit organizations, donations). By building a sophisticated model of how sales actually react to different spending levels, the company can determine exactly how big the marketing budget must be to achieve its sales targets. Companies without such models tend to rely on rule-of-thumb budgeting methods that do not directly correlate spending with sales, such as the percentage-of-sales method, the competitive-parity method, and the objective-and-task method.

With **percentage-of-sales budgeting,** management sets aside a certain percentage of dollar sales to fund marketing programs, based on internal budgeting guidelines or previous marketing experience. Although this is simple to implement, one disadvantage is that sales are seen as the source of marketing funding, rather than as the result of budget investments. Another is that the company may have no justification (other than tradition) for choosing the percentage devoted to marketing. Finally, if the budget is continually adjusted based on month-by-month sales, lower sales may lead to a lower marketing budget—just when the company needs to maintain or even increase the budget to stimulate higher sales.

When companies use **competitive-parity budgeting,** they fund marketing by matching what competitors spend (as a percentage of sales or specific dollar amount). Again, this is a simple method, but it ignores differences between companies and doesn't allow for adjustments to find the best spending level for achieving marketing plan objectives.

PLANNING TIP

Don't match what competitors spend, but be aware of their budget priorities.

With the widely used **objective-and-task budgeting method,** marketers add up the cost of completing all the marketing tasks needed to achieve their marketing plan objectives. In the absence of a proven model showing how sales levels respond to marketing spending, the objective-and-task method provides a reasonable way to build a budget by examining the cost of the individual programs that contribute to marketing performance—as long as the appropriate objectives have been set.

BUDGETS WITHIN THE MARKETING BUDGET   Once the overall budget has been established, marketers start to allocate marketing funding across the various activities in the time period covered by the marketing plan. Then, when they implement the marketing plan, they can input actual expenditures for comparison with planned expenditures. The marketing plan usually includes the following:

- *Budgets for each marketing-mix program.* These budgets list costs for each program's tasks or expense items, presented month by month and with year-end totals. Depending on the company's preferred format, marketing-mix budgets also may show expected sales, gross or net margins, and other objectives and profitability measures. Tracking expenses by program reinforces accountability and helps management weigh expected costs against actual costs—and results.
- *Budgets for each brand, segment, or market.* Creating these types of budgets forces companies to understand their costs and returns relative to individual brands, segments, and markets.
- *Budgets for each region or geographic division.* Budgeting by region or geography focuses attention on the cost of marketing by location and allows easy comparisons between outlays and returns.

- ***Budgets for each division or product manager.*** These budgets help divisional and product managers track costs for which they are responsible, compare spending with results achieved, and pinpoint problems or opportunities for further investigation.
- ***Budget summarizing overall marketing expenses.*** This summary budget may be arranged by marketing program or tool, by segment or region, or by using another appropriate organizing pattern. Typically, this budget shows month-by-month spending and full-year totals; in some cases, companies may project spending for multiple years in one summary budget. And this budget may include expected gross or net margins and other calculations based on sales and expenditures.

All these budgets serve as checkpoints against which actual spending can be measured. In this way, marketers can quickly spot overspending and calculate margins and other profitability measures to check on progress toward financial objectives. Given the dynamic nature of the business environment, however, be ready to rethink budgets when unexpected developments cause complications.

New Budget Realities. The recent economic crisis dampened demand for many offerings. With sales lower than forecasts, marketers in many industries had to adjust to new budget realities. Volvo, for instance, reduced its marketing budget and reallocated spending among different media and messages. "You can't get the same reach for the same budgets now as you would this time last year," explained a Volvo marketing official. For that reason, Volvo increased its budget for online activities such as paid search while decreasing its budget for traditional advertising. While Volvo and other competitors were slashing spending, South Korea's Hyundai Motors was among the few auto marketers increasing their marketing budgets to engage car buyers.[24]

Dr Pepper Snapple, too small to outspend rivals Coca-Cola and Pepsi, differentiates itself on the basis of unique flavors. The company considered budget changes during the worst of the recession as sales of carbonated beverages stalled. Then it looked at how consumer product goods companies fared during the 1980s recession—and found that the most successful continued to invest in marketing. Dr Pepper Snapple decided to increase its marketing budget to position its brands for future growth as the economy improved. It also shifted more money into online marketing to reach teenagers, one of its targeted segments.[25]

Scheduling Marketing Plan Programs

The next step is to coordinate the timing of each activity through scheduling. **Schedules** are time-defined plans for completing a series of tasks or activities (milestones) related to a specific program or objective. Scheduling helps you define the timing of these tasks and coordinate implementation to avoid conflicts and measure progress toward completion. To create a detailed program-by-program schedule, list the main tasks and activities for one program at a time and, through research or experience, assign each a projected start and end date. Schedules also identify who is responsible for supervising or completing each task in each program.

PLANNING TIP

Include the timing and progress of multiyear activities in your situation analysis.

Some companies create a series of schedules, based on best-case, worst-case, and most likely scenarios for timing. Estée Lauder, the cosmetics firm, has stepped up its use of scenario planning in the face of rapid changes in economic conditions worldwide. The CEO also asks brand managers three questions: "What must you have? What would you like to keep going? And what can you give up?"[26]

Marketing plans typically include a summary schedule showing the timing and responsibility for each planned program; the appendix or separate documents may show detailed schedules for each program along with Gantt charts, critical path schedules, or other project-management tools. The point is to make the timing as concrete as possible so you can quickly determine whether you're on schedule. Then you can use metrics to monitor key performance-related activities and outcomes.

CONTROLLING MARKETING PLAN IMPLEMENTATION

To implement a marketing plan most effectively, your organization must "own" the plan, support it, and adapt it as needed (see Exhibit 10.8). During the planning process, a manager (or, ideally, a team) inside the company must be responsible for laying out both strategies and details, championing the plan internally, seeing that rewards are based on marketing performance, and involving senior management. The plan needs support during development

PLANNING TIP

You may want to control performance on other financial measures, including costs.

and during implementation—support in the form of sufficient time, funding, and staffing as well as internal marketing. Finally, be persistent and be ready to adapt the plan if metrics indicate that there is room for improvement.

Four types of marketing control can help gauge the effectiveness of plan implementation: annual plan, profitability, productivity, and strategic control. Because marketing plans are generally developed every year, the organization needs **annual plan control** to assess the progress of the current year's marketing plan. This type of control covers broad performance measures, performance toward meeting marketing plan objectives, and performance toward meeting marketing strategy and program objectives.

Profitability control assesses the organization's progress and performance based on key profitability measures. The exact measures differ from organization to organization, but often include return on investment (or other return measures), contribution margin,

EXHIBIT 10.8 Successful Marketing Plan Implementation

and gross or net profit margin. Many companies measure the monthly and yearly profit-and-loss results of each product, line, and category, as well as each market or segment and each channel. As you saw earlier, Malaysia Airlines applies profitability control every day. By comparing profitability results over time, marketers can spot significant strengths, weaknesses, threats, and opportunities early enough to make appropriate changes.

Productivity control assesses the organization's performance and progress in managing the efficiency of key marketing areas such as the sales force, promotions, channels and logistics, and product management. Productivity is so important to the bottom line that some companies appoint marketing controllers to establish standards, measure performance, and boost marketing efficiency without compromising customer satisfaction or other objectives. Firms also measure the productivity of their product development and manufacturing activities as well as order fulfillment and other tasks, knowing that behind-the-scenes inefficiencies can damage customer relationships. Colgate-Palmolive's productivity control includes measuring the number of patents awarded and products launched in a year, compared with previous years.[27]

Strategic control assesses the organization's effectiveness in managing the marketing function, customer relationships, and social responsibility and ethics issues—three areas of strategic importance. Whereas other types of control are applied monthly or more often, strategic control may be applied once or twice a year, or as needed to clarify the organization's performance in these strategic areas.

When Ford, for example, applies strategic control, it also demonstrates its transparency by publicly reporting progress toward a number of key sustainability goals.

Ford. What is the status of Ford's sustainability initiatives? Anyone can check the automaker's progress over the past decade by examining the public reports posted on its Web site. One of Ford's long-term goals is to reduce carbon dioxide emissions of its new U.S. and European models by 30 percent before the end of 2020. To do this, it's introducing more hybrid and all-electric vehicles; by 2013, it will have low-emission EcoBoost engines available for 90 percent of its product lines. Ford is also setting and meeting or exceeding objectives for conserving water. Although the firm doesn't always meet all of its yearly objectives—it recently fell short of its target for cutting energy use in production facilities worldwide—reporting candidly on its progress gives it credibility.[28]

To assess the effectiveness of the marketing function and gauge strengths and weaknesses, companies should conduct a yearly **marketing audit,** a detailed, systematic analysis of marketing capabilities and performance (see this chapter's checklist). After the audit, include a summary of the findings in the internal environmental analysis section of the marketing plan.

Applying Control

The control process, introduced in Chapter 1, is essential for guiding the implementation of any marketing plan. You need it to determine whether programs are working out as planned and to provide information for decisions about changing, continuing, or abandoning marketing strategies—especially important in today's volatile business environment.

After setting the marketing plan's objectives, you'll set standards and measurement intervals (drawn from marketing plan budgets, forecasts, metrics, and schedules) to measure interim progress. Once the plan is implemented, compare actual results with expected results and diagnose any variances. It can be helpful to diagnose results in the context of historic, competitive, or industrywide results and research the macroenvironmental and microenvironmental issues affecting performance.

The final step is to take corrective action, if necessary, by making adjustments or implementing a contingency plan formulated in advance. You may have to change the program, the strategy, or the implementation to achieve the planned results. Or you may decide to change the standards or objectives by which you measure performance. This is appropriate when the variance is not a one-time occurrence and you understand the underlying influence(s) on performance. Although corrective action is the last step in marketing control, it serves as input for next year's situation analysis and for setting or reevaluating objectives at the start of the next control or marketing planning cycle.

Preparing Contingency Plans

Contingency plans are plans that organizations have ready to implement if one (or more) of their original strategies or programs is disrupted by significant, unexpected changes. Lego, the Danish toy manufacturer, develops multiple contingency plans so no matter what direction the economy moves in, the company is prepared.[29] Hospitals, banks, telecommunications firms, and other organizations that must operate without interruption are especially meticulous about contingency planning.

PLANNING TIP

Think about what might significantly disrupt marketing results or activities.

Marketers usually prepare contingency plans showing how their organization will respond in the case of emergencies such as: computer systems outages; prolonged power or telecommunications interruptions; natural disasters; sudden bankruptcy of a major customer or supplier; contamination or other environmental disasters; sudden technological breakthrough by a competitor; major failure of a program or strategy; price war or other extreme competitive development; and significant criminal, sabotage, or terrorist activities. Many organizations have contingency plans to deal with widespread absenteeism due to a pandemic caused by an illness such H1N1 swine flu.

Planning for Pandemic. Professor Amin Mawani, of Toronto's York University, observes that a company with contingency plans to meet customers' needs during a pandemic will be in a good position to take share from firms that slow down or shut down because of employee absenteeism. Stihl, which makes power tools, has contingency plans to manage production levels if assembly-line workers fall ill with influenza. Each unit of Norfolk Southern, which operates railroad lines in 22 states, has identified the most vital business functions to be maintained during a flu pandemic. The units are cross-training employees to fill in where necessary if up to 50 percent of the workforce is out sick. "We don't have any plans to shut down," says an executive.[30]

Contingency plans should be outlined as marketing plans are being developed, then periodically reviewed and updated as the situation changes. When preparing a contingency plan, think creatively about the organization's options, priorities, and resources to come up with alternatives that minimize the impact of the disruption and allow the organization to recover as quickly as possible. Test the plans in advance to be sure they will work and are as complete as possible. And use the lessons learned from dealing with any emergency as input for analyzing the current situation when preparing the next marketing plan.

Summary

As preparation for implementation, marketing plans typically specify four main tools for measuring performance progress: metrics, forecasts, budgets, and schedules. Metrics are numerical measures of performance-related activities and outcomes that marketers apply to determine whether they are moving closer to their objectives. Metrics focus employees on activities that make a difference, set up performance expectations that can be objectively measured, and lay a foundation for internal accountability and pride in accomplishments. Metrics should be examined in the context of expected outcomes, previous results, competitive/industry outcomes, and environmental influences.

A forecast is a future projection of what sales and costs are likely to be in the months and years covered by the plan. Budgets are time-defined allocations of financial outlays for specific functions, programs, customer segments, or geographic region. Schedules are time-defined plans for completing a series of tasks or activities (milestones) related to a program or objective, used to manage marketing plan implementation. Organizations use four types of marketing control: annual plan, profitability, productivity, and strategic control (including the marketing audit). If results are disrupted by significant, unexpected changes, the organization should have contingency plans ready for implementation.

Your Marketing Plan, Step by Step

Answering the following questions will help you think through plans for metrics, forecasts, budgets, schedules, and marketing control. Also look at how these tools are discussed in the SonicSuperphone sample plan (see Appendix) and in a few of the Marketing Plan Pro *sample marketing plans. When you have decided on how you will gauge interim progress and control implementation, note your ideas in your written plan or using* Marketing Plan Pro.

1. Look at the financial, marketing, and societal objectives you previously set for your marketing plan. For each objective, list at least one metric for measuring progress toward achievement; also list an appropriate interval (such as daily, weekly, monthly, quarterly, yearly) for measuring progress. Refer back to Exhibits 10.4 and 10.6 for ideas as you answer this question.
2. Review your market and customer analyses. If you haven't already done so, forecast sales and costs for your market(s) and targeted segment(s). If possible, do this for each offering or product line, for the cost of sales, and for each channel. For background, read the opinions and forecasts of industry

insiders, competitors, analysts, academic experts, and others knowledgeable about your type of offering in secondary research collected from sources such as:
   a. business and news media
   b. academic, professional, and industry trade groups
   c. government agencies
   d. competitors' annual reports, Web sites, and public statements
   e. financial analysts and industry consultants
3. Using the objective-and-task budgeting method, prepare a basic budget with estimated costs for all marketing activities in your plan. If possible, go into more detail to define budgets for each brand or

offering and each marketing program or campaign. How can you link the investment represented by your budget(s) to the returns represented by your objectives?

4. Develop a basic schedule showing when each key marketing activity or program will begin and end. Also show who will be responsible for each activity. Note the overall pattern of activities and consider the circumstances under which you might need to revise your schedule. For example, if a particular activity doesn't end on time, will that affect the start or end date of another activity? How might departures from the schedule affect your ability to achieve your objectives on time?

5. What standard(s) will you use for determining whether progress has been made after the plan is implemented? For instance, do you expect to move 10 percent closer to a particular objective every month? What historical, competitive, or industrywide standards will you choose for a context in which to understand interim results? What environmental forces, if any, have special significance for each metric?

6. If interim measurements indicate progress isn't being made at the rate you expect, indicate what corrective action would you consider taking (and when) to get back on track toward your most important objectives. What types of control are appropriate for your plan? Do you need contingency plans for certain extraordinary situations that might disrupt implementation? Outline the main points of a contingency plan you would develop to address one particular situation.

Endnotes

1. Jonathan Birchall, "Procter & Gamble Raises Market Growth Forecast," *Financial Times*, October 30, 2009, www.ft.com; A.G. Lafley, "The Work of the CEO: What Only the CEO Can Do," speech to the *Harvard Business Review McKinsey Prize Awards Dinner*, March 24, 2009, p. 5; Ellen Byron and Joann S. Lublin, "Appointment of New P&G Chief Sends Ripples Through Ranks," *Wall Street Journal*, June 11, 2009, www.wsj.com.

2. Lee Kian Seong, "Lower Jet Fuel Prices a Help for Airlines amid Tougher Environment," *The Star Online (Malaysia)*, November 2, 2009, http://biz.thestar.com; Jeeva Arulampalam, "MAS: No Plans to Lay Off Staff," *New Straits Times Press*, June 23, 2009, www.btimes.com; "Turning Around a Struggling Airline," *The McKinsey Quarterly*, November 2008, www.mckinseyquarterly.com.

3. Josh Bernoff, "Measure What Matters," *Marketing News*, December 15, 2008, p. 22.

4. Paul W. Farris, Neil T. Bendle, Phillip E. Pfeifer, and David J. Reibstein, *Marketing Metrics: 50+ Metrics Every Executive Should Master* (Upper Saddle River, NJ: Wharton School Publishing, 2006), p. 331.

5. Laura Patterson, "Bridging the Gap: Unlock the Power of Your Marketing Dashboard (Part 1)," *Manage Smarter*, November 20, 2008, www.salesandmarketing.com.

6. Jeff Zabin, "Recessionary Times Call for Recessionary Marketing," *E-Commerce Times*, March 26, 2009, www.ecommercetimes.com.

7. Elisabeth A. Sullivan, "Measure Up," *Marketing News*, May 30, 2009, pp. 8–11.

8. For more about financial and non-financial metrics, see "When Art Meets Science: The Challenge of ROI Marketing," *Strategy + Business*, December 17, 2003, www.strategy-business.com/press/sbkw2/sbkwarticle/sbkw031217.

9. Neil Goldman, "The Real Value Behind Net Promoter Score: Action Items It Uncovers," *Credit Union Journal*, January 12, 2009, p. 7; Justin Martin, "Get Customers to Sell For You," *Fortune Small Business*, May 27, 2008, www.cnnmoney.com. For a critical analysis of NPS, see Timothy L. Keiningham, Lerzan Aksoy, Bruce Cooil, and Tor Willin Andreassen, "Linking Customer Loyalty to Growth," *MIT Sloan Management Review*, Summer 2008, pp. 51–57.

10. For more about market share as a metric, see "The 'Myth of Market Share': Can Focusing Too Much on the Competition Harm Profitability?" *Knowledge@Wharton*, January 24, 2007, http://knowledge.wharton.upenn.edu/article.cfm?articleid=1645.

11. Ed See, "Bridging the Finance-Marketing Divide," *Financial Executive*, July–August 2006, pp. 50+; Kate Maddox, "ANA Explores Marketing Accountability," *BtoB*, August 8, 2005, p. 3.

12. Geralda Miller, "Big Brothers Big Sisters Celebrates Anniversary," *Reno Gazette-Journal (Nevada),* June 4, 2009, www.rgj.com; "Arby's Collecting Donations for Big Brothers Big Sisters," *Green Bay Gazette,* June 20, 2009, www.greenbaypressgazette.com; Big Brothers Big Sisters of America 2008 Annual Report; www.bbbsa.org.

13. "The Big Question: Given the State of the Economy, What Changes Have You Made in Your Lead-Generation Tactics?" *BtoB,* May 27, 2009, p. 10.

14. Brad Reed, "Sprint Makes Big Leap Forward in Customer Satisfaction Survey," *NetworkWorld,* May 20, 2009, www.networkworld.com.

15. Amanda Finnegan, "Zappos CEO Talks Company Culture at Marketing Conference," *Las Vegas Sun,* November 11, 2009, www.lasvegassun.com; Tom Steinert-Threlkeld, "The Real Case in Social Media: Zappos CEO Not All Atwitter About Twitter," *ZDNet,* June 23, 2009, http://blogs.zdnet.com/BTL/?p=20196.

16. Gordon A. Wyner, "The Right Side of Metrics," *Marketing Management,* January–February 2004, pp. 8–9.

17. "Coming Soon to a PlayStation 3 Near You: Netflix Streaming," *Los Angeles Times,* October 26, 2009, http://latimesblogs.latimes.com; Nick Wingfield, "Netflix Boss Plots Life After the DVD," *Wall Street Journal,* June 23, 2009, www.wsj.com; "Redbox's Vending Machines Are Giving Netflix Competition," *New York Times,* June 22, 2009, www.nytimes.com.

18. Nicholas Kolakowski, "Barnes and Noble's Nook E-Reader Delayed," *E-Week,* November 9, 2009, www.eweek.com; "Amazon's Kindle DX Sells Out Quickly," *InformationWeek,* June 15, 2009, www.informationweek.com; Heather Green, "Amazon Profits Amid Recession," *BusinessWeek Online,* April 24, 2009, www.businessweek.com.

19. John Lippert, Alan Ohnsman, and Kae Inoue, "Toyoda Asks How Many Times Toyota Errs Emulating GM Failures," *Bloomberg,* June 22, 2009, www.bloomberg.com.

20. Susan Berfield, "Coach's New Bag," *BusinessWeek,* June 29, 2009, pp. 40–43.

21. See David B. Whitlark, Michael D. Geurts, and Michael J. Swenson, "New Product Forecasting with a Purchase Intention Survey," *Journal of Business Forecasting* vol. 12, Fall 1993, pp. 18–21.

22. Gary L. Lilien and Arvind Rangaswamy, *Marketing Engineering,* 2nd ed. (Upper Saddle River, NJ: Prentice Hall, 2003), p. 253.

23. Loren Gary, "Why Budgeting Kills Your Company," *HBS Working Knowledge,* August 11, 2003, www.hbsworkingknowledge.hbs.edu.

24. Moon Ihlwan, "Samsung Widens the Gap with Sony in TV," *BusinessWeek,* April 3, 2009, www.businessweek.com; "Sui Genesis," *The Economist,* March 7, 2009, p. 71.

25. Natalie Zmuda, "Dr Pepper Ups Marketing Spend, Readies for Growth," *Advertising Age,* May 4, 2009, p. 18; "Volvo Restructures Marketing Budget to Focus on Digital," *New Media Age,* April 30, 2009, p. 3.

26. Matthew Boyle, "The Budget Knives Come Out," *BusinessWeek,* October 13, 2008, p. 30.

27. Matthew Boyle, "05 Still the King of Dental Care," *BusinessWeek,* April 6, 2009, p. 48.

28. John Gartner, "Ford on the Right Track with Sustainability Efforts," *Reuters,* June 16, 2009, www.reuters.com; "Ford on Track to Cut Vehicle Emissions, Lags on Energy Efficiency," *Reuters,* June 15, 2009, www.reuters.com.

29. "Managing in the Fog," *The Economist,* February 28, 2009, p. 67.

30. Amin Mawani, "Fever, Chills . . . and Losses: More Companies Should Be Preparing for an Influenza Pandemic," *Wall Street Journal,* June 22, 2009, www.wsj.com; Philip Walzer, "Is Your Office Ready to Deal with a Swine Flu Pandemic?" *The Virginian-Pilot,* June 22, 2009, http://hamptonroads.com.

APPENDIX

Sample Marketing Plan: SonicSuperphone

Sonic, a hypothetical start-up company, is about to introduce a new multimedia, multifunction smartphone, a cell (mobile) phone handset with unique features and functions. This product is entering a U.S. market crowded with offerings from Nokia, BlackBerry, Apple, and numerous other rivals. Yet significant profit potential exists for cutting-edge products that can deliver the specific benefits most valued by targeted segments. The following sample marketing plan shows how Sonic is preparing to launch its first product.

EXECUTIVE SUMMARY

Early next year, Sonic will introduce a new product in the fast-maturing U.S. market for smartphones. Competing against well-established multinational rivals, we plan to launch a high-quality, slim handset combining a number of useful, innovative features that eliminate the need for users to carry multiple devices. We are targeting specific segments in the consumer and business markets, matching our features to the benefits sought by these customers. After our initial product is established in the U.S. market, we plan to market it in Canada and Europe.

We will differentiate this first product, the SonicSuperphone, on the basis of innovation and versatile communication, convenience, easy of use, and multiple entertainment capabilities. Our marketing priorities include building brand awareness among affluent consumers and targeted business customers, reaching specific sales levels, breaking even by the end of the second year, and operating in an environmentally friendly manner.

Sonic's core capabilities of technical expertise, design experience, and efficient assembly procedures will minimize variable costs and enable us to react quickly to market trends and technological advances. For the product's introduction, we will use a push strategy aimed at channel members combined with a pull strategy aimed at customer segments.

SITUATION ANALYSIS

Sonic was founded 18 months ago by two entrepreneurs with extensive high-tech experience and a creative design for a new smartphone, to be called the SonicSuperphone. To power this phone, the cofounders developed the SuperSolar battery, a compact, eco-friendly power source that can run the handset for 12 hours of talk time without recharging.

The founders arranged an industry-exclusive license for Wireless Communication Commander software, which makes the handset compatible with Wi-Fi, Wi-Max, and all other wireless communication standards. In addition, they licensed voice recognition software to manage all of the handset's functions, including entering contacts and other data; accessing the Web, text messages, social media, and e-mail; working with video, audio, and Webcam files; and managing business files and data. Moreover, they acquired a special biometric security system to prevent unauthorized access and protect data stored on SonicSuperphone units.

The SonicSuperphone is designed to be light, slender, and user-friendly, with a touch-screen handset and virtual keyboard that can be projected onto a flat surface as needed. The handset will work with any cell-phone carrier or plan, including free plans such as Skype. It comes with a handy docking station for synchronizing data with personal computers or laptops, downloading media files, and backing up phone data. The SonicSuperphone will have a standard 5-megapixel camera and will be able to record, store, play, upload, and download photos, videos, and MP3 music files (with 250 GB of storage capacity). As a result, our product's features and functions deliver significantly more benefits than most competing units (see Table A.1).

TABLE A.1 SonicSuperphone Features, Functions, and Benefits

Feature or Function	Benefits
Voice-activated control of all functions	Built-in, hands-free operation for on-the-go users
Dock to personal computer or laptop	Convenient access to downloadable media; ability to make free international phone calls; one-button backup of phone data
SuperSolar battery	Environmentally friendly battery powers phone up to 12 hours without recharging
Compatibility with all wireless communication and peripheral connection standards	Phone, e-mail, text messaging, and Web access possible from any location; Bluetooth or other technologies can be used for headsets or other peripherals
Exclusive Wireless Communication Commander software	Automatically chooses among wireless options for best quality, least expensive Internet or phone connection in each location
Touch-screen technology plus "virtual" keyboard for data entry	Simplifies operation by eliminating need for separate pen or input device; no external keyboard, because software projects keyboard image and follows user's keystrokes
Live Webcam video capture and display as well as integrated 5-megapixel camera	Record and monitor home, children, pets, and business areas in real time
Video/photo/audio recording, downloading, uploading, storage, playback	Convenient for entertainment purposes and fully compatible with all operating systems; large 250 GB storage capacity to accommodate large multimedia files
Biometric security device	Fast and convenient identity recognition to prevent unauthorized access
Smart Apps store	Downloadable, free or inexpensive consumer and business applications to enhance all aspects of smartphone functionality

We will face intense competition. The top companies in the smartphone market are well established and have years of experience in new-product innovation. They have also learned to differentiate their products with features valued by our targeted segments. Nonetheless, our exclusive software license, our long-lasting green battery, and our core skills in technology, design, and production should provide an important edge (see the SWOT analysis). Moreover, as the following sections explain, the product's launch will be based on favorable market trends; advanced technology; penetration pricing; selective distribution; extensive knowledge of our markets, customers, and competitors; and tight marketing control.

Market Needs and Trends

The SonicSuperphone can meet a wide variety of customer needs, replacing multiple gadgets and enabling consumers and businesspeople to carry only one device. These needs include the following:

1. ***Communication.*** Stay in touch on the go by voice, e-mail, text and multimedia messaging, photo and video images, Webcam, file exchange, social media updates. Make long-distance and international phone calls without charge using special docking station and software.
2. ***Convenience.*** Easy-to-use voice-recognition system, touch-screen handset, and virtual keyboard simplify operation; exclusive Wireless Communication Commander software automatically selects the highest-quality and lowest-price wireless method, guided by preset user preferences.

3. ***Store and manage information securely.*** Receive and access documents and files; make changes or record data; store files; and transmit to home or office systems through voice commands, touch screen, or virtual keyboard. Easy, fast, secure backup to home or office computer systems. In particular, adequate storage for large audio and video files is a growing need that our model will fill. Biometric security system eliminates need for passwords and protects data against unauthorized access.

4. ***Monitor from a remote location.*** With Webcam, watch and listen to what happens in a child's room, anywhere in a home, in a pet's enclosure, or within a business building.

5. ***Entertainment.*** Record, download or upload, store, play, organize video, photo, music, and ringtones; share files on choice of Windows or Apple operating systems.

In addition, many of our targeted customers are interested in protecting the environment. Unique among leading smartphones, our product will have an environmentally friendly SuperSolar battery for 12 hours of talk time between charges.

Targeted Segments

Within the consumer market, our primary target segment is middle- to upper-income professionals who want one portable device to communicate with family and colleagues while on the go. This segment wants to access wireless connections from different locations, have the convenience of a single multifunction device for entertainment and daily organizational use, and monitor home or family security. Consumers in this segment are well educated (attended or completed college or graduate school), and have annual household incomes above $75,000.

A secondary target segment is young adults, aged 18–30, who are early adopters of (and can afford to buy) new electronics; this segment will be particularly interested in the SonicSuperphone's entertainment and imaging features and the ability to add video game units or other peripheral devices. This segment is also particularly interested in green products and inclined to favor products that feature an innovative, earth-friendly power source.

Within the business market, our primary target segment consists of executives, entrepreneurs, and small-business owners who travel; want to access company files and use basic software via a hands-off operation; need to stay in touch with customers and coworkers; and value software that will automatically choose the best-quality, lowest-cost phone and Internet services in any particular location. With our docking station, this segment can make free international phone calls, an extra benefit for those who travel beyond U.S. borders. An additional business segment is being considered for second-year entry: medical users, doctors, and nurses who want to access and update patients' medical records; photograph, video, or remotely monitor patients; and consult reference materials stored in expanded memory.

Market Growth

Global sales for smartphone handsets are expected to grow steadily over the next few years (see Table A.2). Although demand will not be as strong as in the past five years, smartphone sales will continue to increase at the expense of sales of cell phones with few functions and limited wireless capabilities. Worldwide, the number of all cell phones sold last year was 1.2 billion, and sales are projected to continue increasing in developing markets, in particular. The smartphone market, however, will grow much more rapidly, which is why we are focusing on it.

Other market trends point to positive acceptance of our SonicSuperphone. Widespread media attention to developments in the smartphone industry has increased awareness and interest among targeted segments. Also, reviewers have focused on the specific advantages and disadvantages of new smartphone models, providing us with clues to competitive weaknesses that we can exploit through marketing. Green products are gaining acceptance, and our ability to produce a smartphone with solar battery is unmatched in the industry. Although we are targeting only the U.S. market at this time, we are preparing for expansion into other markets.

TABLE A.2 Worldwide Smartphone Sales

2010 (actual)	2011 (projected)	2012 (projected)
145 million units	160 million units	175 million units

SWOT ANALYSIS

In taking advantage of growth opportunities in the U.S. market, Sonic can build on several powerful strengths, including our exclusive licenses for Wireless Communication Commander software (a feature unmatched by competitors at this time), among others; our in-house solar battery design and engineering expertise; and our ability to produce quality handsets cost-efficiently. We expect that most competitors will have voice-recognition systems for all handset functions within 6 months and will be able to match the Commander software within 12 months; still, our head start should provoke positive brand associations and contribute to strong sales. Our solar battery is another important strength as customers seek out green products in every category.

Our major weakness is the lack of brand awareness and image; we also lack the financial resources and global sourcing contacts of the largest handset manufacturers. Moreover, the Smart Apps store will open with only a few thousand offerings, a possible competitive weakness. We see opportunities in higher demand for multimedia, multifunction phones; wider availability of chips for multifunction devices; wider availability of high-capacity storage for smartphones; and frequent media coverage of technologies for personal and business use. We see potential threats from intense competition, pressure to keep prices low, and future obsolescence of wireless standards. Table A.3 summarizes these strengths, weaknesses, opportunities, and threats.

TABLE A.3 SWOT Analysis for SonicSuperphone

Strengths (internal capabilities that support achievement of objectives)	Weaknesses (internal factors that might prevent achievement of objectives)
1. Exclusive licenses for software to manage wireless connections, compatibility, and international calling	1. Lack of brand awareness and image
2. In-house engineering of solar battery technology for eco-friendly power and extended talk time	2. Relatively few applications available at opening of Smart Apps store, which may become an issue for buyers
3. Production quality and efficiency	3. More limited resources than competitors
Opportunities (external circumstances that may be exploited to achieve objectives)	**Threats (external circumstances that might interfere with achievement of objectives)**
1. Higher demand for multimedia, multifunction phones that can operate worldwide	1. Intense domestic and international competition
2. Availability of smaller, faster chips to power multifunction devices and higher-capacity storage for multimedia files	2. Downward pricing pressure due to maturing market and competitive forces
3. Media interest in technologies for everyday use	3. Existing wireless connection standards may become obsolete

TABLE A.4 Top 3 Global Competitors in Smartphones

Competitor	Estimated Worldwide Share
Nokia	38 percent
Research in Motion (BlackBerry)	19 percent
Apple	17 percent

COMPETITION

On the broadest level, our SonicSuperphone will compete with all smartphone products in the global market. These competitors have formidable resources, high brand recognition, and extensive experience in product development and management.

As shown in Table A.4, Finland's Nokia dominates in smartphones, with a 38 percent share of the worldwide market. Canada's Research in Motion, which makes the popular BlackBerry smartphones, has the second-largest share. Apple, the California-based maker of the highly popular iPhone products, has the third-largest share. Two other key competitors in the U.S. market are Motorola, which was hit hard by the recent economic downturn, and Palm, which markets the Pre smartphone. Because we plan to expand internationally within a short time, we are tracking worldwide share more closely than domestic share.

Some competing handsets allow voice-recognition dialing and other voice activation features; none offers voice activation of every function, including data input, file access, storage, and exchange. This feature has special appeal for our targeted segment of business customers. No other handset is equipped with Wireless Communication Commander software, which facilitates connection through any wireless technology and automatically chooses the best-quality, least-expensive method in a given location. No competitor has a long-lasting solar battery as standard equipment. According to our research, both consumers and business customers place a high value on the benefits of these unique features. Most important, no competing product has the exact mix of features and benefits offered by the SonicSuperphone.

CRITICAL ISSUES AND ENVIRONMENTAL FACTORS

One issue critical to our success is proper promotion of the Wireless Communication Commander software that Sonic has licensed. Potential buyers may be skeptical that the software is actually compatible with all wireless communication standards and can select the best-quality, least-expensive connection available at any location. Therefore, we will join with the software firm to demonstrate the benefits through a public relations campaign. Also, we will launch a product-specific radio advertising campaign and post informal YouTube videos taken during the recording sessions, showing celebrities voicing a variety of commands as the SonicSuperphone responds.

One of our print campaigns will show how quickly SonicSuperphone users can accomplish tasks and access functions using voice recognition. Another will focus on Wireless Communication Commander. A third will showcase the eco-friendly solar battery. All campaigns will be posted on our Web site and our Facebook brand page, and provided to retail partners for online and in-store use. Finally, we will give SonicSuperphones to certain opinion leaders as a way of stimulating buzz and positive word-of-mouth communication. We plan to tweet comments, questions, and updates to keep consumers, business users, suppliers, and others informed and interested.

Macroenvironmental factors likely to affect Sonic include demographics (such as trends in household income), economic issues (such as the purchasing power of targeted segments), technology (such as changes in wireless communication standards and alternative power sources), laws and regulations (such as state and federal rules governing telecommunications), ecological concerns (such as being able to recycle product parts), and cultural trends (including the increased popularity and status factor of smartphones as current users upgrade from older cell phones).

Microenvironmental factors likely to affect Sonic include suppliers (especially our industry-exclusive Wireless Communication Commander license), marketing intermediaries (such as relations with retailers and with phone-service providers), competitors (particularly their new-product innovations), and customers (including their perceptions of the SonicSuperphone and the value of its benefits).

MARKETING STRATEGY

SonicSuperphone's positioning will be based on superior innovation, top quality, and high utility. We will segment our consumer and business markets using demographic factors such as income, behavior, and benefits sought. Through differentiated marketing, we will target selected segments for initial entry and add secondary segments (such as medical users) later.

Using all elements of the marketing mix, supported by service and internal marketing, we will educate the market about our product's features and benefits to motivate purchases by first-time users as well as by consumers and businesspeople who switch from competing handsets. Although television advertising is not affordable in our start-up situation, we will use creative messages on radio, in magazines, on the Internet, and in other media to reach targeted segments. Penetration pricing will help us establish our brand. We will attract many first-time buyers new to the smartphone market. We will also appeal to value-conscious buyers who are replacing outdated handsets or trading up to gain more functionality without overspending.

Mission, Direction, and Objectives

Sonic's mission is to make innovative electronics that help consumers and businesspeople become more productive, connected, informed, and entertained in their daily lives. We will pursue rapid growth through the achievement of the following objectives:

- *Marketing objectives.* Achieve first-year unit sales volume of 240,000, gain 40 percent brand awareness among targeted consumer segments and 50 percent among targeted business segments by the end of next year, and establish strong channel relationships with electronics retailers and major phone service carriers within 90 days.
- *Financial objectives.* Restrict first-year losses on the SonicSuperphone to less than $15 million, reach the break-even point within 23 months of introduction, and earn an annual ROI of 15 percent within the first four years.
- *Societal objectives.* Earn the U.S. government's Energy Star designation for power efficiency by the time of introduction, popularize the high-efficiency solar battery as an alternative power source for smartphones, recycle 25 percent of the product's parts after its useful life is over, and build community relations by offering deeply discounted SonicSuperphones to not-for-profit organizations and charitable groups.

Product Strategy

As shown in Table A.1, our product will have features and functions that deliver a number of benefits highly valued by the targeted segments. Some of these features are exclusive to our initial model, although competitors may be able to match one or two key features in a matter of months. We are partnering with a major accessories manufacturer to provide a full line of SonicSuperphone branded accessories. All products carrying our brand must meet rigorous quality and technical standards, as verified by an independent testing laboratory. Moreover, our solar battery will be more efficient than the standard batteries in competing models, offering the dual benefits of longer use when charged and minimal environmental impact.

Depending on market needs, competitive pressure, and demand, we will lengthen the product line by introducing a language-translation-enabled model within 18 months of launching our first model. This new product will reinforce our innovation positioning, encourage business customers who travel internationally to trade up to the new model with more features, and support longer-term market-share objectives. It also will solidify channel relationships and satisfy additional needs of certain targeted segments. We are currently interviewing designers as we decide whether to create limited-edition fashion handsets soon after our first model is introduced.

The SonicSuperphone brand name will be presented in lettering suggesting speed, linked with a stylized, iridescent lightning bolt logo on the product and all accessories, store displays, Web pages, social media profile pages, and other communications. We will cobrand models sold through our phone service providers to show channel support and reinforce customer recognition. All brand elements will be carefully coordinated to contribute to salience, distinctiveness, and image.

(In an actual marketing plan, the product strategy section would include more information about branding, product design and features, packaging and labeling, product compatibility, and other details. Such information is not included in this sample plan.)

Pricing Strategy

Our financial pricing objectives are to achieve profitability within 23 months of introducing the new product and achieve a fourth-year ROI of 15 percent. We aim to hold first-year losses at $15 million or less, including product-development and production expenses as well as communication and channel costs related to the introduction. We will use a penetration pricing strategy to establish our brand in this highly competitive market. The first SonicSuperphone model will carry an average wholesale price of $125 and an average retail price of $199. Thus, first-year revenues are projected to be $30 million based on sales of 240,000 units.

Customers have become price sensitive in recent years as Apple and other competitors have reduced the initial price of new smartphone products. Often carriers bundle handsets with phone-service contracts, another reason for lower handset prices. Product prices and features vary widely, as the following brief competitive sample of smartphones indicates:

- Apple iPhone 3GS ($199 with contract from carrier) has voice control capabilities, video recording function, and a 3-megapixel camera. It weighs 4.8 oz. and the battery lasts up to 30 hours during music playback (up to 9 hours of Wi-Fi talk time).
- Palm Pre ($199 with contract from carrier) has built-in GPS, organizational capabilities to help users manage multiple calendars and voice/e-mail/social media contacts, a built-in camera with flash, and a slide-out keyboard for convenience.
- Blackberry Tour ($199 with contract from carrier) has GPS, a 3.2-megapixel camera, video recording and playback functions, a full keyboard, and an integrated trackball. It weighs 5.2 oz, and the battery will power five hours of talk time.
- Nokia E72 ($469 unlocked for use with any carrier) has built-in Wi-Fi networking, expandable memory, a 5-megapixel camera with flash, a video for video calls, GPS, and a compass. It weighs 4.5 oz., and the battery will power more than 12 hours of talk time.
- Motorola Droid ($199 with contract from carrier) features 5-megapixel camera with DVD quality video recording, large touch screen, GPS, wireless e-mail and web access, voice recognition, full keyboard. It weighs 6 ounces and uses the Google Android operating system.

Our research shows that business customers who pay for a smartphone with a data-service bundle are more likely to remain loyal. Therefore, we are researching optimal price points for bundling the SonicSuperphone with subscriptions to various data storage and transmission services.

(In an actual marketing plan, the pricing strategy section would include more information about the expected break-even volume, fixed and variable costs, pricing by channel, promotional pricing, segment price sensitivity, in-depth data about competitive pricing, and other details. Such information is not shown in this sample plan.)

Marketing Communications and Influence Strategy

Two marketing objectives for our communications strategy are to generate 40 percent brand awareness within the consumer target market and to generate 50 percent brand awareness within the business target market by the end of next year. To achieve these objectives, we will create a multimedia brand-building campaign that differentiates the product from competing handsets and engages customers in ongoing dialogue.

We will also use trade sales promotion to support our distribution strategy and hold high-profile launch events to stimulate publicity and media coverage in consumer media. With retail partners, we will deliver customized product information packages via e-mail to prospects with a specific demographic and behavioral profile. Highlights of our initial six-month promotion activities are shown in Table A.5.

We will soon begin pretesting message and creative elements for specific target audiences. During the launch period, we will advertise in magazines such as *Fortune* to reach high-income consumers and business segments. Also, we will use cooperative advertising to have the

TABLE A.5 Highlights of Communications and Influence Activities

Month	Activity
January	• Start trade campaign to educate channel partners for push strategy supporting product launch. • Give SonicSuperphones to selected product reviewers, bloggers, tweeters, opinion leaders, media representatives, and celebrities as part of public relations strategy. • Train sales personnel to explain Sonic's features, benefits, and competitive advantages. • Post professional product reviews on company and retailer Web sites, as well as on branded Facebook page. Invite customers to post reviews and respond to questions and comments online. • With phone service providers, plan sales activities targeting businesspeople. • With Wireless Communication Commander software firm, plan sales activities targeting consumers.
February	• Begin integrated print/radio/Internet/social media pull campaign targeting professionals, businesspeople, and affluent consumers. Allow for response to customer feedback. • Distribute point-of-sale materials and schedule in-store demonstrations. • With retailer partners, e-mail product information to high-potential prospects. • Hold a launch party with simultaneous Webcast to spark media coverage and buzz.
March	• Rotate messages as consumer advertising campaign continues. • Add sales promotions such as discounting accessories to encourage switching from competing handsets. • Distribute new in-store displays. • Arrange additional targeted e-mail promotions through retail partners.
April	• Announce trade sales contest for May–June. • Launch a trade campaign focusing on May–June sales opportunities. • Temporarily reduce frequency of consumer ad messages but continue online dialogues through social media, company blog, etc.
May	• Roll out new radio commercials, print ads, and YouTube videos featuring celebrities and well-known businesspeople using the SonicSuperphone. • Send retailers display blow-ups of new print ads.
June	• Exhibit at semiannual electronics industry show. • Provide channel partners with new feature/benefit sales aids. • With retailers, plan year-end holiday promotions and sales contests.

SonicSuperphone featured in high-traffic store areas and on the front page of retailers' Web sites. We are fine-tuning our media plan to deal with clutter, competitive advertising, and audience fragmentation. In addition, we are working with channel partners to develop policies for communicating pricing by market.

(In an actual marketing plan, the communications strategy section would include more information about integrated messages and media, specific tools to be used, exact timing of campaign activities, and additional details. Such information is not shown in this sample plan.)

Channel Strategy

We are using selective distribution to market the SonicSuperphone through two main channels during its first year. One channel consists of major retailers such as Amazon.com and Best Buy, which are known for their selection of electronics and technology products. These retailers have extensive customer databases that we can leverage for customized, product-specific promotions. They also are known for good prices and good customer service, a combination that complements our penetration pricing strategy.

The second channel consists of cell-phone-service providers. We have reached agreement to offer the initial model through Verizon Wireless, which gives us access to their stores in major markets and opportunities for cobranded promotions. During the second year, we will use agreements to expand sales through two other phone-service providers. We will negotiate with non-U.S. carriers when we expand to global markets.

Although channel costs are a factor, we have decided to emphasize customer service and logistical efficiency to build our brand image among channel members. Buyers will place orders, track shipments, and handle other functions online through our secure systems. Our suppliers will have sufficient parts and components ready for peak production periods, and our flow of goods will ensure proper inventory levels during the introduction. On the other hand, we do not want to have excess inventory, because of the threat of technological obsolescence.

(An actual marketing plan would include more information about channel functions, criteria for selection and evaluation, customer requirements, competitors' channel strategies, and other details. Such information is not shown in this sample plan.)

Service and Internal Marketing

As part of our customer service strategy, the SonicSuperphone will carry a one-year warranty on parts and labor. In the United States, repairs will be handled by a nationwide firm whose technicians have been trained by our engineers. We will receive weekly reports so we can pinpoint any problems to be addressed through manufacturing or design adjustments. To ensure that customers receive the expected level of warranty service, we will conduct quarterly customer satisfaction surveys and monitor social media for reviews, complaints, and comments posted by users.

Sonic will provide comprehensive training and point-of-sale service for channel partners. Customers and retailers will be able to obtain service support 24 hours a day, 7 days a week, on the Web, on a toll-free hotline, or by pressing the "Service" button on the SonicSuperphone. They will also be able to log onto branded, moderated forums in social media to exchange ideas, post reviews, discuss problems, and suggest improvements. Because we are establishing a new brand, we have high service standards and will measure results to ensure that we consistently meet those standards. We will survey a sample of customers monthly and annually to track satisfaction and plan improvements.

To build internal support and improve product and customer knowledge, our internal marketing activities will include monthly staff meetings, weekly e-mail bulletins, beta-testing by staff and channel members, coordination of marketing and production schedules, and recognition rewards for meeting sales and customer-satisfaction objectives.

MARKETING RESEARCH

Sonic's use of marketing research includes the following:

- ***Product development.*** Through concept testing, surveys, focus groups, and market tests, we have identified the features and benefits that targeted segments most value in enhanced phones and related electronics. We are collecting additional data on usability, quality, and value perceptions, and new features of interest to medical users.
- ***Marketing communications and influence.*** We plan to measure brand awareness before, during, and after our campaigns to determine the effectiveness of each medium in reaching the targeted audience and stimulating the desired response. We also want to analyze customers' attitudes toward competitors' campaigns and learn how customers receive and interpret our messages so we can refine our communications and media as needed.
- ***Customer satisfaction.*** We are planning comprehensive studies to gauge customer satisfaction and identify product defects or other issues that require immediate attention. We will also solicit feedback from retail partners and phone-service providers.

FINANCIALS AND FORECASTS

Total first-year revenue for the SonicSuperphone is projected at $30 million, based on sales of 240,000 units at an average wholesale price of $125. We anticipate first-quarter sales of $6 million, second-quarter sales of $4 million, third-quarter sales of $8 million, and fourth-quarter sales of $12 million. These projections assume cumulatively higher business sales and a spike in year-end consumer sales. Table A.6 shows unit forecasts by market and channel.

Investments in product development, communications, and channel support will mean a first-year loss of up to $15 million. However, we should reach the break-even point just before the end of the second year, a realistic objective given our ability to rapidly lower production costs as volume increases. Once we introduce a second model, we plan to slash the wholesale price of the first model—in line with standard industry practice—to reduce the retail price and dramatically increase sales volume. Our first-year marketing budgets cover advertising, sales materials, point-of-purchase displays, consumer and trade sales promotions, public relations, online marketing, channel costs, marketing research, sales training and support, shipping, and customer-service support.

(In an actual marketing plan, each action program would carry its own financial assumptions, management assignments, and schedules. The full marketing plan would also include a detailed profit-and-loss analysis; month-by-month forecasts by product and channel; and summary and detailed budgets by program and activity, market/segment, region, and manager. None of these is shown in this sample plan.)

TABLE A.6   First Year Sales Forecasts

By Market	Unit Sales
Consumer	88,000
Business	152,000
Total	240,000

By Channel	Unit Sales
Online/store retailers	180,000
Phone service carrier(s)	60,000
Total	240,000

METRICS AND MARKETING CONTROL

We plan stringent control activities to monitor quality and customer service satisfaction so we can respond immediately to any problems. We are also monitoring customer-service communications and online product reviews to detect any early signs of customer concern or confusion.

Metrics to be monitored during implementation include weekly and monthly sales (to gauge progress toward revenue and unit sales objectives), weekly and monthly costs (to gauge progress toward the break-even point), quarterly awareness levels (to gauge progress toward brand awareness targets), weekly and monthly sales by channel (to gauge progress in channel relationships), and the number of not-for-profit organizations making special purchases (to gauge progress toward community-relations objectives). Quarterly financial measures will include return on marketing investment, return on sales, and return on sales by channel. In addition, we are tightly controlling schedules to ensure timely implementation.

A contingency plan has been developed to deal with severe downward pricing pressure, which may occur if a major competitor initiates a price war or develops a lower-cost technology. Our contingency plan calls for introducing a significant but short-term price promotion such as a rebate to remain competitive while gauging the price sensitivity of different segments. Based on the outcome of this short-term promotion, we would revise the marketing plan as necessary to defend market share while retaining a minimally acceptable level of profitability.

(An actual marketing plan would include detailed schedules and management assignments by program and activity. For control purposes, the plan also would allow for month-by-month comparison of actual versus projected sales and expenses; and it would summarize any contingency plans. None of these is shown in this sample plan.)

Sources for Appendix

Some background information for the fictional sample plan was adapted from: Lance Whitney, "Apple Overtakes Nokia in Phone Profits," *CNet News,* November 11, 2009, http://news.cnet.com; Martin Perez, "Smartphones Sales Continue Rise," *InformationWeek,* November 11, 2009, www.informationweek.com; Steve Hamm, "Smartphone Roulette for App Makers," *BusinessWeek,* June 22, 2009, p. 28; "The Wireless World," *BusinessWeek,* June 22, 2009, p. 62; David Zeiler, "Smartphone Sales in U.S. Up 68 Percent in 2008," *Baltimore Sun,* February 7, 2009, www.baltimoresun.com; Matt Richtel, "Can the Cellphone Industry Keep Growing?" *New York Times,* February 4, 2009, www.nytimes.com; Connie Guglielmo, "Apple Releases Faster iPhone as Competition Escalates," *Bloomberg,* June 19, 2009, www.bloomberg.com.

GLOSSARY

affordability budgeting Method of budgeting for marketing in which the company plans to spend what it believes it can afford. (Chapter 10)

annual plan control Type of marketing control used to assess the progress and performance of the current year's marketing plan. (Chapter 10)

attitudes An individual's lasting evaluations of and feelings toward something. (Chapter 3)

auction pricing Type of pricing in which buyers submit bids to buy goods or services. (Chapter 7)

B2B marketing Business-to-business marketing. (Chapter 1)

benefits Need–satisfaction outcomes that customers desire from a product offering. (Chapter 6)

brand equity Extra value perceived in a brand that enhances long-term loyalty among customers. (Chapter 6)

brand extension Putting an established brand on a new product in a different category, aimed at a new customer segment; also known as *category extension*. (Chapter 6)

branding Using words, designs, or symbols to give a product a distinct identity and differentiate it from competing products. (Chapter 6)

break-even point Point at which revenues cover costs and beyond which a product becomes profitable. (Chapter 7)

budget Time-defined allocation of financial outlays for a specific function or program. (Chapter 10)

business market Companies, not-for-profit organizations, and institutions that buy products for operations or as supplies for production—also known as the *organizational market*. (Chapter 3)

buzz marketing More intense, company-stimulated word-of-mouth communication about a product or brand, which can spread and fade quickly. (Chapter 9)

cannibalization Allowing a new product to cut into sales of one or more existing products. (Chapter 6)

cause-related marketing Marketing a product or brand through a link to benefiting a charitable cause. (Chapter 5)

channel The set of functions and the structure of organizations performing them outbound on the value chain to make a particular offering available to customers, also known as the *distribution channel*. (Chapter 8)

competitive-parity budgeting Method in which the company creates a budget by matching what competitors spend, as a percentage of sales or a specific dollar amount. (Chapter 10)

concentrated marketing Focusing one marketing strategy on one attractive market segment. (Chapter 4)

consumer market Individuals and families that buy products for themselves. (Chapter 3)

contingency plan Plan that is ready to implement if significant, unexpected changes in the situation disrupt the organization's strategy or programs. (Chapter 10)

cost leadership strategy Generic competitive strategy in which the company seeks to become the lowest-cost producer in its industry. (Chapter 2)

crowdsourcing Generating new product ideas or marketing materials by having customers and others outside the organization submit concepts, designs, content, or advice. (Chapter 6)

customer churn Turnover in customers during a specific period; often expressed as a percentage of the organization's total customer base (Chapter 6).

customer-influence strategies Strategies for engaging customers through marketing communications and influencing how they think, feel, and act toward a brand or offering. (Chapter 9)

customer lifetime value Total amount a customer spends with a company over the course of a long-term relationship. (Chapter 6)

derived demand In B2B marketing, the principle that demand for a business product is based on demand for a related consumer product. (Chapter 3)

differentiated marketing Creating a separate marketing strategy for each targeted segment. (Chapter 4)

differentiation strategy Generic competitive strategy in which the company creates a unique differentiation for itself or its product based on some factor valued by the target market. (Chapter 2)

diversification Growth strategy of offering new products to new markets through internal product-development capabilities or by starting (or buying) a business for diversification purposes. (Chapter 5)

dynamic pricing Approach to pricing in which prices vary from customer to customer or situation to situation. (Chapter 7)

emotional appeal Message strategy that relies on feelings rather than facts to motivate audience response. (Chapter 9)

features Specific attributes that enable a product to perform its function. (Chapter 6)

financial objectives Targets for performance in managing specific financial results. (Chapter 5)

fixed pricing Approach to pricing in which prices do not vary; the customer pays the price set by the marketer. (Chapter 7)

focus strategy Generic competitive strategy in which the company narrows its competitive scope to achieve a competitive advantage in its chosen segments. (Chapter 2)

forecast Future projection of what sales and costs are likely to be in the period covered by the plan. (Chapter 10)

frequency How many times, on average, the target audience is exposed to the message during a given period. (Chapter 9)

goals Longer-term performance targets for the organization or a particular unit. (Chapter 1)

integrated marketing communication Coordinating content and delivery so that all marketing messages are consistent and support the positioning and direction in the marketing plan. (Chapter 9)

internal marketing Marketing that targets managers and employees inside the organization to support the marketing mix in the marketing plan. (Chapter 5)

keyword search advertising Form of online advertising in which the company pays to have its site listed in the search results for specific words or brands, also known as *paid search*. (Chapter 9)

lifestyle The pattern of living that an individual exhibits through activities and interests. (Chapter 3)

line extension Putting an established brand on a new product added to the existing product line. (Chapter 6)

logistics Managing the movement of goods, services, and related information from the point of origin to the point of sale or consumption and balancing the level of service with the cost. (Chapter 8)

macroenvironment Largely uncontrollable external elements that can potentially influence the ability to reach goals; these include demographic, economic, ecological, technological, political-legal, and social-cultural forces. (Chapter 2)

market All the potential buyers for a particular product. (Chapter 3)

market development Growth strategy in which the company identifies and taps new segments or markets for existing products. (Chapter 5)

market penetration Growth strategy in which the company sells more of its existing products to customers in existing markets or segments. (Chapter 5)

market segmentation Grouping customers within a market according to similar needs, habits, or attitudes that can be addressed through marketing. (Chapter 4)

market share The percentage of sales in a given market held by a particular company, brand, or product; can be calculated in dollars or units. (Chapter 3)

marketing The activity, set of institutions, and processes for creating, communicating, delivering, and exchanging offerings that have value for customers, clients, partners, and society at large. (Chapter 1)

marketing audit A detailed, systematic analysis of an organization's marketing capabilities and performance. (Chapter 10)

marketing control The process of setting goals and standards, measuring and diagnosing interim results, and taking corrective action when needed to keep a marketing plan's performance on track. (Chapter 1)

marketing dashboard A computerized, graphical presentation enabling management to monitor marketing results by tracking important metrics over time and spotting patterns that signal deviations from the plan. (Chapter 10)

marketing objectives Targets for performance in managing specific marketing relationships and activities. (Chapter 5)

marketing plan A document that summarizes marketplace knowledge and the strategies and steps to be taken in achieving the objectives set by marketing managers for a particular period. (Chapter 1)

marketing planning The process of determining how to provide value to customers, the organization, and key stakeholders by researching and analyzing the market and situation; developing and documenting marketing objectives, strategies, and programs; and implementing, evaluating, and controlling marketing activities to achieve the objectives. (Chapter 1)

mass customization Creating products, on a large scale, with features tailored to individual customers. (Chapter 6)

metrics Numerical measures of specific performance-related activities and outcomes. (Chapter 10)

microenvironment Groups that have a more direct effect on the organization's ability to reach its goals: customers, competitors, channel members, partners, suppliers, and employees. (Chapter 2)

mission Statement of the organization's fundamental purpose, its focus, and how it will add value for customers and other stakeholders. (Chapter 2)

mobile marketing Getting coupons, information, directions, and other messages to customers via cell phones. (Chapter 9)

motivation What drives the consumer to satisfy needs and wants. (Chapter 3)

negotiated pricing Type of pricing in which buyer and seller negotiate the price. (Chapter 7)

niche Smaller segment within a market that exhibits distinct needs or benefit requirements. (Chapter 4)

North American Industry Classification System (NAICS) Method of classifying businesses according to industry designation, used in the United States, Canada, and Mexico. (Chapter 3)

objective-and-task budgeting Method in which the budget is determined by totaling the cost of all marketing tasks needed to achieve the marketing plan objectives. (Chapter 10)

objectives Shorter-term performance targets that support the achievement of an organization's or unit's goals. (Chapter 1)

paid search Also known as *keyword search advertising*, a form of online advertising in which the company pays to have its site listed in the search results for specific words or brands. (Chapter 9)

penetration pricing Pricing a product relatively low to gain market share rapidly. (Chapter 7)

percentage-of-sales budgeting Method of budgeting in which the company allocates a certain percentage of sales revenues to fund marketing programs. (Chapter 10)

perception How the individual organizes environmental inputs such as ads and derives meaning from the data. (Chapter 3)

personas Detailed but fictitious profiles representing how individual customers in a targeted segment behave, live, and buy. (Chapter 4)

positioning Using marketing to create a distinctive place or image for a brand or product in the mind of customers. (Chapter 1)

price elasticity of demand Percentage change in unit sales of demand divided by the percentage change in price; where customers are price sensitive and demand changes considerably due to small price changes, the demand is elastic. (Chapter 7)

primary research Research conducted specifically to address a certain situation or answer a particular question. (Chapter 3)

product development Growth strategy in which the company sells new products to customers in existing markets or segments. (Chapter 5)

product life cycle The stages of introduction, growth, maturity, and decline through which a product moves in the marketplace. (Chapter 6)

product line Group of products made by one company that are related in some way. (Chapter 6)

product mix Assortment of all product lines marketed by one company. (Chapter 6)

productivity control Type of marketing control used to assess the organization's performance and progress in managing the efficiency of key marketing areas. (Chapter 10)

profitability control Type of marketing control used to assess the organization's progress and performance based on profitability measures. (Chapter 10)

psychographic characteristics Variables used to analyze consumer lifestyle patterns. (Chapter 3)

pull strategy Using marketing to encourage customers to ask intermediaries for a product, thereby pulling it through the channel. (Chapter 9)

push strategy Using marketing to encourage channel members to stock a product, thereby pushing it through the channel to customers. (Chapter 9)

quality How well a product satisfies customer needs. (Chapter 6)

rational appeal Message strategy that relies on facts or logic to motivate audience response. (Chapter 9)

reach How many people in the target audience are exposed to the message during a particular period. (Chapter 9)

schedule Time-defined plan for completing work that relates to a specific purpose or program. (Chapter 10)

secondary research Research data already gathered for another purpose. (Chapter 3)

segments Groups within a market having distinct needs or characteristics that can be effectively addressed by specific marketing offers and programs. (Chapter 1)

service recovery How an organization plans to recover from a service lapse and satisfy its customers. (Chapter 5)

skimming pricing Pricing a new product high to establish an image and more quickly recover development costs in line with profitability objectives. (Chapter 7)

social media Online media designed to facilitate user interaction. (Chapter 9)

societal objectives Targets for achieving specific results in social responsibility. (Chapter 5)

stakeholders People and organizations that are influenced by or that can influence an organization's performance. (Chapter 1)

strategic control Type of marketing control used to assess the organization's performance and progress in the strategic areas of marketing effectiveness, customer relationship management, and social responsibility and ethics. (Chapter 10)

subcultures Distinct groups within a larger culture that exhibit and preserve distinct cultural identities through a common religion, nationality, ethnic background, or lifestyle. (Chapter 3)

sustainable marketing Forming, maintaining, and enhancing customer relationships to meet all parties' objectives without compromising the achievement of future generations' objectives. (Chapter 1)

SWOT analysis Summary of an organization's strengths, weaknesses, opportunities, and threats in preparation for marketing planning. (Chapter 2)

target costing Using research to determine what customers want in a product and the price they will pay, then finding ways of producing the product at a cost that will accommodate that price and return a profit. (Chapter 7)

target market Segment of the overall market that a company chooses to pursue. (Chapter 4)

targeting Decisions about which market segments to enter and in what order, and how to use marketing in each. (Chapter 1)

undifferentiated marketing Targeting all market segments with the same marketing strategy. (Chapter 4)

value The difference between total benefits and total price, as perceived by customers. (Chapter 1)

value-based pricing Approach to setting prices that starts with customers' perspective of a product's value and the price they are willing to pay; marketers then work backward to make the product at a cost and profit that meet the company's objectives. (Chapter 7)

value chain The series of interrelated, value-added functions and the structure of organizations that perform these functions to get the right product to the right markets and customers at the right time, place, and price; also known as *supply chain*. (Chapter 8)

word-of-mouth communication People telling other people about an organization, a brand, a product, or a marketing message. (Chapter 9)

CREDITS

CHAPTER 1

Exhibit 1.1   Marketing Zappos

Zappos print ad

Copyright 2009 Zappos.com, Inc.

Exhibit 1.4   Six Approaches to Growth

Adapted from Alan R. Andreasen and Philip Kotler, *Strategic Marketing for Non-Profit Organizations*, 6th ed. (Upper Saddle River, NJ: Pearson Prentice Hall, 2003), p. 81.

Exhibit 1.6   The Marketing Mix

Adapted from Gary Armstrong and Philip Kotler, *Marketing: An Introduction,* 8th ed. (Upper Saddle River, NJ: Pearson Prentice Hall, 2007), p. 53.

CHAPTER 2

Exhibit 2.3   Judging Organizational Strengths and Weaknesses

Mary K. Coulter, *Strategic Management in Action* (Upper Saddle River, NJ: Pearson Prentice Hall, 1998), p. 141.

Exhibit 2.5   Mission Statements

www.target.com; www.southwest.com; www.terex.com; www.brooklynpubliclibrary.org; www.guggenheim.org.

Exhibit 2.8   Competitive Forces Affecting Industry Profitability and Attractiveness

Michael E. Porter, *Competitive Advantage* (New York: Free Press, imprint of Simon & Shuster, 1985), reprinted with permission.

CHAPTER 4

Exhibit 4.5   Assessing Segment Attractiveness

Adapted from Graham Hooley, John Saunders, and Nigel Piercy, *Marketing Strategy and Competitve Positioning*, 3d ed. (Harlow, Essex, England: FT Prentice Hall, 2004), p. 354.

CHAPTER 5

Exhibit 5.2   Options for Marketing Plan Direction

Marian Burk Wood, *Marketing Planning: Principles into Practice* (Harlow, Essex, England: Pearson Education, 2004), p. 124.

Exhibit 5.4   The Ad Council

Screen grab: http://www.adcouncil.org/default.aspx?id=82

Exhibit 5.6   Strategy Pyramid

Adapted from Tim Berry and Doug Wilson, *On Target: The Book on Marketing Plans* (Eugene, OR: Palo Alto Software, 2001), p. 107.

CHAPTER 6

Exhibit 6.6   Marketing Advantages of Strong Brands

Philip Kotler and Kevin Lane Keller, *Marketing Management*, 12th ed. (Upper Saddle River, NJ: Pearson Prentice Hall, 2006), p. 277.

Exhibit 6.7   Marketing Tabasco

TABASCO® is a registered trademark for sauces and other goods and services; TABASCO, the TABASCO bottle design and label designs are the exclusive property of McIlhenny Company, Avery Island, LA, USA 70513. www.TABASCO.com

Exhibit 6.8   Pyramid of Brand Equity

Kevin Lane Keller, *Strategic Brand Management*, 2nd ed. (Upper Saddle River, NJ: Pearson Prentice Hall, 2006), p. 76, Fig. 2.5.

CHAPTER 7

Exhibit 7.3   Auction and Fixed Pricing

www.usa.gov/shopping/supplies/supplies.shtml

Exhibit 7.5   Cost-Based versus Value-Based Pricing

Thomas Nagle and John Hogan, *Strategy and Tactics of Pricing*, 4th ed. (Upper Saddle River, NJ: Pearson Prentice Hall, 2006), p. 4.

Exhibit 7.8   Break-Even Analysis

Tim Berry and Doug Wilson, *On Target: The Book on Marketing Plans* (Eugene, OR: Palo Alto Software, 2000), p. 163.

Exhibit 7.9   Skim Pricing and Penetration Pricing Compared

Roger J. Best, *Market-Based Management*, 4th ed. (Upper Saddle River, NJ: Pearson Prentice Hall, 2005), pp. 242, 248.

Exhibit 7.10   Alternative Reactions to Competitive Price Cuts

Philip Kotler, *Framework for Marketing Management* (Upper Saddle River, NJ: Pearson Prentice Hall, 2001), p. 231.

CHAPTER 8

Exhibit 8.3   Channel Levels

Philip Kotler and Gary Armstrong, *Principles of Marketing*, 12th ed. (Upper Saddle River, NJ: Pearson Prentice Hall, 2008), Fig 12.4, p. 344.

CHAPTER 9

Exhibit 9.2   Push and Pull Strategies

Philip Kotler and Gary Armstrong, *Principles of Marketing*, 12th ed. (Upper Saddle River, NJ: Pearson Prentice Hall, 2008), p. 415.

Exhibit 9.3   Models for Audience Response

Adapted from Michael R. Solomon, *Consumer Behavior*, 5th ed. (Upper Saddle River, NJ: Prentice Hall, 2002), pp. 200–202.

Exhibit 9.5   Marketing Massachusetts: Massachusetts Uses Multiple Media to Reach Its Target

http://www.mass.gov/?pageID=mg2topic&L=3&L0=Home&L1=Visitor&L2=Visitor+Resources&sid=massgov2

Exhibit 9.6   The Media Mix

Kenneth Clow and Donald Baack, *Integrated Advertising, Promotion, and Marketing Communications*, 3rd ed. (Upper Saddle River, NJ: Pearson Prentice Hall, 2007), Fig. 8.5, p. 260.

CHAPTER 10

Exhibit 10.3   Main Categories of Marketing Metrics

Farris, Paul W., Bendle, Neil T., Pfeifer, Phillip E., Reibstein, David J., *Marketing Metrics: 50+ Metrics Every Executive Should Master*, 1st Edition, © 2006, p. 5. Reprinted by permission of Pearson Education, Inc., Upper Saddle River, NJ.

Exhibit 10.5   The CDC Markets Public Health

Centers for Disease Control and Prevention
www.cdc.gov

Exhibit 10.8   Successful Marketing Plan Implementation

Roger J. Best, *Market-Based Management*, 4th ed. (Upper Saddle River, NJ: Pearson Prentice Hall, 2005), p. 453.

INDEX

Note: Bold locators refer to definition of key terms. Notation "b" and "ex" refers to box and exhibits cited in the text.